HOW TO WALK
IN THE
FOOTSTEPS
OF
JESUS
AND
THE PROPHETS

A scripture reference guide
for Biblical sites in
Israel and Jordan

Hela Crown-Tamir

JERUSALEM ♦ NEW YORK

Typesetting: Marzel A.S. - Jerusalem.
Cover Design: Studio Paz, Jerusalem.

Edition 9   8   7   6   5   4   3   2

Gefen Publishing House   Gefen Books
6 Hatzvi St.   600 Broadway
Jerusalem 9438, Israel   Lynbrook, NY 11563, USA
972-2-538-0247   1-516-593-1234
orders@gefenpublishing.com   orders@gefenpublishing.com

www.israelbooks.com
Printed in Israel   *Send for our free catalogue*

_____

Library of Congress Cataloging-in-Publication Data
Crown-Tamir, Hela, 1943-
How to Walk in the Footsteps of Jesus and the Prophets: A Scripture
Reference Guide for Biblical Sites in Israel and Jordan
      p.   cm.
ISBN 965-229-229-X

1. Israel—Description and travel. 2. Jordan— Description and
travel. 3.Palestine —Gazetteers. 4. Jesus Christ —Journeys. I.
Title.
DS107.5.C76 1999
220.9'1—dc21

                              99-045133
                              CIP

Contents

THE OLD TESTAMENT
NAMES AND ORDER OF THE BOOKS

Genesis	Proverbs
Exodus	Ecclesiastes
Leviticus	Song of Solomon
Numbers	Isaiah
Deuteronomy	Lamentations
Joshua	Ezekiel
Judges	Daniel
Ruth	Hosea
1 Samuel	Joel
2 Samuel	Amos
1 Kings	Obadiah
2 Kings	Jonah
1 Chronicles	Micah
2 Chronicles	Nahum
Ezra	Habakkuk
Nehemiah	Zephaniah
Esther	Haggai
Job	Zechariah
Psalms	Malachi

THE NEW TESTAMENT
NAMES AND ORDER OF THE BOOKS

Matthew	1 Timothy
Mark	2 Timothy
Luke	Titus
John	Philemon
Acts	Hebrews
Romans	James
1 Corinthians	1 Peter
2 Corinthians	2 Peter
Galatinas	1 John
Ephesians	2 John
Philippians	3 John
Colossians	Jude
1 Thessalonians	Revelation
2 Thessalonians	

Dedicated to
my beloved husband Fred
and
all the wonderful tour guides
in Israel

May all who walk behind us
*find us faithful!**

* "Find us Faithful" – 1987 Birdwing Music / Jonathan Mark Music.
Words and Music by Jon Mohr

*"Remember to magnify His work
of which men have sung."*

Job 36:24

INTRODUCTION COMMENTS

These Biblical sites are both ancient and present sites in Israel and Jordan, with a few in Egypt's Sinai Peninsula. The purpose of this book is to enable the reader, my fellow guides and the travelers to walk, visit and explore these sites today. The explanations are short and concise. The sites are the birthplaces, homes, Biblical and historical places named in the Bible, in both the Old and New Testament. They are sites from the time of Abraham (2200 BC) until the time of Jesus of Nazareth (4BC-30AD), including the early church and Mishnah period, up until the second century. This book will enable one to look up the site quickly in its alphabetical form, read the Biblical references, and travel to the site from most major cities in Israel and Jordan. The section named 'Specific Sites where Jesus walked' is after the main entries.

I invite the reader to explore the 'Land of the Bible' in connection with its Biblical history, and I use the name "Prophet" on the title page to include the Patriarchs, Abraham, Isaac, Jacob and their families and descendants who are mentioned specifically in the Bible. It also includes all those who were divinely inspired and honored and called Prophets in the Bible. You will walk in the modern and ancient sites as these forefathers of Biblical history did.

The alphabetized sites are listed by the names they are known by today or the ancient name, with an explanation. Different names were used to refer to the same site in different time periods. I have made a cross reference to all the names when necessary. I have attempted to give exact names with the Hebrew in parenthesis. The Hebrew translation is always understood. Some entries have Greek, Latin, Arabic or Aramaic translations, as indicated. The entry tells the current status of the site and its description, then its location and a further explanation, if necessary. Some entries are modern cities, and the ancient cities, or tels are nearby and are indicated, such as Arad and Tel Arad. See Tel in main entry. A few entries are explanations of the parables that Jesus used in speaking to the multitudes. He pointed to people, places and things to illustrate a point. For example, see Eye of the Needle Gate and the Mustard Seed Site. The geographical landmarks are included, and the scripture references that are in brackets are from the Old and New Testament, using the Open Bible, the New King James version, the Open Bible Expanded Edition, Thomas Nelson Publishers. At the end of the entry, you are invited to see another entry site, for further information in connection with the site you looked up. The distances from each site are in kilometers. To change kilometers into miles you multiply by six and divide by ten. Most of the sites are accessible and distanced from Jerusalem, Israel's capital city, or another major city. Some sites are in Jordan and Egypt today, as indicated.

There are actually two types of sites that can be located with reasonable accuracy. Some sites have not been exactly identified or are no longer visible. I have included them, as they are Biblical sites and perhaps will be uncovered and explored in the future. One of my professors in guide school suggested that there are over 6000 archaeological sites in Israel, and only 250 have been excavated and explored. Many of these Biblical sites are still active digs and "...the hidden treasures in the sands are still coming to light" [Deut. 33:19].

I have used the term 'The Promised Land' in all references to Israel, as opposed to the land of Canaan. The Israelites are called 'The children of Israel.' Both ancient and modern maps can be found at the end of these entries. Look at the specific section on the Tribes of Israel for distinguishing the borders as given by God to Moses. The map of Ezekiel's vision of the Holyland gives you an interesting insight. The ancient gates of

Jerusalem's Old City are also illustrated and outlined for further reference. You will find the prayers for the '14 Stations of the Cross' under the Via Delorosa entry at the back of this book.

Please see the Bibliography at the back of this book. My main source of information is the Bible, from which I have derived endless hours of study and enjoyment. The Bible is my handbook as I guide individuals and groups all over the land of Israel. As a licensed, official tour guide in Israel I carry and use the Bible daily, reading and relating the scriptures as we walk on these Biblical sites throughout the land. The Bible stories come alive here in the land where they occurred, as we walk in the footsteps of Jesus and the prophets. One Christian minister once commented to me that walking in the land of the Bible is the fifth gospel. I invite you, the reader, to comment or offer corrections on any of these entries, and again, I invite you to come walk in and through the land, using this small work as a reference.

Thank you.

Hela Crown-Tamir
Jerusalem 1999 / 5759

"The Land of Israel, scene of divine revelations, home of the People of the Book, background of the marvels recorded in the Bible... a land sacred to Jew, Christian and Moslem, visiting Israel, retracing the footsteps of Jesus and the Prophets, is more than just a journey, it is a pilgrimage to the very source of faith."

"Beautiful for situation, the joy of the whole earth..."

Psalm 48:2

BIBLICAL SITES

Ab'arim   (regions beyond) Mountain range **E** of the Dead Sea in Jordan. This was the second to last stopping place for the children of Israel where, with Moses, they encamped "before Mt. Nebo" *[Numbers 33:47]*. Mt. Nebo, in the northern part of the Abarim range, is across from Jericho. God commanded Moses to "look at the land of Canaan which I give to the Israelites for a possession," *[Deut. 32:49 Amplified Bible]* from the top of Mt. Nebo.

Abel   (watercourse) Site near Bet Shemesh where the Philistines set the Ark of the Covenant when they returned it to Israel *[I Samuel 6:7-18]*. 27 kms. **W** from Jerusalem.

Absalom's Pillar Monument   (ab'sa-lom; father of peace) David's rebellious son Absalom, set up a pillar for himself located in the King's Valley, in the Kidron Valley (in front of Gethsemane) in Jerusalem *[II Samuel 18:18]*. See Valley of Shevah. Some Archaeologists say the present pillar of Absalom is a replacement for the one that was originally built by Absalom.

Abel Bayt-Maachah   (meadow of the house of Maachah) This city, attacked by Ben-Hadad, who was King of Syria *[I Kings 15:20]*, is identified with the village of Abil el-Qamh, 20 kms. **N** of the Hula Lake in the northern Galilee.

Abel Kera'mim   (watercourse of the vine) City **E** of the Jordan River where Jephthah defeated the Ammonites with a great slaughter *[Judges 11:33]*. An archaeological ruin bearing the name Bet Ha Kerem (house of the vine), **N** of Kerak city in the country of Jordan marks the site.

Abel Meholah   (meadow *[brook]* the dancing) In the Jordan Valley, birthplace of Elisha where he was anointed by Elijah, the Prophet *[I Kings 19:16]*. Gideon's army of 300 men followed God's instructions, causing the Midianites to kill one another with a great slaughter ensuing *[Judges 7 :22]*. Present day Tel el-Maqlub near Jordan River, **S** of Beth Shean.

Abel-Mizraim (the mourning of Egypt) The scene of the great lamenting over Jacob by Joseph, his brothers and the Egyptian household *[Genesis 50:10-11]*. The entire mourning party traveled from Egypt to Hebron. This site was the threshing floor of the Canaanites called Atad. See Atad and Hebron.

Abel Shittim (meadow *[brook]* of acacia trees) The last holding place of the children of Israel camping in the country of Jordan on the plains of Moab opposite Jericho *[Numbers 33:48,49]*. Israel was lured into idol worship and other sins here, resulting in God's punishment and the death of 24,000 Israelites by plague *[Numbers 25:1; Joshua 2:1; Micah 6:5]*. You can still see the upper terraces, as you look eastward over Jordan from the Jericho plain and the green of the acacia trees as you head **S** along the Dead Sea road. Present day Khirbet Kefre in Jordan.

Abomination of Desolation See Temple Mount

Abro'nah (passage) Near present day Eilat (Ezion-geber) The 31st site where the children of Israel encamped, enroute from Egypt to the Promised Land. It is called Ebrona in the KJV *[Numbers 33:34]*.

Abu-Dis (father of the stone) The 'Stone of Meeting'. On the **E** side of the Mt. of Olives, just beyond the city of Bethany. A Greek Orthodox Chapel marks the site of Martha's meeting with Jesus after Lazarus' death *[John 11:20-21]*. 2.2 kms. **E** from Jerusalem's Old City. See Bahurim and Bethphage.

Abu Ghosh (father of Ghosh, Arabic family name) see Kiryat-jearim *[I Samuel 7:1; II Samuel 6:3-4]*. Located off the Jerusalem/Tel Aviv Hwy. 8 kms. **W** from Jerusalem City Center.

Abu Tor (father of the ox) Presently active Jewish and Arab community off of the Hebron Road, **E** of the Jerusalem Railway Station. Also called Bet Hananiya (house of Hananiya) Possible first home village of high priest, Caiaphas, during the time of Jesus *[Luke 3:2]*. Border of the southern slope of the Jebusite City of Jerusalem. When Caiaphas became the High Priest, he moved to Mt. Zion in order to be near the Temple *[Matthew 26:3,57]*. See Peter of Galicantu.

Acco See Akko

Acel'dama　(field of blood, Potter's Field) Eastern end of one of the southern slopes of the Valley of Kidron as it meets the Valley of Hinnom. Called today "Hak ed-damn" meaning a bloody field. Judas betrayed Jesus, repented and returned the 30 pieces of silver to the Chief Priests. They bought the field with this 'blood money' in order to bury strangers here *[Matthew 27:1-10; Acts 1:16-19]*. St. Onuphrius Greek Orthodox Monastery built in 1892 stands at the site. See Potter's Field

Ac'hor (troubles) Valley of　SW of Jericho on the plains of Qumran, presently known as el-Buqeiah. Achan and his entire household were brought here and punished by Joshua *[Joshua 7:24]*. God promised that the Valley of A'chor would be a door of hope, as announced by the Prophet Hosea. He prophesied good results from godly discipline and a time of restoration *[Hosea 2:15]*.

Ach'zib, Ach'ziv　(falsehood, deceit) A city on the border of the Asher tribe, near the Mediterranean Sea Coast, 6 kms. N of Akko *[Joshua 19:29; Judges 1:31]*. It is now a deserted tel. Micah, the prophet, said this city would "be a lie to the kings of Israel," *[Micah 1:14]*. A Roman milestone was discovered, together with a large number of tombs from the Israelite period.

Adadah　A city in the southern limits of Judah, presently deserted *[Joshua 15:22]*.

Adam　(red, earth, ground) Presently Tel ed-Damieh on the bank of the Jordan River, near the mouth of the Jabbok and 25 kms. N of Jericho, site where the waters rose in a heap allowing the children of Israel to cross over. A town near the Jordan close to Zaretan bears this name *[Joshua 3:16]*.

Ad'amah　(earth, ground) Fenced city of Naphtali *[Joshua 19:36]*. Presently Tel ed-Damiyeh, 10 km. W of the city of Tiberias on the Sea of Galilee.

Ada'mi-Nekeb　(a hollow, narrow passage) Halfway between Tiberias and Mt. Tabor, this town was formed as a border marker for the tribe of Naphtali. Currently deserted *[Joshua 19:33]*.

Ad'mah   (red earth) One of the border cities of the family of Canaan, descendants of Noah. City in Sidim Valley, Dead Sea Valley. Destroyed with Sodom and Gomorrah. Not identifiable today *[Genesis 10:19; Deut. 29:23]*.

Adora'yim   (two hills) Presently an Arab village in SW of Judah, 8 kms. **SW** of Hebron. It was a Judean city fortified by Rehoboam *[II Chronicles 11:9]*. Archaeologist Robinson identified it as "Dura" where ancient buildings and cave tombs can be seen today.

Adul'lam   (Canaanite city) Presently Tel esh-Sheikh Madhkur 18 kms. **SW** of Jerusalem and 3 kms. **NE** of Beit Jibrin, which became part of Judah's inheritance. One of the resident cities of the Canaanite kings *[Joshua 12:15; 15:35]*. David fled to a cave in this Canaanite city when he was a fugitive, though anointed for kingship, when escaping from King Saul *[I Samuel 22:1; II Chronicles 11:7]*. An alternative name is "the rock of David" *[I Chronicles 11:15]*. See entry below.

Adul'lam Region   A Jewish settlement region between Bet Shemesh and Bet Guvrin, opposite the Hebron Hills, built near and over the ruins of the ancient city. See above. In 1957, land development and settlement began here for more protection along the Israel-Jordan border. Some ruins are visible and identified as Hurvot Adullam.

Adum'im   See Ma'ale Adum'im, Site of the Good Samaritan Inn

Aenon   (springs; fountain GK) – northern site. The Medaba Map has two locations named Aenon. One is in the **N** and located by Eusebius, "seven and a half miles **S** (12 kms.) of Bet Shean". John's gospel describes it as being **W** of the Jordan "in the land of Judea" and "near Salim" *[John 3:22, 23]* This Jordan Valley site fits the description of one of the places where John baptized the repentant *[John 3:23; Matthew 3:13]*. See Bethabara and Medaba.

Aenon   (springs; fountain GK) – southern site. The Medaba Map places the second site where the Jordan empties into the Dead Sea. Traditionally, the place of Jesus' baptism is held to be 9 kms. **N** of the entry point of the Jordan River into the Dead Sea, near Wadi el-Charrar *[Mark 1:9]*. A Greek Orthodox Monastery of St. John stands a short distance from the river. See Bethabara and Medaba.

Afek, Aphek   (strength, fortress) It is identified as Rosh Ha'ayin, near the Yarkon River, just **N** of Petah Tikva, 20 kms. **NE** of Joppa. The Philistines encamped here, drawing a battle line during the time of the Prophet Samuel, defeated Israel *[I Samuel 4:1; 29:1]*. The Ark was captured by the Philistines here *[I Samuel 4:11]*. Although not mentioned in Acts, Paul would have stopped here on his way to Caesarea for trial, as it was near Antipatris, a Roman headquarters *[Acts 23:31]*. See Antipatris.

Ai   (the ruin) Today, thought to be identified as Et-Tel, about 3 kms. **E** of Bet-el, where Abraham pitched his tent and built an altar *[Genesis12:8]*. From Ai, Joshua's army spied out the land *[Joshua 7:2]*. Joshua and the children of Israel won their first great victory within the Promised Land here. Ai was burned by Joshua and became a heap of ruins *[Joshua 8:28]*. The present tel reveals a habitation on the site from 2200 B.C. Archaeologists differ as to the evidence of it being a city or a military outpost from the Israelite period.

Ai'jalon, Ai'jalon, Ayyalon Valley   (place of deer or gazelles) A Levitical city of Dan and a city of refuge *[Joshua 19:42;21:24]*. Throughout history and currently, it was referred to as "the valley", named after this valley town where Joshua, in gaining the victory over the Amorites, commanded the sun and the moon. He ordered, "Oh sun, stand still at Gibeon, and Oh, moon, in the valley of Ai'jalon" *[Joshua 10:12]* The valley lies in the route from the Coastal Plain to the mountain ridge: through Sha'ar Ha Gai and Ma'ale Bet Horon. Today, it is believed to be modern city of Yalo (Yalu) within Canada Park, 28 kms. **W** from Jerusalem in the Judean foothills.

Akeldama   See Aceldama, Field of Blood

Akko   Known as Ptolemais (hot sands GK.) the ancient Greek and Roman name. The site is at Tel-el-Fukhar on northern Mediterranean coast, 53 kms. **S** of Tyre and 173 kms. **N** from Jerusalem. built by Ptolemy, king of Egypt in 100 BC. Akko has the only natural harbor on the coast S of Phoenicia. The apostle Paul arrived here from Tyre and greeted the brethren *[Acts 21:7]*. 13 kms. **N** of the Carmel headland.

Akrabbim, Akravim   (Scorpion's Way) Also known as The Ascent of Akrabbim because of its very steep, winding pathway. Located in the Negev Desert mountains, on the southern border of the Promised Land, this area was also the boundary of Judah's allotment, as appointed by God to the Children of Israel, through Moses *[Numbers 34:4; Joshua 15:3]*. See map of the southern end of the Dead Sea for route.

Alexander Nievsky Church (church of the Russian Saint Nievsky) This Russian church and compound is built partly over Golgotha and part of the rock of Golgotha can be seen inside the church *[Matthew 27:33,59-60; Mark 15:22,46;16:8; Luke 23:33,53; John 19:17;20:1-8]*. It is **E** of the Church of the Holy Sepulcher in the Christian Quarter of Jerusalem's Old City and in its basement can be seen remains of one of the Roman gates that led into the city. See Holy Sepulcher Church.

Allon-Bacuth (oak of weeping) Below Bet-el, the burial place of Devorah, Rebekah's nurse *[Genesis 35:8]*. See Bet-el.

Allon-Melech (oak of the king) The town included in the territory of Asher *[Joshua 19:26]*. See Tribes at back of this book.

Al'mon-Diblatha'im (prim. root to conceal; hiding place of fig sacks) In the wilderness **E** of the Dead Sea, the 51st station of the children of Israel as they journeyed from Ai *[Numbers 33:46,47]*. Some scholars differ and believe this is Riblah in the wilderness, as mentioned by Ezekiel *[Ezekiel 6:14]* and located somewhere in the N of Israel and not near the Dead Sea.

A'lush (crowd) This site along the eastern side of the Red Sea was the second stopping place for the children of Israel after they left the wilderness of Zin. It is identified as being next to Rephidim; the exact location is unknown. There was no water to drink at this encampment and they moved on to Rephidim, where the murmuring took place *[Numbers 33:13,14]*. See Rephidim.

Am'mah (cubit) On the road to the wilderness of Gibeon, close to tel-Jib, 10 kms. **NW** of Jerusalem. Site reached by Joab and Abishai at sundown, while in pursuit of Abner *[II Samuel 2:24]*.

Am'man See Rabbah

Anab, Anav   (grapes) 23 kms. **SW** of Hebron, on the mountains of Judah where Joshua destroyed the Anakim (giants) of Anab, Debir, Hebron and their towns *[Numbers 13:33; Joshua 11:21]*. It is presently called Kiryat Anab, an Arab village and has a tel that extends over 15 dunam with caves, winepresses and the remains of a Byzantine church.

Anata   See Anathot

Anatot   (answers i.e. to prayers) In the land of Benjamin, the priestly inheritance and a city of refuge *[Joshua 21:18]*. The birthplace and hometown of the Prophet Jeremiah, 4 kms. **NE** of Jerusalem, a Levite city *[Jeremiah 1:1; 11:21-23]*. This strong walled city, located on this broad ridge of hills, overlooks the Jordan Valley and the northern part of the Dead Sea. An Arab village called Anata may be sitting on the ruins of ancient Anatot, or indicate its proximity thereof. Presently a modern Jewish village on site.

A'nim   (fountains) A city in the mountains of Judah, 18 kms. **SW** of Hebron, most likely Kiryat Gurwein at Tahta. Joshua allotted A'nim as one of the several cities in the hill country of Judah *[Joshua 15:50]*.

Antipatris   (instead of his father, LT.) Presently Tel Afek and Rosh Ha'Ayin, on main road that the Romans built from Caesarea to Jerusalem, 20 kms. **NE** of Joppa. Herod the Great founded this new city in 20 BC, in honor of his father Antipater. Remnants of a wide Roman paved street, bordered with shops have been excavated. Roman soldiers brought Paul here at night under cavalry escort, to prevent enactment of a death plot against him in Jerusalem *[Acts 23 :31]*. Today we see a Turkish fort built in 1571. See Afek.

Antonio's Fortress, Antonia   (fortress named in honor of Antonius or Mark Anthony) This strong fortress was built by Herod the Great and housed the Roman soldiers. It was located on the **NW** corner of the Temple Mount with a secret passage to the Second Temple. The soldiers kept order in the Temple courts and were continually spying on the Jews. Jesus was arrested, brought here and delivered to Pontius Pilate *[Matthew 27:2; Mark 15:1-8; Luke 23; John 19:5]*. Also spoken of as the army barracks *[Acts 21:37]*. Paul addressed the crowds, after his arrest, from the safety of this fortress *[Acts 22:1-21]*. Remains can be seen at the Sisters of Zion

Convent in the Old City, Moslem Quarter. See Barracks and Ecco Homo

Antonio's Fortress Barracks (army camp, GK) The Roman army camp building in the Antonio next to the Second Temple in Jerusalem. Paul was brought here when he was arrested *[Acts 21:34,37;22:24; 23:10,16,32]*. The exact location today is not clear but most scholars favor the remains underneath the Ecco Homo convent run by the Sisters of Zion. See Ecco Homo

Aphek See Afek

A'qaba (gulf) Jordanian name for Gulf of A'qaba, while in Israel, it is called the Gulf of Eilat at the northern arm of the Red Sea where Solomon's seaport, Etzion Geber, lay. In Solomon's time, this was all part of his kingdom; now it belongs to Jordan *[I Kings 9:26]*. See ancient maps and note that today it is the southern most city in the land of Israel.

Arad (fugitive) A Modern urban city center, recently rebuilt on the bare desert of an upper plateau of the Judean Hills, 45 kms. **E** from Beersheva and about 25 kms. from Zohar by the Dead Sea. Likely, a place passed often by Abraham, Isaac and Lot with their herds. See the surrounding mountains encircled round and round by goat tracks, multi-millennial in age. It is easy to imagine the sun-bronzed, weather-beaten faces of shepherds watching from lower levels of the mountains as the herds scrambled to the top. See the Biblical Tel Arad below.

Arad, Tel Arad (fugitive) Twin tels, 30 kms. **ENE** of Beersheva and 25 kms. **S** of Hebron. See a continuous archaeological record from the period of the Judges to the destruction of the First Temple. Evidence of habitation goes back to 2650 BC but that Arad was destroyed and abandoned before the Israelite Exodus from Egypt and entry into the Promised Land. The western tel has remains of the walled Canaanite City; the eastern one has foundations of a series of Israelite fortresses. The King of Arad and Canaanites attacked the children of Israel *[Numbers 21:1-3; 33,40]*. Joshua conquered Arad *[Joshua 12:14]*.

Arava, Ar'abah (desert) The southern desert and long valley located between the Dead Sea and Eilat, about 178 km. in length *[Deut. 1:1; 2:8; 3:17; 4:49]*. Here King Zedekiah tried to escape Nebuchadnezzar *[II Kings 25:4]*. Isaiah said "the desert shall blossom like a rose" *[Isaiah 35:1]*. He will make a road in the wilderness *[Isaiah 43:19]*. Traveling **S** in the Arava from the Dead Sea, we see the desert blossoming under Israeli technology. We come to the copper mines of Punon. Because of the availability of water, the mines operated and were a source of great wealth for the Edomites and the Nabateans. Ruins can be seen.

Arau'nah's Threshing Floor   (Araunah's 'Jebusite name', even place) This Jebusite, a descendant of the Canaanites from Ham, was also called Ornan and owned a threshing floor on Mt. Moriah. It was an even spot on top of the rock where the sheaves were spread out and beaten. It was considered valuable and guarded all night *[Ruth 3:3-6]*. Araunah (Ornan) sold it to King David as the site for the altar and future First Temple of Israel. King David insisted upon paying for it with the currency of that time although Araunah offered it as a free gift *[II Samuel 24:24; I Chronicles 21:25]*. David's purchase became the site of the Ist and 2nd Temples on the Temple Mount where the Dome of the Rock stands over the threshing floor, in Jerusalem's Old City. See Temple Mount.

Arba   See Kiryat Arba

Arbel, Bet-Arbel   (place of God's ambush) A high ridge, extending very high overlooking the Sea of Galilee, 4 kms. **NW** of Tiberias. Magnificent lookout point. Hosea's prophecy...as Shalman plundered Arbel in the day of battle *[Hosea 10 :14]* Tradition tells us that Dinah, the daughter of Jacob, is buried here. Caves here were occupied by the Jewish zealots fighting Herod in 39 BC. There appears to have been a thriving Jewish community on these hills during the Roman and Byzantine times. Jesus could have visited this synagogue, the remains of which have been dated by a coin found from 106-73 BC, indicating the synagogue was built prior to Jesus' time. Moshav Arbel, on site next to the nature reserve, extends over 1500 dunam (425 acres) and takes its name from this ancient site. See remains of the fortress and synagogue from Roman times.

Archaeological Garden   See Ophel

Arimathea   (city name, translation unclear) A city near Jerusalem. The birthplace and home of Joseph of Arimathea, who was a devoted, wealthy and secret Jewish disciple of Jesus. The body of Jesus was buried in Joseph's personal new tomb which was in Jerusalem *[Matthew 27:57, Mark 15:43, Luke 23:51, John 19:38]*. It is identified as Ramataim, (Ramatayim) also home of Samuel the Prophet, situated just 9 kms. **NW** of Jerusalem in the hill country of Ephraim. See Ramah of Samuel.

Armaged'don   (Har Magedon) See Megiddo and Revelation 16:16

Armenian Quarter of the Old City   The **SW** section of the Old City of Jerusalem occupied by the Christian Armenian people, located on Mt. Zion. See Cathedral of St. James for scripture reference.

Armon Hanatziv   (castle of the representatives) See Mount of Abraham

Ar'non   (rushing torrent) This river rises in the mountains of Gilead, **E** of Jordan River and reaches the Dead Sea and the Dead Sea valley. There is an enormous trench (ditch) adjacent to the valley, known as Wadi Mojib (dry river bed), which runs across the plateau of Moab in Jordan. This deep wadi runs along the eastern side of the Dead Sea opposite Ein Gedi and formed the southern border of the territory of the tribe of Reuven *[Deut. 3:12,16]*. The children of Israel took possession of this area under Joshua and it became the border between Israel and Moab *[Numbers 21:13, 26. Joshua 12:1]*. Isaiah the prophet spoke against Moab *[Isaiah 16:2]*. 72 kms. **E** from Jerusalem in Jordan. See Salt Sea.

Ar'oer   (nudity) One of the three cities that Gad built on the bank of the Arnon River (see above) *[Numbers 32:34; Joshua 13:9]*. Israelites lived here 300 yrs. under the time of the Judges (1380 BC-1045 BC) *[Judges 11:26]*. One of David's 'mighty men' came from here *[II Chron. 11:44]*. Forsaken city as prophesied by *[Isaiah 17:2]*. Now called Khirbet Arair in Jordan, 20 kms. **E** of Dead Sea where a fortress from the Iron Age has been discovered.

Artificial Pool   See Pool of Siloam

Aru'mah   (height) A site a few kms. from Shechem (Nablus) where Abimelech (Avimelech) the son of Gideon dwelt *[Judges 9:41]*. 59 km. **N** of Jerusalem.

Ascension Site   See Mount of Olives

A'shan, Kiryat Ashan   (smoke) A Levitical village in the lowlands of Judah, 8 kms. **NW** of Beersheva, first assigned to Judah, then to Simeon *[Joshua 15:42;19:7]*. It became a priestly village *[I Chronicles 4:32]*. It is identified today at Kiryat Ashan.

Ashdod, Azotus   (Philistine city) Modern port city on Israel's coast, on the ancient Via Maris (the way of the sea), one of five Philistine cities together with Gaza, Gath, Ekron and Ashkelon; the Philistines brought the ark of the covenant here after fighting against the Israelites at the battle of Afek *[I Samuel 5:5,6]*. From the time of King Saul (1020 BC), these cities saw their greatest power through the time of King David and Solomon's monarchy, ending with the destruction of Jerusalem in 586 BC. King Uzziah warred against the Philistines and broke down the wall of Ashdod *[II Chronicles 26:6]*. Amos prophesied against this city *[Amos 3:9]*. The Prophet Zephaniah called for repentance *[Zephaniah 2:4]*. Nehemiah protested against the Israelite men marrying women from Ashdod, who couldn't speak the language of Judah *[Nehemiah 13:23-25]*. Philip baptized the Ethiopian near here and returned here *[Acts 8:26-40]*. Some believe Ein Yael was the site of the Ethiopian's baptism. Ashdod is 66 kms. due **W** from Jerusalem and the tel which is revealed shows 22 strata of settlement, just 3 kms. **S** of the modern city. See Ein Yael.

Ashdod, Port of   Solomon used this port of entry for receiving and then transporting the wood, the cedars of Lebanon and cypress logs, from here to Jerusalem. These logs floated down from Lebanon, by sea, to be used for the construction of the First Temple *[I Kings 6:6, 9-10; II Chronicles 2:8-9]*. See Ashdod above.

Asher, tribe of   (happiness) The area allotted to the tribe of Asher was on the seashore from Carmel northward with Manasseh on the **S** and Zebulun and Issachar on the **SE** and Naphtali on the **NE**. See *[Joshua 19:24-31; 17:10-11; Judges 1:31-32]*. Anna, a prophetess, who rejoiced to see the baby Jesus, was of the tribe of Asher *[Luke 2:36]*. See map of tribes in back of book.

Ash'kelon   (scallion; Philistia city) One of five principal cities of the Philistines. See Ashdod above. Name derived from 'escallot' (scallion) a vegetable grown there in abundance.

Among the important events was the revolt against Ramses II (1280 BC) Judah's conquest of Ashkelon *[Judges 1:18]*. The Prophets, Jeremiah and Zechariah, prophesied against this city, that it would be cut off. *[Jeremiah 47:5,7; Zechariah 9:5]*. Herod the Great was born here and his sister Salome, lived here, therefore, Herod took a personal interest in beautifying it with impressive colonnaded courts (20 BC). It is 71 kms. **SW** from Jerusalem and boasts a modern archaeological park containing the tel of Ashkelon within the city itself.

Ash'tarot, Tel Ashtarot (to be smooth or shiny) Located 34 kms. **E** of the Sea of Galilee in a well-watered plain in Jordan. This ancient site of Bashan was in the allotment for the half tribe of Manasseh *[Deut. 1:4; Joshua 9:10]*. In the capital of Og, the inhabitants were giants and their idol worship to their gods was extremely lewd *[Numbers 21:33]*. God commanded the Israelites to annihilate them, *[Deut. 3:2-6]*. The armor of Saul and his three sons was taken to the temple in Ashtaroth before their bodies were taken to Beth Shean and hung on the walls *[I Samuel 31:10]*.

Atarot (crowns) Allotment to the tribe of Gad, favorable land for livestock, **E** of the Jordan River, 10 kms. from the northeastern shore of the Dead Sea in Jordan *[Numbers 32:3,34]*. Boundary of allotment to Joseph's children *[Joshua 16:2]*.

Atarot Addar (wide crowns) Boundary of Ephraim on the E side *[Joshua 16:5]*. Southern border of Benjamin *[Joshua 18:13]*. 6 kms. **SW** of Beth-el.

Atad (thorn) threshing floor of Ancient city and threshing floor, where Joseph came with his brothers and a great multitude of servants from Egypt as they were enroute to Hebron, to the Cave of Machpelah, to bury their father, Jacob. Seven days of great mourning transpired and the Egyptians named the place Abel Mizraim (mourning of Egypt) *[Genesis 50:10,11]*. In present day Jordan, a thorny locality but not identifiable.

Atarim A caravan route in the Negev followed by the Israelites on their way to the Promised Land. The Canaanites fought against the Israelites and took some prisoners *[Numbers 21:1-3]*. The location is between Mt. Hor and Arad some 30 kms. **S** of Hebron.

Avit, Avith　(to take or seek refuge) An Edomite city, capital of King Hadad before there were kings in Israel *[Genesis 36:35, I Chronicles 1:46]*. In present day Jordan.

Azariyeh　See Bethany and Lazarus' Tomb

Aze'kah　(tilled) A strong town in the plains of Judah where Joshua won a great victory over the Amorites *[Joshua 10:10]*. Boundary of Judah *[Joshua 15:35]*. The Philistines encamped here when David defeated Goliath *[I Samuel 17:1]*. Rehoboam, son of Solomon, strengthened the cities of Judah here *[II Chronicles 11:9]*. After the return from captivity, during Nehemiah's time, there was a resettlement by the Jews *[Nehemiah 11:30]*. See Socoh. Located 18 km **SW** of Hebron, presently Wadi el-Khalil.

Az'mon, Atzmon　(bonelike) A site on the southern border of Israel between Hazaraddar and the 'brook of Egypt, Shihor' *[Numbers 34:4-5]*. Presently in Egypt, 60 kms. **SW** of Arad and 10 kms. N of the Rafiah border crossing.

Azotus　See Ashdod

Ba'alah　(mistress) Called also Kiryat-jearim. A border village of the tribe of Judah on the **N** *[Joshua 15:10]*. David and all of Israel came up here with the ark of God *[I Chronicles 13:6]*. See Kiryat-jearim, 12 km. **N** of Jerusalem.

Ba'alat, Ba'alath　(mistress) A town of the tribe of Dan near Sorek River, 15 kms. **E** of Ashdod *[Joshua 19:44]*. This city was fortified by King Solomon *[I Kings 9:18; II Chronicles 8:6]*.

Ba'ale-Judah　(lords of Judah) Perhaps the same as Ba'alah, from which place David had the ark carried to Jerusalem *[II Samuel 6:2]*. See Ba'alah above.

Ba'ale-Gad　(lord of fortune) A Canaanite city at the foot of Mt. Hermon in the **N**. Therefore, also called Ba'ale Hermon *[Joshua 11:17, 12:7; Judges 3:3]*.

Ba'ale-Hamon　(lord of the multitude) The site where Solomon had a vineyard where caretaker tenants worked *[Song of Solomon 8:11]*. The location is most likely near the Palace in Jerusalem, in the gardens near Kidron.

Ba'ale-Hatzor   (landlord owning a village) Site near Ephraim on the **N** border of the Samaritan Hills, 10 kms. **NE** of Ramallah and 20 kms. **NE** of Jerusalem, where Absalom, David's son, had a sheep farm and where he murdered Amnon, his brother *[II Samuel 13:23]*. Today called Tel Asur, on the summit of the hill of 1000 meters (3320 ft.) above sea level. There are many ancient trees here and houses, also a church from the Byzantine period.

Ba'ale-Hermon   (lord of Hermon) The mountain range **E** of Lebanon. A city also called Ba'ale-Gad (see above) where the Israelites tried to expel the Hivites from the land *[Joshua 13:5; Judges 3:3]*. 220 kms. **N** from Jerusalem. See Hermon.

Ba'ale-Me'on,   (house, lord of the dwelling) Town located
Beth Ba'ale Meon   15 kms. **E** of the Dead Sea in Jordan, rebuilt by the Reubenites with the name changed to Bet Meron *[Numbers 32:38; Joshua 13:17]*. Presently known as Ma'in, a modern Jordanian village 7 kms. **SW** of Madeba which is built on these ancient ruins. Remains from a Byzantine church, with interesting mosaics of Holyland sites, can be seen here.

Ba'ale-Perazim   (possessor of breaches) Called Mt. Perazim *[Isaiah 28:21]*. An old Canaanite sanctuary where David fought the Philistines in his attempt to conquer Jerusalem *[II Samuel 5:20; I Chronicles 14:11]*. The exact location is unknown but it appears to be in Jerusalem, possibly the village of Shurafat or Abu Tor, near the Valley of Rephraim.

Ba'ale-Shalisha   (lord of the Shalisha, a foreign god, "triangular") Also called Shalilsha, a district next to Mt. Ephraim, **W** of Gilgal *[II Kings 4:38,42]*. A man was sent with provisions for Elisha, the prophet, from here *[I Samuel 9:4]*. 2 kms. **NW** from Jericho or 15 kms. N from Jerusalem.

Ba'ale-Tamar   (lord of the date palm trees) 5 kms. **NE** of Jerusalem. The site of the palm trees of Deborah where she judged Israel *[Judges 4:4-5; Judges 20:33]*. It is present day Erhah.

Babylon   (babal, to confound) The ancient city state on the plain of Shinar. The children of Israel were dispersed here after the destruction of Jerusalem and the Temple by Nebuchadnezzar, in 586 BC. Many New Testament Christians see Babylon as a "great harlot" and prefigures political Babylon, which some Christians see will be the political situation on the earth in the end times. They see this great 'harlotry' being destroyed as a prerequisite to the return of Jesus Christ *[Revelation 16:19,17:5-18, 17:15-18,18:2-21]*. Present day Iraq. See map in back of this book.

Bahurim   (young men) A village of Judah on the road from Jerusalem to Jordan, **E** of Mount Olivet *[II Samuel 3:16]*. In David's encounter with Shimei, Saul's relative, he was cursed and stones were thrown at him *[II Samuel 16:5,6]*. David's spies hid here *[II Samuel 17:18]*. Now, it is the Arab village Ras et-Tmim, just **E** of Mt. Scopus and some scholars believe it is the ancient city of Bethphage, also called Abu Dis. See Bethphage.

Ba'moth, Ba'moth-Ba'al   (heights of Baal) The 47th station of the children of Israel, in the country of Moab (Jordan), as they made their way to the Promised Land *[Numbers 21:19-20]*. The boundary of Reuven *[Joshua 13:17]*. It is **E** of the Jordan River and the Arnon River. 72 kms. **E** from Jerusalem in Jordan.

Banias   See Ba'ale Gad and Caesarea Phillippi.

Barracks   (army camp GK) See Antonio Fortress

Ba'shan   (smooth; rockless plain AK) Moses gave this vast, fertile territory, from Gilead in the **S**, to Hermon in the **N**, as a possession to the half tribe of Manasseh *[Joshua 22:7]*. This large region included the area **E** of the Jordan River, Lake Hulah and the Kinneret (Sea of Galilee); 11,200 sq. kms. Og, the king of Bashan, was a giant and was defeated by the Israelites *[Deut. 3:11]*. "A mountain of God is the mountain of Bashan, a mountain of many peaks," *[Psalm 68:15; Jeremiah 50:19]*. The psalm most likely refers to Mt. Hermon. 225 kms. **N** from Jerusalem. See Ashtaroth.

Bashan-Havvoth Jair   See Havvoth Jair

Basilica of the Agony   See Gethsemane

Beatitudes   See Mount of Beatitudes, the Sermon on the Mount *[Matthew 5,6,7]*.

Beautiful Gate   See Eastern Gate

Be'er Lahai Roi   (well of him that lives and sees or the well of the vision of life) The well between Kadesh and Bered, 20 kms. **S** of Beersheva, where the Lord found Hagar weeping and in great distress *[Genesis 16:14]*. Isaac prayed at the well and meditated in the field before he looked up and saw Rebekah coming to him *[Genesis 24:62]*. Isaac and Rebecca dwelt here after Abraham's death *[Genesis 25:11]*. The exact location is not known.

Be'ersheva   (well of the oath) The modern town lies 4 kms. **SE** of the Biblical town. It is the Capital of the Negev, a modern settlement dating from 1900. See below.

Be'ersheva, Tel   (the hill of the well of the oath) Midway between the Mediterranean Sea and the southern part of the Dead Sea. Abraham made a covenant here with Abimelech *[Genesis 21:31]*. Both Abraham and Isaac had their homes here. They dug a well here *[Genesis 26:33]*. Jacob offered sacrifices to God here on his way to Egypt *[Genesis 46:1-5]*. Samuel's sons were judges in Beersheva *[I Samuel 8:2]*. We say FROM DAN TO BE'ERSHEVA as a formula for the entire land of Israel. This phrase was a customary designation which began during the days of the Judges *[Judges 20:1; II Samuel 3:10]*. After Elijah fled from Jezebel, he sought refuge in Be'ersheva *[I Kings 19:3]*. 77 kms. **SW** from Jerusalem.

Beit Sahour   See Shepherd's Field *[Luke 2:8-21*

Bela   See Zoar

Bene Brak   (sons of lightning) One of the cities of Dan *[Joshua 19:45]*. Presently Ibn Abrak, 7 km. **E** of Jaffa.

Ben-Hinnom, Valley of   See Hinnom Valley

Benjamin Gate   (son of joy or right hand gate) See Sheep Gate

Benjamin Tribe Area   (son of joy or right hand) The border went from the **S** side of Luz (Bet el) and descended to Ataroth Addar, near the hill that lies on the **S** side of Bet Horon *[Genesis 49:27; Joshua 18:11-28]*. See maps of tribes, back of book.

Berachah, Valley of   (blessing) See Johosh'aphat, Valley of

Be'red   (hail, hailstones) A site 20 km. **S** of Beersheva where the well Lahai-roi (the well of him who lives and sees) is located near Kadesh. See Beer Lahai-roi.

Besor   (to bear tidings, news) A brook flowing into the Mediterranean Sea, 9 kms. **S** of Gaza. The place where David's weary troops remained behind, while he pursued the Amalekites *[I Samuel 30:9, 10, 21]*. Presently called Wadi Gaza.

Bet-She'arim   (house of gates; Besara GK) After the monarchy of Solomon was divided, settlement probably began here. It is located in lower Galilee on the southern slope of a hill near Kiryat Tivon, 131 kms. **N** from Jerusalem, 20 kms. **SE** from Haifa. It is only mentioned in the NT in connection with Bernice (the daughter of Agrippa I and sister of Agrippa II) as her estate was here *[Acts 25:13,23]*. After the destruction of Jerusalem by Titus in 70 AD, Bet-Shearim became the head of the Sanhedrin and reached a position of great importance. In the second century the great Rabbis, like Judah ha-Nasi and others took up residence and are buried here.

Beten   (belly, hollow) City on the border of the tribe of Asher **E** of Mt. Carmel *[Joshua 19:25]*. Presently called Abtum, a village 152 kms. **N** from Jerusalem.

Bethab'ara   (house of the ford) Bethany beyond the Jordan site. Gideon captured the Midianites here and their water holes *[Judges 7:24]*. The place on the **E** bank of the Jordan River where John the Baptist was baptizing *[John 1:28]*. The 6th C. Medeba map shows this site. Plans are being made by the Israel Ministry of Tourism to set up a baptismal site here in the near future, as a joint project between the Ministry of Tourism of Israel and Jordan. 38 kms. **E** from Jerusalem.

Beth-anat   (house of the goddess) The modern city of Anat, 20 kms. **E** of Akko. It retains the name of the fortified city of Naphtali, named with Beth Shemesh *[Joshua 19:38]*. The Canaanites remained here during Joshua's time *[Judges 1:33]*.

Beth-anot   (house of the goddess Anoth) Just 4 kms. N of Hebron, a town in the mountains of Judah *[Joshua 15:59]*. 35 kms. from Jerusalem.

Beth'any   (house of misery, poverty) Located on eastern slope of Mt. Olivet on the Mt. of Olives, 2 kms. **NE** from the Old City Jerusalem. It was called the house of misery because of its lonely site and the many disabled people who came here. Simon the leper lived here. It was the home of Martha, Mary and Lazarus. Jesus visited their home often *[Matthew 21:17; Matthew 26:6; Mark 11:1, Mark 14:3, Luke 10:38, Luke 19:29]*. Jesus raised Lazarus from the dead at Bethany *[John 11:1-44]*. Presently called El Eizariyya in Arabic (place of Lazarus), an inhabited Arab village with several churches.

Bethany beyond the Jordan   See Bethabara, Matthew 3

Beth Barah   (house of the ford, shallow part of a body of water) A chief ford of the Jordan River, near the ford, Jabbok, over which Jacob crossed *[Genesis 32:22]*. The site of Gideon's fantastic victory over the Midianites *[Judges 7:24]*. Jephthah slew the Ephraimites on this site *[Judges 12:5]*. See Oreb, rock of. Exact location is uncertain, perhaps 38 kms. from Jerusalem **NE** on the Jordan River, 9 kms. **E** of Jericho. Possibly the same as Bethab'ara.

Beth Dagon   (house of Dagon, the fish god) A site in the low country of Judah 9 kms. from Lydda and **S** of Tel Aviv off the Ramla Rd. Boundary of the tribe of Asher near Philistia *[Joshua 15:41; 19:27]*. The village that was called Kiryat Dajun and now, a memorial to the fallen soldiers from the War of Independence marks the spot. After 1948, the village was renamed Bet HaKerem Ha Kayemet.

Beth E'ked   (house of the binding of the shepherds, shearing house) A place on the road between the Jezreel Valley and the hills of Samaria, 23 kms. **NE** from Samaria. Jehu was on his way to Samaria as he was intent on killing all those who remained of the house of the wicked Ahab. He killed 42 members of the royal family of Judah here *[II Kings 10:12-14]*. The exact location is unknown.

Beth'el, Bet-el   (house of God) 17 kms. **N** of Jerusalem and 4 kms. **NE** of Ramallah, also known as Luz *[Genesis 28:19]*. Here Abraham encamped *[Genesis 12:8;13:3]*. Jacob dreamed and saw a heavenly ladder. Jacob said, "How awesome is this place, …house of God, gate of heaven." *[Genesis 28:10-22]*. The Lord appeared to Jacob here *[Genesis 35:9,13-15]*. Joshua assigned it to the tribe of Benjamin. It was the place where the ark was brought after the Israelites assembled together at Shiloh *[Joshua 18:1; Judges 20:26-28]*. Samuel held court here *[I Samuel 7:16]*. Jeroboam sinned and set up an altar here *[I Kings*

12:29]. Josiah removed Jeroboam's altar and restored true worship *[II Kings 23:15-20]*. The tel is presently next to the modern Arab village of Beitin 880 meters (2886 ft.) above sea level) on the low, rocky ridge between two wadis. A new Jewish settlement, named Bet-el, stands on a nearby site.

Bethes'da (healing place; house of grace, GK) Next to the Sheep Gate. In Jerusalem's Old City, a spring-fed pool with 5 porches, where invalids used to come to be healed *[John 5:2-4]*. Here, on a Sabbath day, Jesus healed a man by this pool, who was crippled for 38 years *[John 5:1-9]*. This pool can be seen next to St. Anne's Crusader church, and the ruins of a church from the 4th century. Located in the Moslem Quarter of the Old City near St. Stephen's Gate (Lion's Gate). See Pool of the Kings.

Beth-ezel (a near place) Town in southern Judah, 5 kms. **E** of Tel Bet Mirsim. Prophet Micah sounded judgment on Judah and said Beth-ezel would mourn *[Micah 1:11]*. Now Deir el'Asa, (monastery of honey) a small Arab village 17 kms. **SW** of Hebron. Remains from the Bronze Age and Roman Period can be seen.

Beth-Gamul (house of recompense) City in Moab, 10 kms. **E**. of Dibon, between the Arnon and Ummer Rasas. The prophet Jeremiah spoke words of judgment against Beth-Gamul *[Jeremiah 48:23]*. Site identified as Kiryat Jemeil in Jordan. See Moab.

Beth-Gilgal (house of Gilgal) See Gilgal.

Beth-HaKerem (house of the vineyard) A Judean town. The leader of Beth-HaKerem, Malchijah repaired the 'Refuse Gate' (misnamed the Dung Gate) under Nehemiah *[Nehemiah 3:14]*. King Jehoiakim, one of the last kings of Judah (609-587 BC) built a large palace here *[Jeremiah 22:13-17]*. Jeremiah warned the children of Benjamin concerning the coming destruction of Jerusalem. "...set up a signal fire in Beth HaKerem," *[Jeremiah 6:1]*. Now it is identified as Ramat Rachel, in the southern suburbs of Jerusalem and a modern kibbutz hotel is on the site; 4 kms. from city center.

Beth-Haggan (house of the garden) The place from which King Ahaziah fled from Jehu *[II Kings 9:27]*. This house stood some distance from the city of Jezreel itself. The exact site is not identified. 95 kms. **N** from Jerusalem near Jezreel Valley.

Beth-Hannanya   See Abu Tor

Beth-Haram   (house of the height) A town **N** of the Dead Sea on the boundary of Gad, opposite Jericho, 10 km. **E** of the Jordan River *[Joshua 13:27]*. Named Julias by Herod in honor of the wife of Augustus. Identified as Tel er Ramah, at the mouth of the hot springs where Herod Antipas built a palace. In Jordan today.

Beth-Hoglah   (house of the partridge) A site on the border between the tribes of Judah and Benjamin *[Joshua 15:6,18:19]*. Presently Dir Hijleh next to Ein Hajlah Springs, 6 kms. **SE** of Jericho off the new Jericho-Dead Sea Road. The remains here show Roman and Byzantine remains.

Beth-Horon   (house or place of the hollow) Today the Latrun-Ramallah road runs through this mountain pass, 25 kms. **W** of Jerusalem. This site is on the boundary line between the tribes of Benjamin and Ephraim. Joshua's forces, while defending their allies the Gibeonites, defeated the armies of five attacking Amorite kings of Gibeon and chased down survivors along the road to Beth-Horon *[Joshua 10:10; 11;16:3,5]*. The Philistine raiders came against Israel here *[I Samuel 13:18]*. King Solomon built 2 cities, Upper Beth Horon and Lower Beth Horon and fortified them with walls, gates and bars *[II Chronicles 8:5]*. Presently there are two Arab villages on the sites and can be seen, Upper is 8 kms. from Gibeon called Ur al-Fawqa on the ascent and Lower is opposite Upper Beth-Horon, called Beit Ghur el Fauqa.

Beth-Jamal   (house of lion AK) The village of Gamala which was the hometown of Rabbi Gamaliel, who taught Paul *[Acts 22:3]* 2 kms. **S** from Beth-Shemesh on the Beth-Shemesh-Valley of Elah road. A Greek Orthodox Monastery and agricultural school stands on the site which is entered **E** on a dirt road. Byzantine remains, mosaics and tombs have been discovered.

Beth'lehem, Bet-Lehem   (house of bread) Bethlehem of Judah, (Judea) a more distinctive title. Christian/Moslem Arab city in Judean hills 7 kms. **S** of Jerusalem where Jesus was born as prophesied by the Prophet Micah *[Micha 5:2; Luke 2:1-20; Matthew 2:1]*. In Jacob's time it was known as Ephratha (Efrata) and Jacob buried Rachel here *[Genesis 35:19;48:7]*. Ruth came here with her mother-in-law, Naomi, and the Lord visited her *[Ruth 1:9]*. Ruth married Boaz and gave him a son Obed, who was the great-grandfather of King David *[Ruth 4:13-14]*. David was born and anointed King in Bethlehem and it was sometimes called the City of David (his home town) but not to be confused with Jerusalem *[I Samuel 16:1; 20:6]*. "…unto us a child is born, unto us a son is given *[Isaiah 9:6]*. Joseph, the husband of Mary, was born in Bethlehem and was from the House of David and had to take Mary his wife, who was also from the House of David to register according to the Roman authority *[Luke 1:27; 2:4]*. Christians see Jesus as the 'Bread of Life' so they feel the town is appropriately named. See Church of the Nativity and Shepherds Field. Currently under Palestinian control.

Mary, did you know?

Mary, did you know, that your Baby Boy
will one day walk on water?
Mary, did you know, that your Baby Boy
will save our sons and daughters?
Did you know that your Baby Boy
has come to make you new?
This child that you've delivered
will soon deliver you?
Mary, did you know that your Baby Boy
will give sight to a blind man?
Mary, did you know that your Baby Boy
will calm a storm with His hand?
Did you know that your Baby Boy
has walked where angels trod?
and when you kiss your little Baby
You've kissed the face of God?

Mark Lowry

Beth-Ma'acah   (house of Ma'acah) 1 km. **WNW** of Tel Dan (Laish) and 10 kms. **WNW** of Caesarea Phillippi (Banias), near the sources of the Jordan River. Joab came here in pursuit of Sheba, son of Bichi *[II Samuel 20:14]*. The present site is Tel Abil.

Beth-Mar Caboth   (places of chariots) The southern border town of Judah, in the tribe of Simeon. Some of descendants of Shimei, who was the one who cursed David, dwelt here *[Joshua19:5; II Samuel 16:5; IChronicles 4:31]*. It was one of Solomon's Chariot Cities where he kept his chariots and horses ready for war. The exact location is unclear.

Beth-Milo   (house of Milo) also "the filling" The soldiers of the garrison at this site proclaimed Abimelech their king. The name of the citadel (tower) at Shechem *[Judges 9:6, 20]*. 59 kms. **N** from Jerusalem.

Beth-Pe'or   (house or temple of Peor) A site in Moab, E of Jordan River and famous for its idolatry; allotted to the tribe of Reuben *[Joshua 13:20]*. Moses rehearsed the law of Israel to the congregation in the valley next to Beth-Peor. "...and He (God) buried him in the valley in the land of Moab, opposite Beth-Peor, but no one knows his grave to this day *[Deut. 34:5-6]*. In Jordan, exact location unclear.

Beth'phage   (house of unripe figs) On the Mt. of Olives in Jerusalem, on the old route from Jerusalem to Jericho, close to Bethany. The Triumphal Entry of Jesus began at Bethphage as He entered Jerusalem. The disciples found a colt and Jesus rode on it into Jerusalem *[Matthew 21:1-11]*. Evangelicals see the fulfillment of Zechariah's prophecy in Matthew's description of Jesus' entry into Jerusalem *[Zechariah 9:9; Matthew 21:5]*. Ancient tradition tells us that the Prophetess Hulda is buried here. Presently Arab city of Abu Dis 3 km. **E** of Jerusalem, on the fringe of the Judean desert.

Beth-Re'hob   (roomy house) Northern town near Dan (Laish) in the valley in the upper part of the Hula lowlands. The Israelites built the city and dwelt there during the period of the Judges *[Judges 18:28]*. The central source of the Jordan River flows from springs nearby. The Ammonites took foot soldiers from this site to fight against David *[II Samuel 10:6-8]*. 223 kms. **N** from Jerusalem.

Beth-Sahur   See Shepherd's Field

Bethsa'ida (house of fishing; from Aramaic root) City on the **NE** coast of Galilee on the road to Caesarea Phillippi (Banias), home of Andrew and Philip and often visited by Jesus *[John 1:44;12:21]*. Jesus scolded this town for not receiving Him *[Luke 10:13]*. It was a lonely, desolate place where Jesus fed the 5000 *[Luke 9:10-17]*. He cured a blind man here *[Mark 8:22-26]*. Josephus tells us Philip, the tetrarch, raised it up, renewed it in the Hellenistic style and renamed it Julias, after Julia, wife of Augustus. (Ant. 5 8 20) Philip is buried here. It is identified as Et-tel just **NE** of the Jordan River bank, **N** of the Sea of Galilee. Extensive excavations are going on presently and various remains have been uncovered. See Julias.

Beth-Shean, Bet-Shean, Beth-shan Tel (house of security mount) Perhaps house of the Babylonian god, Shaman, since this is a very ancient site, founded 3000 BC in the valley of Esdraelon (Tel el-Husn) "mound of the fortress." It is 120 meters (390ft.) below sea level. The excavations reveal that it was once a important station for caravans and a center for Egyptian rule some in 1400 BC. Today in the Bet Shean Valley on the road from Jericho to the Sea of Galilee in the Jordan Valley, we find an interesting, restored site from the Roman period, with levels from many periods. One of the most impressive and interesting archaeological sites in Israel, marking the longest, unbroken occupation, with twenty layers of settlement discovered. Saul and his three sons were slain by the Philistines on Mount Gilboa but their bodies were brought here to Beth Shean and hung on the walls *[I Samuel 31:8-10]*. King David conquered the city *[I Kings 4:12]*. Paul makes a point for the 'new man' *[Colossians 3:11]*. The park is 115 kms. **NE** of Jerusalem, by the Jordan Valley road and 37 kms. **S** from Tiberias.

Beth-Shemesh (house of the sun) A city of Dan also called Ir-shemesh on the border of the Judean foothills, 5 kms. **S** of the Shimshon junction and 27 kms. **W** of Jerusalem. It was once a major Canaanite city-state before it was a priestly city with pasture lands *[Joshua 19:41;21:16, I Samuel 6:5, 9-12; I Chronicles 6:59]*. A fierce battle erupted here in which Amaziah and Judah was defeated *[II Chronicles 25:21-23]*. The Ark of the Covenant was returned to this place *[I Samuel 4:6; 5:1-16]*. It is known today as tel er-Rumeileh. It is also a thriving, busy Jewish city, founded in 1950, on the site of the military outpost held by Israel's army during the War of Independence.

Beth-Shittah   (house of the acacia) The town called Shattah (site of a prison) 5 kms. **N** of Bet Shean, just **W** of the Jordan River, where the Midianites fled from Gideon's army *[Judges 7:22]*. 120 kms. **N** from Jerusalem in the Jordan Valley.

Beth-Tappuah   (house of apples) 9 kms. **W** of Hebron, same as Taffuh, boundary of Judah *[Joshua 15:53]*.

Beth-Zur   (house of rock) 7 kms. **N** from Hebron, a fortress city of Rehoboam, Solomon's son *[II Chronicles 11:7]*. Nehemiah, son of Azbuk, was a leader over half of the district of Beth-Zur *[Nehemiah 3:16]*. In 165 BC Judas, the Maccabeus defeated the Greeks here and built strong fortifications on this site.

Beyond the Jordan sites   refers to places on the eastern bank of the Jordan River, formerly called Trans Jordan, in the country of Jordan, but allotted to the Israelites.

Bezek   (lightning) Khirbet Ibziq, 20 kms. **NE** of Shechem inhabited by the Canaanites and the Perizzites and the home of Adoni-bezek who was the King or Lord of this Canaanite city. 10,000 Canaanites were killed here by Judah after the death of Joshua *[Judges 1:4-5]*. Adoni-Bezek was captured and received retributive justice *[Judges 1:5-7]*. Saul gathered his forces (300,000) here before going against Jabesh-gilead *[I Samuel 11:1-11]*. See maps and Ezekiel's vision at back of the book.

Bezer   (to cut off, make inaccessible) **E** of the Jordan River, 14 km. **NE** of Medeba. A Reubenite city now in Jordan and a city of refuge *[Deut. 4:43; Joshua 20:8]*.

Bochim   (weepers) A site **W** of the Jordan River, near Bethel and Shiloh, place named for the tears shed by the unfaithful people upon the Lord's reproving them. The angel of the Lord announces judgment here *[Judges 2:1-5]*. 15 kms. **NE** from Jerusalem.

Borders of Israel   The original and present boundaries and borders of Israel. See border page and maps back of this book. See Ezekiel's vision map at back.

Boz'kat   (to swell, make larger) Located on the border of Judah near Lachish and Eglon *[Joshua 15:39]*. The birthplace of Adaiah who was grandfather of King Josiah *[II Kings 22:1]*. 20 kms. W of Hebron.

Boz'rah   (a fortress, to enclose or gather) **SE** of the Dead Sea near Buseira in Jordan. A city of Edom and residence of Jobab *[Genesis 36:33; I Chronicles 1:44]*. It is identified as the Edomite metropolis city called Buseirah and was famous for its dyed garments. Isaiah pronounced judgment on the Edomites saying that "…the Lord required a sacrifice in Bozrah *[Isaiah 34:6;63:1]* Both Jeremiah and Amos echoed Isaiah's prophecies *[Jeremiah 49:13; Amos 1:12]* 20 kms. **SE** from the southern tip of the Dead Sea and 90 kms. from Jerusalem. A moshav by the same name is in southern Israel near Ra'ananah but has no connection to the ancient site

Broad Wall   Nehemiah was called by God to rebuild the walls of Jerusalem after the destruction of Jerusalem by Nebuchadnezzar (586 BC) and the exile of the Jews from the land. Nehemiah, who was in the court of Persia and won favor there *[Nehemiah 2:6-8]*. He came to Jerusalem (444 BC) to rebuild *[Nehemiah 3:8; 12:38]*. See the remains of this wall, which may be viewed, inside the Jewish quarter of the Old City in Jerusalem on Plugat Ha Kotel Street. See Ancient Gates at the back of this book.

Brook of Cherith   See Monastery of St. George and Wadi Kelt

Brook of Egypt, River of Egypt   (nahal, small river bed) Called Shihor, the southern border as dictated by God through Moses "…the border shall turn from Azmon to the Brook of Egypt and it shall end at the Sea" *[Numbers 34:5; Joshua 15:4,47]*. David gathers all Israel together here *[I Chronicles 13:5]*. King Solomon held a Feast here for 14 days *[I Kings 8:65; II Chronicles 7:8]*. Israel blossoms in the kingdom here and within *[Isaiah 27:12]*. Ezekiel speaks of Israel's boundary extending here *[Ezekiel 47:19;48:28]*. Presently El-Arish, the great wadi (nahal) and it is actually a desert stream that flows rapidly in winter during the rainy season and it is also called the Wadi of Egypt. See the southern border of Israel with Egypt. See maps of borders.

Brook of Mis'rephot   See Misrephot-maim

Ca'bul   (a fetter, sterile, worthless) A city on the **E** border of Asher, 16 kms. **SE** of Akko. Part of the district Solomon gave to Hiram, king of Tyre, in return for his services rendered in building the temple in Jerusalem, but Hiram was displeased and showed his displeasure to Solomon *[I Kings 9:13]*.

Cave of Nicanor   (caver shel Nicanor, GK) In the courtyard of the Hebrew University on Mt. Scopus is a tomb which is in a burial cave. A stone coffin was discovered, engraved in GK: "The bones of Nicanor of Alexandria who built the gate." The wealthy Jewish man Nicanor from Alexandria, Egypt donated the magnificent bronze gates for the Second Temple courtyard." Josephus said that they shone like pure gold. Mt. Scopus in Jerusalem, 3 kms. **E** of City Center.

Caesarea Maritima   (pertaining to the title of the Roman Emperor GK) This site is on the Mediterranean Sea, on the great coast from Egypt to Tyre, 48 kms. **S** of Haifa, 105 kms. **NW** from Jerusalem. Originally called Strato's Tower (90 BC) but rebuilt by Herod in his grand manner and renamed Caesarea in honor of Augustus Caesar. It was a marvel in ancient engineering as this port held an entire Roman fleet. Josephus tells us that Pontius Pilate was resting here, on vacation, when he was suddenly called back to Jerusalem to help quiet an uproar over a young Jewish man whom the Jews wanted to crucify. This man was Jesus. Pontius Pilate remained the governor here from 6 AD. One of the Capitals of the Byzantine Empire after Constantine became a Christian in 325 AD. Philip stopped here at the end of his preaching tour *[Acts 8:40]*. Paul was taken here by the brethren before continuing to Tarsus *[Acts 9:30]*. Cornelius, the Roman centurion had a vision, sent for Peter and received the good news of salvation in Caesarea *[Acts 10]*. Peter came here *[Acts 10:23-24]*. Herod, the King returns here *[Acts 12:19]*. Paul returned here and greeted the church *[Acts 18:22, 21:8,16; Acts. 23:23, 33]*. Paul appears before Festus, King Agrippa and his sister Bernice *[Acts 25:1-14]*. One of the best and most beautiful National Park sites and is presently an active dig with exciting history now emerging from the sands every day.

Caesarea Philippi   (Caesarea of Philippi) This is Banias, once named Pan for the Canaanite god Pan, in northern Israel, 200 kms. **N** from Jerusalem, renamed Philippi by Herod Philip, son of Herod the Great, to distinguish it from Caesarea on the coast. It had been a Canaanite sanctuary for the worship of Ba'al. It was the most northeast of Jesus travels'. He came here with His disciples and asked Peter, the question, "Who do men say that I am?"*[Mark 8:27-33; Luke 9:18]*. From this time on, from Caesarea Philippi, Jesus began to tell the disciples His purpose in continuing to Jerusalem, His plans and His crucifixion *[Matthew 16:21]*. Another beautiful National Park site. See Ba'al Hermon.

The Outdoor Son of God

My Master was a man who knew
the rush of rain, the drip of dew.
He was a man of sun and stars.
He knew the planets and Mars.
That star-trail called the Milky Way,
the crescent moon, the dawn, the day.
To Him there was no sweeter tones
than water washing over stones.
To Him, no splendid symphony like murmuring
Blue Galilee.
His skin, it had the look of one
who knew the blazing balm of sun.
His feet were stained by dusty ways,
His face was tanned as autumn days.
His heart and hair were washed by showers,
He loved the wayside fields and flowers.
The sea and tree, the star and sod;
He was the outdoor Son of God.

William Stidger

Caiaphas House   See Peter of Galicantu.

Caiaphas Tomb   (family name, Aramaic root) Recently excavated 1994, located in the Peace Forest, near the Haas Promenade, in the Abu Tor area of Jerusalem. 4 kms. **S** from city center. Caiaphas was the High Priest of the Jews in the reign of Tiberias Caesar, at the beginning of Jesus' ministry *[Luke 3:2]*. He advocated the condemnation of Jesus and His ultimate death *[Matthew 26:3, 57]*.

Calvary (kranion, skull GK) See Calvary, Garden Tomb, Holy Sepulcher Church

Cana (Cana of Galilee) Arab Christian village of Kfar Cana, 7 kms. **N** of Nazareth on the road to Tiberias. The birthplace of Nathanael, disciple of Jesus *[John 21:2]*. The site of the miracle of changing the water into wine, Jesus' first recorded miracle *[John 2:1,11; John 4:46]*.

Ca'naan (to be humbled) The term is used "the land of Ca'naan" and covers all of Israel **W** of the Jordan River and the Tigris-Euphrates in the **NE** and the Nile River in Egypt in the **S**. The Lord spoke to Moses and said, "When you come into the land of Ca'naan, this is the land which shall fall to you as an inheritance" *[Numbers 34:1-29]*. See maps of ancient borders at back of book.

Capernaum (village of Nahum, village of comfort) Located on the western shore of the Sea of Galilee, Jesus called this Jewish town, 'His hometown'. No doubt He found comfort and solace here. "And leaving Nazareth He came and dwelt in Capernaum."*[Matthew 4:13; 8:5; 11:23,17:24]*. Here He chose Matthew, or Levi and here, the two brothers Simon Peter and Andrew, made their homes by the sea *[Mark 1:21; 2:1; 9:33, Luke 4:31;7:1]*. Simon Peter's mother-in-law lay sick and was healed *[Mark 1:29-31]*. Jesus eventually rebukes Capernaum for its unbelief *[Luke 10:15]*. After the miracle at Cana he came here with his family *[John 2:12]*. The nobleman came from Cana and Jesus healed his son *[John 4:46]*. Jesus walked on the water near here *[John 6:17, 24]*. Of great interest is the limestone synagogue built over the synagogue of Jesus and an octagonal church built over Peter's house. The Franciscans run the site. See below. 157 kms. **N** from Jerusalem.

Capernaum Octagon Church A Roman Catholic church named for Peter stands between the synagogue and the seashore and experts agree that it is built over the ruins of Peter's house *[Mark 1:29]*. Jesus gives the disciples a lesson in servitude *[Mark 9:33]*. He enters Simon's Peters' house *[Luke 4:38-39]*.

Capernaum Synagogue See part of the Ist C. synagogue here. The limestone structure, dated 400 AD, stands on top of the ruins of the synagogue of Jesus. Jairus, one of the rulers of the synagogue begged Jesus to heal his daughter *[Mark 5:22; Luke 8:41-48]*. Jesus casts out demons *[Luke 4:31-37]*. Jesus teaches the disciples and the multitudes *[John 6:24-59]*. "These things He said in the synagogue as He taught in Capernaum"*[John 6:59]*. See Capernaum above.

Cardo (heart) The name cardo itself doesn't actually appear in the Bible but it was a Roman term used just after Jesus' time and was the main street in the Old City of Jerusalem, running **N** to **S**, called the Cardo Maximus. The Cardo itself is from the Roman period, after the destruction of Jerusalem and the Temple in 70 AD. See it in the Jewish Quarter of the Old City in Jerusalem. See the Medeba mosaic map on display in the Cardo.

Carmel (vineyard, field park garden) This prominent mountain range in the **N** fell to the tribe of Asher, bordered by the Bay of Akko in the **S** and running out almost to the Mediterranean sea. It abruptly ends on its eastern side with a steep bluff. Its average height is 1500 feet (546 meters). The Canaanites worshipped Ba'al on these gardenlike mountains. King Jokeam of Carmel was conquered by Joshua *[Joshua 12:22]*. Saul set up a "monument" here after his victory over Amalek *[I Samuel 15:12]*. It is most famous for its story connected to the life of Elijah and the prophets of Ba'al *[I Kings18:20-40]*. Here Elisha received the woman whose dead son he was to restore *[II Kings 4:25]*. Isaiah compares the coming kingdom to the excellence of Carmel *[Isaiah 35:2]*. These mountains still are full of great forests and a Nature Reserve. Drive 157 kms. N along coastal road from Jerusalem.

Carmel of Nabal (vineyard, field, park garden belonging to Nabal) The vineyard of Nabal is just **S** of Hebron, 38 kms. **S** from Jerusalem. Here was the residence of Nabal and his disdain for David which resulted in his death and the subsequent marriage of his widow, Avigail, to King David *[I Samuel 25:2-42]*.

Cathedral of St. James (large church named after James, brother of Jesus) Located in the Armenian quarter of the Old City of Jerusalem on Mt. Zion, it is the largest and holiest place of worship for the Armenian community. The Armenians are the first group of people to adopt Christianity as a whole nation. This site is believed to be the spot where James, the brother of Jesus, was beheaded by

Herod Agrippa I, grandson of Herod the Great, in the year 44 AD, as related in Acts *[Acts. 12:1-2]*.

Cave of Adullam   See Adullam *[I Samuel 22:1]*

Cave of Machpelah,   (machpelah, to double) Sarah lived
Cave of the Patriarchs   127 years and she died, Abraham bought this burying cave for the full price from the sons of Heth *[Genesis 23:9-20]*. Abraham died and his sons buried him here *[Genesis 25:9]*. Jacob charged his sons to bury him in this cave *[Genesis 49:29-30]*. Jacob is buried here *[Genesis 50:13]*. See Hebron in Judean Hills, 36 kms. **S** from Jerusalem. Hebron, one of Judaism's four holy cities together with Jerusalem, Safed and Tiberias. See Hebron and Kiryat Arba.

Cenacle   See Upper Room (Room of the Last Supper on Mt. Zion)

Chamber of the Last Supper   See Upper Room

Chapel of the Madonna   See Grotto of Gethsemane

Chariot Cities   (city of merkab; to mount, ride) A city where ancient horse drawn two wheel carriages were kept for use in war. These were actually stations, stables or depot cities which were built by King Solomon on the boundaries of his kingdom such as in Beth-Marcaboth which means 'house of chariots" *[II Chronicles 1:14; I Kings 9:11-13, 19; 10:26]*. The Psalmist exhorts us not to trust in chariots *[Psalm 20:7]*. The Lord makes the clouds His chariots *[Psalm 104:3]*. See Beth-Marcaboth.

Cheesemakers Valley   See Tyropoeon Valley

Chephirah   (village, hamlet) A City in Benjamin belonging to the Gibeonites *[Joshua 18:26]*. Now Kefireh, a small village, 12 kms. **NE** from Jerusalem. Joshua made peace with its people *[Joshua 9:17]*. The members of the tribe of Benjamin returned here after the exile of 586 BC *[Ezra 2:25; Nehemiah 7:29]*.

Cherith, the Brook Cherith   (to cut off or cut down) The brook where Elijah fled in order to hide and escape from Ahab and Jezebel, **E** of the Jordan River near Gilead. The Lord fed Elijah miraculously by the ravens of the air *[I Kings 17:2-8]*. The brook runs down to Wadi Kelt which runs into the Jordan Valley. The site of the brook's northern course is opposite Beth Shean, called Wadi Yabis, about 116 kms. **NE** from Jerusalem, then runs down to Wadi Kelt along the Old Jericho Road approached by Jericho, 27 kms. **NE** from Jerusalem. See Monastery of St. George.

Chidon   See Perez-uzzah

Chinnereth, Cinnereth   (kinor; harp shaped) See Sea of Galilee

Chorazin   (unclear translation) City on **NW** coast of the Sea of Galilee in the vicinity of Bethsaida and Capernaum where Jesus spoke out against the inhabitants, again for their unbelief *[Matthew 11:21]*. It is 5 kms. **N** of tel Hum also called Kerazeh. The excavated synagogue from 3rd C is similar to the one in Capernaum. 162 kms. **N** from Jerusalem to the Sea of Galilee.

Church of All Nations   See Gethsemane

Church of Dormition   See Dormition Abbey

Church of John, the Baptist   (church of Yochanan, the Immerser) John the Baptist was born to Elizabeth and Zacharias in En-Kerem *[Luke 1:57-66]*. This Spanish Franciscan Church and Monastery is built over the site of the birthplace of John. A small grotto which is a natural cave bears an inscription from Byzantine time *[Luke 1:68]*. 6 kms. **SW** of Jerusalem. See Church of the Visitation, En-Kerem and Qumran.

Church of Holy Sepulcher   See Holy Sepulcher Church

Church of Multiplication   See Tabgha

Church of the Nativity   (church of the birth) See also Bethlehem, the church built over the site of the birth of Jesus. The Persians entered the Holyland in 614 AD and destroyed most Christian sites, but they fell short of destroying this church because when they entered the courtyard, they saw a grand mosaic of three men; the wise men who had come from the **E** who were Persians, consequently it was not destroyed. This church remains the oldest in the world from the fourth century *[Luke 2:1-20; Matthew 2:1]*. In the courtyard of St. Catherine's next to the Nativity Church, see the statue of St. Jerome. There is a tradition that connects Genesis

3:15 with this statue, as Jerome is seen standing on the skull, referring to the belief that death was 'swallowed up in victory' by the ministry of Jesus Christ. Satan was defeated by Jesus' death on the cross. See the 'Eye of the Needle Gate' as you enter the original church *[Matthew 19:24]*. 7 kms. **S** from Jerusalem. See Bethlehem.

Church of St. Mark   (church of Marcos GK.) This small church is on the narrow alley in the Old City of Jerusalem, off of St. Mark's Street and parallel to David Street, between the Armenian and Jewish quarters. The Mother of Mark, one of Jesus' disciples, had a home here, according to tradition. Peter is said to have escaped from the Roman guards and hid here after he was arrested by King Herod Agrippa I *[Acts 12:3-17]*. The Church is Syrian Orthodox and their tradition holds this site to be the Upper Room where Jesus gathered with His disciples. See Upper Room.

Church of the Eight Apostles   (messenger church, one sent on a mission GK.)This interesting Greek Orthodox church with its 8 bright red domes is on the shore of the Sea of Galilee next to Capernaum. Here is the traditional site of the first calling of Jesus to His disciples *[Matthew 4:18-22; Mark 1:16-20]*. **N** 160 kms. from Jerusalem to the Sea of Galilee.

Church of the Synagogue, Church Synagogue   (church of Bet Knesset, gathering) A very short distance up the hill, through the shuk, from the Church of the Annunciation in Nazareth, brings one to the site of the Greek Catholic church. It is believed that it is built over the Jewish Orthodox synagogue from the time of Jesus. Here Jesus, Joseph and His brothers would have come with family and friends to worship. Jesus returned here to the town where He grew up and came into the synagogue but seemed to antagonize the members *[Isaiah 61:1; Luke 4:16-30]*. If the door is locked, ring the bell and someone will come. They are very hospitable.

Church of Viri Galilaei   (church of the men of Galilee LT.) Here is another site of the ascension of the Lord. The men of Galilee gazed up into the heaven *[Acts 1:11]*. This Greek Orthodox church is in the Arab village of A-Tur on the Mt. of Olives, 2 kms. **E** from the Old City.

Church of the Visitation   (church of the visit) Mary, while pregnant with Jesus, came here to visit her cousin, Elizabeth, who was herself pregnant with John the Baptist *[Luke 1:39-56]*. Mary spoke the 'Magnificat', (Mary's hymn of thanksgiving to the Lord LT.) *[Luke 1:46-55]*. This site is in En-Kerem, 6 kms. **SW** from Jerusalem and a Franciscan church stands over the site of the home of Elizabeth and Zacharias *[Luke 1:5]*. The courtyard has an arcade on one side and is beautifully decorated with ceramic plaques with this 'Magnificat' prayer in 42 languages. See Church of John the Baptist and En-Kerem.

Cistern of Malchiah   See Jeremiah's Pit

Citadel of David   See Tower of David Museum

City of Refuge   See Kedesh; Shechem; Kiryat Arba (Hebron); Bezer; Ramoth and Golan in Bashan *[Numbers 35:9-34; Joshua 20:8]*.

City of David   (the city of King David) The ancient portion of the city of Jerusalem, the eastern slope which was inhabited by the Jebusites. David bought the threshing floor from Araunah for the full price *[II Samuel 24:24]*. King Asa rested with his fathers and is buried in the city *[I Kings 15:24]*. David came to Jerusalem from Hebron, which was then occupied by the Jebusites and he took the stronghold of Zion (that is the City of David) *[I Chronicles 11:5]*. David built houses for himself and he brought the ark of the covenant from the house of Obed-Edom to the City of David *[I Chronicles 15:25-29]*. The Jewish Kings are buried here in the City of David *[II Chronicles 24:16; 25:28; 27:9]*. Presently the Arab village of Silwan. The gospel writer, Luke, refers to the City of David, meaning the city where David was born, which is Bethlehem *[Luke 2:4]*. Today, the entire city of Jerusalem is commonly called the City of David.

City of God   See Jerusalem *[Psalm 46:4; 48:1,8]*

City of Palms   See Jericho *[Judges 1:16; 3:13]*

Cities of Refuge   (asylum, sanctuary) "Now among the cities you give to the Levites, appoint 6 cities of refuge…"*[Numbers 35:6]*. As dictated by God to Moses, they were Kedesh in the Galilee *[I Chronicles 6:76]*. Shechem in Ephraim *[Joshua 21:21]*. Hebron in Judah *[Joshua 21:11; II Samuel*

5:5]. Bezer, **E** of the Jordan River on the plains of Moab *[Deut. 4:43; Joshua 21:38]*. Bashan in the Golan *[Joshua 21:27]* and Ramoth in Gilead *[Deut. 4:43, Joshua 21:38]*. These cities afforded the man slayer, who killed a person by accident, a place to escape and hide. See individual cities listed for further description and locations.

Coenaculum   See Upper Room

Common lands   (pasture lands) In Shiloh Eleazar, the priest reminded Joshua that the Lord promised the children of Israel cities to dwell in, with their common lands for the livestock *[Joshua 21st chapter]*. There were 48 cities *[Joshua 21:41]*.

Corner Gate   (pinnah, chief) King Joash (835-796 BC) tore down the wall and gates *[II Chronicles 25:23]*. King Uzziah (790-740 BC) built towers in Jerusalem at the Corner Gate and the Valley Gate located in the **NW** corner of Jerusalem's Old City *[II Kings 14:13; II Chronicles 26:9]*. Jeremiah spoke of the rebuilding of the gates *[Jeremiah 31:38]*. Zechariah foretells a day when Jerusalem will remain unto the Corner Gate *[Zechariah 14:10]*. See Jerusalem Gates and Towers at the end of this book.

Corruption, Mount of   See Destruction, Mount of

Court of the Gentiles   (place for goyim, nations, non-Jews) The non-Jews could not enter the main courtyard of the Temple and see the altar. Jesus quoted Isaiah and said, "His house was a house of prayer for all nations (goyim) *[Isaiah 56:7]*. In the last book of the NT in Revelation, the writer sees a new heaven and a new earth and there will be an area in the new temple reserved for the nations *[Revelation 11:2]*. See Model of the Second Temple in the Holyland Hotel, West Jerusalem.

Court of the Guard   See Jeremiah's Pit

Court of the Women   (ezrat nashim) Jewish women were not allowed to advance beyond this court, which was the outermost court. The procession of the High Priests and the 'Festival of the Water Libation Ceremony' took place here on the day of Atonement *[Exodus 30:17-21]*. See Model of the Second Temple in the Holyland Hotel, West Jerusalem.

Dalmanu'tha   (Gk. gold, fountain) Site on the **W** coast of the Sea of Galilee where Jesus sailed in a boat with His disciples *[Mark 8:10]*. Presently el-Mejdel. 155 kms. **N** from Jerusalem to the Sea of Galilee.

Dan, Laish   (judge) The city taken by the Danites, the tribe of Dan. The northern border of the northern kingdom *[Judges 20:1]*. Abraham pursued the men who had taken Lot captive as far as Dan *[Genesis 14:14]*. Samson was stirred by the Spirit of the Lord at Mahaneh Dan *[Judges 13:25]*. "And they called the name of the city Dan... formerly was Laish," *[Judges18:29]*. All Israel from Dan... knew that Samuel had been established prophet by the Lord *[I Samuel 3:20]*. Under Solomon's reign Judah and Israel dwelt safely from Dan to Beersheva *[I Kings 4:25]*. Jeroboam, Solomon's son sinned and built an altar here *[I Kings 12:29-30]*. Jeremiah proclaimed destruction for Dan *[Jeremiah 4:15; 8:16]*. Ezekiel proclaimed the division of the land *[Ezekiel 48:2, 32]*. Presently Tel Dan is an exciting Israel Park Nature Reserve with an interesting archaeological site. 223 kms. N from Jerusalem.

Dan, Tribe of   See *Joshua 19:40-48* and Tribes at the back of this book.

David's Tomb   (tomb of King David) From Crusader times the traditional site is on Mt. Zion underneath the Upper Room. The Upper Room which is also called Coenaculum, has both Roman and Byzantine ashlars lining the lower part of the wall of David's Tomb. "So David rested with his fathers, and was buried in the City of David," *[I Kings 2:10; Acts 2:29]*. Today it is a synagogue and one of the holiest sites for prayer in Judaism. Many scholars tend to believe that David is buried in the Valley of the Kings. Enter through Zion Gate in the Old City of Jerusalem.

Dead Sea   (yam ha-melech) See Salt Sea as referred to in the scriptures, also called Sea of the Aravah.

Dead Sea Valley   (emek yam ha-melech, valley of the salt sea) Notice great groves of palm trees being irrigated by the water from wells in the hills. As they did in Elim, the children of Israel found refreshment with date palms and water *[Exodus 15:27]*. Isaiah also speaks of streams of water in a dry place *[Isaiah 32:2]*. See Valley of Siddim where the Canaanite kings came together *[Genesis 14:3,8]* 40 kms. **SE** from Jerusalem. See Dead Sea, Jordan Valley, Ein Gedi.

Debir, Kiryat-sepher (book town) A highland city 20 kms. **SW** of Hebron. It was fully conquered by Joshua and he hung the kings on this site *[Joshua 10:38-40]*. It is identified as tel Beit Mirsim and shows it was originally a Hyksos city. The Hyksos were a mixed race, Semitic who invaded and took control of Egypt and some invaded Israel. They occupied this site from 2200 BC but after the destruction from Babylonian king Nebuchadnezzar in 586 BC, it was never rebuilt.

Decapolis ("ten cities" GK.) Jesus traveled here to this district of ten cities in the **NE** part of Galilee, near the Sea of Galilee. They were originally built by Alexander the Great in 330 BC then rebuilt in 65 BC by the Romans. They were typical Greco-Roman cities with forums, pagan temples, bath houses, theaters and were repulsive to the Jews because of their 'fleshly' lifestyle. Jesus traveled in all of Galilee and great multitudes followed Him from the ten cities of the Decapolis *[Matthew 4:23-25. Mark 5:20; Mark 7:31]*.

Decision, Valley of See Jehoshaphat, Valley of

Desert Plain (misur shel midair) Moses addressed all Israel here on this side of the Jordan in the wilderness on the desert plain *[Deut. 1:1-4]*. See Moab in Jordan.

Destruction, Mount of (mountain of ruin, trap, death) This small rise or 'high place' was also called the Hill of Corruption where King Solomon sinned and gave in to his wives and worshipped foreign gods *[II Kings 23:13-14]*. It is just **S** of the Mount of Olives opposite the Old City of Jerusalem.

Diblah (translation unclear) In the **N** on one of the extreme borders of the land where Ezekiel prophesies against the land and its desolation *[Ezekiel 6:14]*. Exact location is uncertain, most likely on the border with Syria in the present Golan Heights.

Di'bon, Dibon-gad (pining) The children of the tribe of Gad set up this town on the **E** side of the Jordan. Noted for its rich pasture lands *[Numbers 32:3,34; 33:45-46]*. It was capital of the Moabite kingdom and both the prophets, Isaiah and Jeremiah refer to this city *[Isaiah 15:2; Jeremiah 48:18,22,24]*. It is located 20 kms. **E** of the Dead Sea, S of the capital of Amman in Jordan.

Dim'nah (dunghill) One of the Levitical cities with common lands which was located in Zebulun *[Joshua 21:35]*. The exact location is unknown.

Di'mon, Waters of (unclear translation) In Moab, a small stream E of the Dead Sea where Isaiah cursed the waters and prophesied against the land of Moab *[Isaiah 15:9]*. The exact location is unknown.

Dimo'nah (unclear translation) A city in the **S** of Judah belonging to the tribe of Judah *[Joshua 15:22]* Presently this is an interesting Negev development town, 35 kms. **S** of Beersheva. Israel's Nuclear Power Plant is located here.

Dome of the Rock See Moriah, land of

Dominus Flavius Church (church of the Tear Drop, the Lord wept LT.) Jesus descended from the Mount of Olives and came to this spot and He wept over the city of Jerusalem *[Matthew 23:37; Luke 13:34]*. "He drew near and He saw the city and He wept over it" *[Luke 19:41]*. "For the days will come upon you when your enemies will build an embankment around you, surround you and close you in on every side"*[Luke 19:43]*. This site is halfway down the Mt. of Olives, just off of the Palm Sunday Path, as one is heading down the path from **E** to **W**, opposite the Golden Gate in the Old City of Jerusalem. Many remains here from the Byzantine time, both Jewish and Christian burial caves and mosaics from the original church from the 4th C. can be seen here.

Dor, Tel Dor (dwelling) In the book of Joshua this Canaanite city is referred to as "the heights of Dor"*[Joshua 11:2;12:23]*. It was the capital of one of Solomon's administrative districts *[Judges 1:27; I Kings 4:11]*. It prospered under the Romans and is identified as Khirbet el-Buri and is 13 kms. **N** of Caesarea on the coast of the Mediterranean Sea. Extensive excavation is still in progress and remains found from 1500 BC. A modern Israeli Moshav (farm) and Hotel Nachsholim rests at its shore.

Dormition Abbey (place of rest) This site is an outstanding German Catholic Church building on Mt. Zion and hems the skyline over Mt. Zion for miles. It is the site where Mary, the Mother of Jesus 'fell asleep' or died and is buried. This site has been honored from the 4th C. High up in the apse of the church is the scripture from Isaiah, the Prophet, in Latin. "Behold, a virgin shall conceive, and bear a son and shall call His name Immanuel." *[Isaiah 7:14]*. The Benedictine Monks live here and operate the church and its facilities. See Mt. Zion.

Do'than (two wells, the pit of Joseph) This site is 100 kms. directly **N** from Jerusalem, an upland plain on the old caravan route from Syria to Egypt. Excellent pasture fields, 20 kms. **N** of Shechem where Joseph was sold by his brothers *[Genesis 37:17]*. The pit that has been found next to the well on the site is called 'the pit of Joseph'. Elisha had a vision of the mountain full of horses and chariots *[II Kings 6:13-17]*. Twenty layers of settlement have been identified on the tel dating from 3000 BC to 1400 AD. Presently this excavation site has yielded one of the richest tombs found in Israel and over 3200 pottery vessels.

Dragon's Well, Serpents Well Nehemiah returned from exile to rebuild the walls of Jerusalem. He came by night to this well next to the Gihon Spring on the **W** side of the Old City in Jerusalem. Here he viewed the broken walls *[Nehemiah 2:13]*.

Dumah See Edom

Dura See Adorayim

Eastern Gate (gate of Old City facing E) One of the 8 gates of the Old City of Jerusalem. It is the only one presently closed, blocked and has been since the 15th Century (1541). According to tradition, the Turks closed it because they feared the Jewish Messiah would enter here. It is also called the Golden Gate, the Mercy Gate, the Jericho Gate, for it is on the road to Jericho, Gate of Repentance and the Shushan Gate. During the time of Jesus, He would have walked through this gate, though on a lower level, in order to get to the Mt. of Olives, which He so often frequented. The prophet, Ezekiel, speaks about the return of the Glory of God to the Temple. "And behold the glory of the God of Israel comes from the east…" *[Ezekiel 43:1-2; 44:1-2]*. Jesus came from the Mt. of Olives to the Temple (through this gate) *[Luke 19:45]*. Peter and Paul healed the lame man *[Acts 3:1-11]*, then called the Beautiful Gate. See Ancient City Gates at the back of this book.

Ebal (Mt. Ebal) "to be bare, stone") The mountain opposite Mt. Gerizim, **N** of Shechem known as the Mt. of Cursing *[Deut. 11:29]*. From here the Law of Moses was recorded and read by Joshua and he built an altar *[Joshua 8:30-35]*. *[Deut. 27:4]*. Presently, it is Jebel Eslamiyeh 59 kms. **N** from Jerusalem.

Eben-ezer (stone of the helper) Between Mizpeh and Izbet Sartah, half a kilometer **E** of Aphek. All Israel encamped here against the Philistines *[I Samuel 4:1]*. This stone was set up by the Prophet Samuel after the battle and defeat of the Philistines. It is a memorial to the help received from God Jehovah *[I Samuel 7:12]*.

Ecco Homo (Behold the man, LT.) We see part of the Arch from the Antonio Fortress here spanning the Via Delorosa (Way of the Cross) in Jerusalem's Old City, Moslem Quarter, that was part of the praetorium of Pilate where the Roman soldiers would have gathered." ...Jesus came out wearing the crown of thorns and a purple robe. And Pilate said "...Behold the Man," *[John 19:5]*. Convent of the Sisters of Zion in Old City on site. Located on the Via Delorosa, the Way of Sorrows. See Antonio's Fortress. See Pilate's judgment Seat.

Edom (red; also called Dumah or Idumaea GK.) The name of the country settled by the Edomites, the descendants of Esau, who settled **SE** of Israel and is in present day Jordan. The average elevation of the mountain peaks is 664 meters (2000 ft) above sea level and along the eastern slope a ridge sinks into the plateau of the Arabian Desert *[Numbers 20:14-21;24:18; Joshua 15:1; II Samuel 8:14]*. This country lay along the route of the children of Israel in their wanderings from the Sinai to Kadesh-barnea onto Eloth (Eilat) *[Deut 1:2; 2:1-8]*. King Jehoram fought against the Moabites and went by the way of Edom *[II Kings 3:8]*. Both Prophets Jeremiah and Ezekiel spoke of the fall and destruction of Edom *[Jeremiah 49:7,17; Ezekiel 25:12-14]*. See Mount Seir. **SE** of the Dead Sea in Jordan.

Ed'rei (mighty) Site of one of the metropolitan towns of Bashan beyond the Jordan River where King Og was defeated by the Israelites *[Joshua 12:4; 13:12; Deut.3:10; Numbers 21:33-35]*. The city fell to Manasseh *[Joshua 13:31; Numbers 32:33]*. It was an important Amorite town. Presently Ed-Dera'ah 18 kms. **N** of Ramoth-gilead on the eastern tributary of the Yarmuk River in Jordan.

Eglon (calf like) This is an Amorite city in the western lowlands that was captured by Joshua *[Joshua 10:3, 23; 12:12;15:39]*. 32 kms. **SW** of Jerusalem.

Egypt, Brook of See Brook of Egypt (El-Arish)

Eilat, Elat See Elath, it's Biblical name.

Ekron (extermination) One of the capital cities of the Philistines, and according to the latest archaeological excavations, appears to be Tel Miqne just 48 kms **W** of Jerusalem. It has been occupied since the early Bronze age (1200 BC) and an urban center was founded here. The last fortified city was destroyed by Sennacherib of Assyria in 701 BC. It belonged to Judah and Dan *[Joshua 13:3;19:43]*. The Philistines took the ark here and the people were afraid! *[I Samuel 5:10-11]*. The men of Israel and Judah pursued the Philistines to the gates of Ekron *[I Samuel 17:52]*. It is called Tel Miqne today. It is the largest Iron Age site in Israel.

Ein Gedi (spring of the wild goat) Also called the 'City of Palm Trees' "Hazazon-tamar" *[Genesis 14:7; II Chronicles 20:2]*. On the **W** shore of the Dead Sea, 50 kms. SE of Jerusalem *[I Samuel 23:29]* David was in the wilderness hiding out from King Saul, although he was already anointed king *[I Samuel 24:1-22]*. The Prophet Ezekiel speaks of a time when fish will swim here at Ein Gedi *[Ezekiel 47]*. The 'Waterfall of David' is seen here and a Chalcolithic Temple from 3500 BC. Wonderful Natural Reserve and National Park *[Psalm 104:18; Song of Sol. 1:14]*.

Ein Ha'rod See Ha'rod

Ein Sheva (seven springs) See Tabgha

Ein Yael (spring of the deer) An ancient farm here by Ein Yael, on the road leading from Jerusalem to Gaza, has an abundance of water. This way was paved in Roman times and may have been suitable for chariots. Perhaps this was the site of the conversion and baptism of the minister of Ethiopia's Queen Candace, as recorded by Philip, the evangelist *[Acts 8:26-40; Isaiah 53:7-8]*. Byzantine remains on the site indicate that a monastery stood here. An ancient icon from this site depicts Philip and the Ethiopian being baptized. There were two desert roads to Gaza and this was one of them. 30 kms. **SW** from Jerusalem enroute to Bet Guvrin. See Gaza.

Elah   See Valley of Elah *[I Samuel 17:2]*

El Arish   See Brook of Egypt

El Bethel   See Bethel

El Muhraka   See Muhraka

Elath, Eloth   (great trees, Ezion Geber) Port on the Gulf of Eilat on Israeli side and Gulf of A'qaba on the Jordanian side. The Children of Israel passed along here on their trek **N** from the Sinai *[Deut.2:8]*. Because of its strategic stopping place for caravans from Arabia, this site passed back and forth between the Edomites and the Jews in the two centuries between David and King Uzziah *[II Kings 14:22;16:6]*. Solomon had a great economic operation here and built a navy from this point. *[I Kings 9:26; II Chronicles 8:17]*. King Jehoshaphat also built many ships on this site *[II Chronicles 20:36]*. Modern resort, tourist town of Eilat founded in 1951.

El-Bethel, El-Elohe Israel   ("the mighty God of Israel") Jacob built an altar here, near Shechem and gave glory to the God of Israel *[Genesis 33:20]*. 59 kms. **N** from Jerusalem but the exact site is not identifiable.

El-Eizariyya   (AK) See Bethany and Lazarus' Tomb

Elim   (trees) The site of the second station of the children of Israel in the desert where they camped for 30 days *[Exodus 15:27; Numbers 33:9]*. Here were 'twelve springs of water and seventy palm trees," *[Exodus 16:1]*. It is located at Wadi Gharandel but the exact location in the Sinai Desert, Egypt is unknown.

Elisha's Fountain   (God, His salvation fountain) Near Jericho and the water source of the Springs of Jericho. In Arabic it is called Ain-es Sultan, the spring of the Sultan. Elisha healed the waters and sweetened them, using salt by the hand of the Lord *[II Kings 2:19-22]*. 36 kms. **SE** of Jerusalem. It is a fine, copious spring with its source coming from a large filled pond and is still in use today.

Elon-Moreh   (oak of the teacher or teaching oak) Jewish settlement in the Samarian Hills, 5 kms. **E** of Shechem on the hill Jebel el Kabir. Abraham's first stop here in the Land of Promise *[Genesis 12:6-8]*. Here was the promise of God "...to your descendants I will give this land,"*[Genesis 12:7]*.

Mitzpeh Elon-Moreh has a wonderful view of the land spreading in all directions. 64 kms. N from Jerusalem. See Mitzpeh Elon Moreh.

El-Paran   (oak of Paran, prayer to God) Also called Castle of the Palm, here King Chedorlaomer crossed the desert in the wilderness and came to a standstill before entering the land of Canaan. Abraham rescues Lot near here *[Genesis 14:5-6]* Ishmael dwelt here in this wilderness when he and Hagar went out from Abraham and Sarah *[Genesis 21:21]*. In the Sinai desert in Egypt, 90 kms. S of Beersheva.

Emek Israel   Emek Jez'reel, See Jez'reel Valley

Emek-Ke'ziz Valley of Ke'ziz   (to cut off, deep) This site in Benjamin is still a wadi called Wadi-el-Ke'ziz on the ancient road from Jerusalem to Jericho *[Joshua 18:21]*. 36 kms. S from Jerusalem.

Emek-Rephaim   (valley of the giants) See Valley of Rephaim.

Emmaus   (hot baths) A town 13 kms. W from Jerusalem off the Jerusalem Tel Aviv Highway. After Jesus rose from the dead He revealed Himself to many and on the road to Emmaus is where He met two men *[Luke 24:13-32]*. Today the ruins of Emmaus are a part of the JNF Canada Park on the eastern edge of the Ayyalon Valley.

Enaim, Enam   (fountain, spring) Site near Timnah in the S, one of the cities of Judah in the lowlands *[Joshua 15:34]*. Tamar, the widowed daughter-in-law of Judah sat here before her father-in-law came by *[Genesis 38:12-21]*. 25 kms. N from Eilat.

En'dor   (fountain or spring of Dor, dwelling) Town 6 kms. S from the foot of Mt. Tabor. Saul came here to inquire of the medium when the Lord did not answer him. *[I Samuel 28:7]*. A plea to God to destroy Israel's enemies *[Psalm 83:10]*. There are numerous caves in the area today which suggest a dwelling for a person such as the witch of Endor. Presently called Khirbet Safsafa.

Eneg'laim   (fountain of two calves) The Prophet Ezekiel sees this area in his vision. It appears that he sees the Dead Sea as 'holy waters' *[Ezekiel 47:10]*. It is identified as Ain

Hajlah just 3 kms. **N** of the Dead Sea next to the Jordan River on its **W** coast.

En-Gan'nim   (fountain of gardens) The city given to the Levites in the territory of Issachar located 22 kms. **S** of Mt. Tabor, 122 kms. **N** from Jerusalem and is identified as the place where Ahaziah escaped from Jehu *[II Kings 9:27]*. It is identified today as Jenin, an Arab village which served as a Turkish-German army base during the First World War.

Enge'di   See Ein Gedi

En-Harod   (spring of trembling) See Harod, Spring of

En-Kerem   (spring of the vineyards) Just 6 kms. **SW** of Jerusalem, lovely, sleepy pleasant village which was the home of Zechariah and Elysheva (Elizabeth) the parents of John the Baptist *[Luke 1:23]*. Miriam (Mary) the mother of Jesus came here to visit her cousin, Elysheva (Elizabeth), who was 6 months pregnant with the baby, John the Baptist *[Luke 1:39]*. A spring here still emerges from a rock over which an old mosque stands. This is the site by tradition, believed to be where Mary washed the baby Jesus when she came to visit her cousin Elizabeth.

En-Hak'kore   (fountain of the crier or caller) God made this Spring burst forth *[Judges 15:19]* It is identified as Ayun Kara near Zoreah (Zorah) in Lehi 20 kms. **W** from Jerusalem. See Lehi.

En-Mishpat   (fountain of judgment) See Kadesh-Barnea

En-Rimmon   (fountain of the pomegranate) Site 15 kms. N from Be'ersheva where the returning exiles came after the destruction of the First Temple *[Nehemiah 11:29]*. Now called Umm er-Rummamin. The same as Ain and Rimmon *[Joshua 15:32]*.

En-Rogel   (fountain of the treaders, foot mountain) In Jerusalem just below the junction of the valley of Hinnom and the valley of Kidron, **SE** of the Op'hel hill. It is not the Gihon Spring but one of the ancient water sources, near Shiloah Pool near Kidron Spring. Here the fullers, the washerwomen worked and cleansed their garments *[Joshua 15:7; 18:16; I Kings 1:9]*. The site where Adonijah, David's rebellious son, declared himself King *[I Kings 1:5-10]*. The Arabic name is Job's well, 'Bir Aiyub'.

E'phes-Dam'mim   (boundary of blood) The site of the bloody battles between Israel and the Philistines, also called Pasdammim *[I Samuel 17:1; I Chronicles 11:13]*. It is modern Beit Fased (house of bleeding) located between Socoh and Azekah, 18 kms. **SW** of Hebron.

Ephraim, City of   (city of covering, bandage) Site in the Judean Wilderness where Jesus sought refuge with His disciples when they were being threatened by the priests in Jerusalem *[John 11:54]*. It is identified as Taiyibeh 12 kms. **NE** of Beth-el and 20 kms. **NE** from Jerusalem.

Ephraim, Forest of   (forest of covering, bandage) Site just **E** of the Jordan River near Mahanaim, **E** of Rosh Pina, where David's army was forced to attack his son, Absalom *[II Samuel 18:6]*. Absalom was killed and cast into a large pit in this place *[II Samuel 18:17]*. An area of grape vineyards in great profusion *[Judges 8:2]*. 10 kms. **E** from the Jordan River in Jordan today.

Ephraim, Gate of   (gate of covering, bandage) This is present day Damascus Gate on the **N** side of the ancient city of Jerusalem which also stood during the period of the Kings *[II Kings 14:13; II Chronicles 25:23]*. See charts of Gates at end of this book.

Ephraim, Mountain of   (mountain of covering, bandage) In the hill country of central Israel. This was the earliest name given to the "hills" or "mountains of Samaria," Timnath-heres on the **N** side of Mt. Gaash where Joshua is buried *[Judges 2:9]*. The whole plateau was also called Mt. Judah *[Joshua 11:21]*. Saul passed through here while he was searching for his lost donkeys *[I Samuel 9:4]*. Jeremiah says Israel will be restored when the watchmen cry aloud on Mount Ephraim *[Jeremiah 31:5-6]*. "Assemble on the mountains of Samaria" was the cry of the Prophet Amos *[Amos 3:9]*. Located 9 km. **S** Shechem.

Ephraim, Tribe of   See Joshua 16:8-10. See chart on the Tribes of Israel at the end of this book.

Eph'ratah   (fruitfulness, fruitful) The ancient name of Bethlehem (house of bread) during the time of the Patriarch, Jacob, also the birthplace of Jesus *[Genesis 35:19]*. It was the home of Naomi's family who are described as Ephrathites *[Ruth 1:2; 4:11]*. The psalmist wrote, "Beloved, we heard of it in

Ephratha" *[Psalm 132:6]*. 7 kms. **S** from Jerusalem. See Bethlehem, Church of the Nativity and Rachel's Tomb.

E'phron, City of   (fawn like) Here King Abijah and the army of Judah took this city from Jeroboam *[II Chronicles 13:19]*. It was the ancient city of Ophrah in the tribe of Benjamin and is near Taiyibeh just **E** of Bethel. 20 kms. **NE** from Jerusalem.

E'phron, Mountain of   (fawn like mountain) Here is a steep mountain ridge on the **W** side of the valley of Terebinith which formed the northern border of the tribe of Judah *[Joshua 15:9]*. 3 kms. **N** from Jerusalem.

Esdrae'lon, Plain of   (God sows, GK) This plain is located in the Jez'reel Valley and is often referred to by the same name. It is 38 kms. long and 21 kms. wide. It is a fertile plain due to the rich soil that rolls down from the Galilee mountains and the highlands of Samaria. The Wadi Kishon, from the River Kishon, drains from here to the Mediterranean Sea. The battle of Deborah was fought here *[Judges 4:7;5:21]*. Elijah the Prophet conducted his contest with the priests of Ba'al here next to Mt. Carmel *[I Kings 18:40]*. Megiddo and Beth Shean were built along the edge of the plain by the Canaanite chariot kings. Many believe the last great battle of the earth will be fought on this plain and in this valley. See Jez'reel and Megiddo.

E'sek Well   (well of contention) In the valley of Gerar this well was dug by the herdsmen of Isaac but the herdsmen disputed over possession of the well. Isaac dug many wells; this was one of them *[Genesis 26:20]*. It was a Philistine city and identified today as tel-Jemmeh, some 12 kms. **S** of Gaza. See Gerar.

Esh'col Valley   See Valley of Esh'col

Esh'taol   (from pinion, hold fast or the wing of a bird) This site 21 kms. **NW** of Jerusalem, at Eshwa near Zorah, was first assigned to Judah, then to the tribe of Dan *[Joshua 15:33;19:41]*. Samson was born here *[Judges 13:24-25]*. From here the sons of Dan started their expedition to conquer more land *[Judges 18:2]*. 20 kms. **NW** from Jerusalem.

Etam, City of   (hawk ground) This city of Judah was fortified by King Rehoboam *[II Chronicles 11:6]*. The source of water here identifies this to be where Solomon's Pools, near

Bethlehem, and Tekoa are located. Solomon's aquaduct came from here to his gardens in Jerusalem, into his palace and the First Temple. It is el-Eurak, 7 kms. **S** from Jerusalem and 4 kms. **S** from Bethlehem. Some scholars believe it was only built from Herod's time, while others believe Herod built over three existing pools built out of the rock to catch the rain water and store the spring water contained therein.

Etam, Rock of   (hawk ground) The 'rock of Etam' is identified near Solomon's Pool near Bethlehem, the place to which Samson retreated after his slaughter of the Philistines *[Judges 15:8]*. The city was fortified by Rehoboam. *[I Chronicles 4:3; II Chronicles 11:6]*. 4 kms. **S** from Bethlehem.

Etham, Wilderness of   See Shur (Numbers 33:8)

Eye of the Needle Gate   A small opening of a gate within a gate. An example of this is in Bethlehem at the main entrance (Crusader period) to the Church of the Nativity. We stoop down in order to enter. Jesus may have been pointing out and referring to gates such as these in His time. Jesus said, "It is easier for a camel to go through the eye of a needle than for a rich man to enter the kingdom of God," *[Mark 10:24]*.

Ezel   (separation, the mound) Near Ramah but the exact location is unknown. It is a memorial stone, the stone of separation between David and Jonathan where they sadly parted from one another *[I Samuel 20:19]*.

Ezion-geber   See Elath, Eilat

Field of Blood   See Potter's Field *[Matthew 27:7,8,10]*

Field of Zophim   See Zophim

First Temple Sites in Jerusalem   We speak of the First Temple, the Temple that Solomon built in 950 BC *[I Kings 5:5; 6:14-38; I Chronicles 28:6-7; 10-11]* The First Temple Period was from 968 BC-586BC. According to the scriptures it took him seven years to complete the First Temple *[I Kings 6:1,37-38]*. See Scottish Church; Broad Wall; Cardo; Temple Mount in Jerusalem.

Fish Gate   (gate where they brought in the fish) King David built this gate near the Ophel on the **W** side of the Gihon Springs, going down to the valley of Gihon in Jerusalem. There may have been a fish market and the fish were brought into the city, thus its name *[II Chronicles 33:14; Nehemiah 3:3;12:39]*. The Prophet Zephaniah sees a day in the future when a mournful cry will come from the Fish Gate *[Zephaniah 1:10]*. Zechariah the Prophet speaks of the kingdom of the Messiah *[Zechariah 14:10]*. See Ancient Gates at the back of this book.

Ford of Jabbok   (water passing) A river **E** of the Jordan River named Jabbok, where this small stream has a hollow place which can be crossed over by foot. Here, Jacob crossed over on his way to meet his brother Esau *[Genesis 32:22]*. It is in present day Jordan, just **E** of the Dead Sea at its northern point, 28 kms. **NE** from Jerusalem.

Foundation Rock   See Rock of Foundation

Fountain of Siloam   See Pool of Siloam

Fuller's Field   (launderer's, washers, washerman's field) The site is just **W** of Jaffa Gate in Jerusalem near Mamila, also known as Birkat-el-Mamila, which is actually the head of the Valley of Hinnom. Water once flowed here which leads us to believe that people came to wash their clothes at this place. The Prophet Isaiah came here to meet Ahaz. There was an ancient aquaduct from the Ist Temple Period, which supplied water to this field *[II Kings 18:17; Isaiah 7:3; Isaiah 36:2]*.

Furnace, Tower of   (tower of a stove or firepot) In the First Temple Period this was one of the towers of the middle, second wall of Jerusalem in the **NW**, adjoining the "corner gate" near the present route of the Via Dolorosa (the Way of Sorrows) and the Street of St. Stephen. Nehemiah returned to rebuild the walls and towers *[Nehemiah 3:11;12:38]*.

Ga'ash   (quaking) See Mount of Ephraim, the place of Joshua's burial. On the **N** side of this hill is Timnah-serah *[Joshua 24:29-30]*. The brooks and valleys of Ga'ash are mentioned as being the place where one of King David's mighty men came from *[II Samuel 23:30; I Chronicles 11:32]*. 18 kms. **N** from Jerusalem in the mountains of Ephraim.

Gad, Tribe of   See Tribes in back of book ; Joshua 13:24-28

Gad'ara   See Gadarenes below

Gadarenes, Gerasenes   (from GK. Gadara, translation unclear) The site of Gadara, the capital of the Roman province of Peraea, **E** of the Jordan River, opposite Tiberias some 9 kms. The inhabitants are mentioned in the account of Jesus healing the demon-possessed men who were coming out of the tombs, the man was healed and restored here *[Matthew 8:28-34; Mark 5:1-20; Luke 8:26-39]*. Also called Gerasene. The present site is called Kursi *[place for sitting down]* on route 92 on the eastern shore of the Sea of Galilee, a National Park site.

Gal'eed   (heap of witness) Laban pursued Jacob and overtook him in the Mountains of Gilead. Jacob named the pile of stone Gal'eed but Laban called it Jegar Sahadutha, an Aramaic name. It was a memorial to the covenant between Jacob and his father-in-law, Laban *[Genesis 31:23-55]*. 72 kms. due **E** from Jerusalem, across the Jordan River in Jordan.

Galicantu   See Peter of Galicantu Church in Jerusalem.

Galilee   "Come to the Galilee and savor the beautiful landscape which so influenced the thoughts of a man, who influenced the thoughts of the entire world." written by a Christian pilgrim.

Galilee, land of   ('galil', circle or circuit) During the time of Jesus, Palestine was divided into the three provinces of Judea, Samaria and Galilee which occupied the upper part of the land, being the **NW** province. The gospel accounts from Matthew, Mark and Luke, are focused mainly on Jesus' ministry in the Galilee. In His three years of public ministry, He spent seventy five percent of His time in the Galilee. He spoke thirty two parables and nineteen were spoken in the Galilee. "The greatest sermon that was ever spoken" said one pilgrim, "was spoken here in the Galilee on the Mount of Beatitudes."

Galilee of the Gentiles   The prophet Isaiah speaks to a people who were in darkness, who will see a great light *[Isaiah 9:1]*. This area may refer to the Gentile or Pagan side of the Sea of Galilee during the time when Jesus preached the gospels. See map at the back of this book for reference.

Galilee, Sea of, Sea of Kinneret (harp-shaped) Heb. kinor (harp) This sea, lake is also called the Lake of Gennesaret, Sea of Tiberias. The most frequently used term by most Israelis is Kinneret; the Christians say "The Sea of Galilee." It is shaped like a harp, 700 ft. or 220 meters below sea level, 20 kms. long (13 miles), 14 kms. wide (8 miles). From this sea comes two thirds of Israel's water source containing eight natural springs. These fresh waters of this Sea are clean with an abundance of fish called St. Peter's, a musht fish, net caught. The Jordan River flows through and provides an additional water supply from the **N**. In Jesus time only Capernaum, Bethsaida, Gennes'aret, Mag'dala and Tiberias are mentioned which stood on the northern and western shores. Here on this Sea, Jesus did many of His most important miracles. He called Capernaum 'home' and referred to it as His 'home town'. He walked on the Sea and called Peter to Him on the Sea of Galilee *[Matthew 14:22-32, Mark 6:45-52; John 6:14-21]*. He made the winds and waves and the tempest obey Him. *[Matthew 8:23-27; Mark 4:35-41; Luke 8:22-25]*. What manner of man is this, they asked, "…that even the winds and the waves obey Him?"

JESUS IN THE GALILEE

Jesus began His ministry, He departed and came to the Galilee *[Matthew 4:12]*. He spoke of the way of the sea, beyond the Jordan *[Matthew 4:15]*. He called His first two disciples here, Simon Peter and Andrew, fishermen *[verse 18]*. He went about in all of Galilee, teaching, preaching, healing *[verse 23]*. Great multitudes from all of Galilee followed Him *[verse 25]*. Near the Sea, He went up on the mountain to pray *[Matthew 15:29]*. He spoke about His death here *[Matthew 17:22-23]*. He departed from Galilee and came to the regions of Judea *[Matthew 19:1]*. All the city was moved, wondering, and saying, "Who is this?" and the multitudes said, "This is Jesus, the prophet from Nazareth in the Galilee," *[Matthew 21:11]*. He told them He would go before them into Galilee after He arose *[Matthew 26:32]*. Many women from Galilee stood by the cross when He died *[Matthew 27:55]*. The angel told the disciples, "He is going before you into Galilee; there you will see Him. Behold I have told you," *[Matthew 28:7]*. The eleven disciples left Jerusalem and went into Galilee to the mountain to which Jesus had appointed them *[Matthew 28:16]*. Jesus came from Nazareth in the Galilee for His baptism *[Mark 1:9]*. His fame spread throughout all the regions of Galilee *[Mark 1:28]*. Jesus withdrew with His disciples to the Sea, multitudes followed *[Mark 3:7]*. After a forty day fast, Jesus returned to the Galilee *[Luke 4:14]*. They accused Him of stirring up the people and teaching throughout all of Judea, beginning from Galilee *[Luke 23:5]*. He was on His way to Galilee and called Philip *[John 1:43]*. He came to Galilee and the Galileans received Him *[John 4:45]*. He went over to the Sea of Galilee also called Sea of Tiberias *[John 6:1]*. He walked in Galilee freely but in Judea they sought to kill Him *[John 7:1]*. Others asked, "Will the Christ come out of Galilee?" *[John 7:41]*. They said, "Search and see for yourself, no prophet comes from Galilee,"*[John 7:52]*

Garden of Agony   See Gethsemane, Garden of

Garden of Gethsemane   See Gethsemane

Garden Tomb   A site in Eastern Jerusalem, **N** of the Old City, near the Damascus Gate. Also referred to as Gordon's Calvary, in honor of a British General Charles George Gordon who came to Jerusalem in 1883 and discovered this garden, cistern and a rock-cut tomb. The shape of the hill, the burial cave and the garden itself seem to fit the New Testament description. This site is honored by many evangelical Protestant Christians as the site of Jesus' burial and resurrection, while others accept only the Church of the Holy Sepulcher. *[Matthew 27:57-65, Matthew 28; Mark 15:42-47; Luke 23:50-55; John 19:38-42]*. See Holy Sepulcher Church.

Gates of Old City, Jerusalem   (sha'arem shel ear-ha atique) There are presently 8 gates, one was closed, the Eastern or Golden Gate, in 1541 under the Ottomon Turks. The following are their present names and former names, traveling from the right, **E** to **S**, **W** to **N** to the E direction. See Gates at the end of the book for other locations and names from former periods. The following are the present gates which we can see and touch.

Eastern Gate: Golden Gate; Mercy Gate; Jericho Gate; Gate of Repentance; Shushan Gate

Dung Gate: "Refuse Gate" Gate of Jeremiah's Pit; Gate of Siloam; Bab Silwan Gate (Arab period)

Zion Gate: The Prophet David's Gate

Jaffa Gate: Gate of David (Crusader period); Oratory Gate; Western Gate; Bab Mihrab David Gate (Arab period); Hebron Gate; Bab-el-Khalil (Turkish Period)

Damascus Gate: Gate of the Column; Bab al Amud; St. Stephen's Gate (Crusader's)

Flower Gate also called Herod's Gate:Babez-Zahra Gate (place where people stay awake to pray) Arab period; Herod's Gate (from Byzantine period)

St. Stephen's Gate also called Lion's Gate: Bab Ariha Gate (Arab period); Gate of Jericho; Gate of Jehoshaphat (Crusader period)

An additional small gate has been constructed next to Dung Gate for the use of pedestrians only.

Gath   (wine press) Philistine city, 15 kms. **E** of Ashdod and 15 kms. **SE** of Ekron. Joshua destroyed all the Anakim in the land, but some remained in Gath *[Joshua 11:21-22]*. The ark of God rested here after it was brought from Ashdod and before going to Ekron *[I Samuel 5:8]*. Goliath came from Gath *[I Samuel 17:4]*. David captured the city *[I Chronicles 18:1]*. Rehoboam, Solomon's son fortified it *[II Chronicles 11:8]*. Amos, the prophet, speaks out a word against it *[Amos 6:2]*. The city seemed to have disappeared by some unexplained disaster.

Gath-He'pher   (winepress of digging) The birthplace of Jonah *[II Kings 14:25]*. The town belonged to Zebulun in lower Galilee located 5 kms. **N** from Nazareth and identified today as Neby-Junas, where a tomb at the top of the hill identifies it also from Roman times *[Joshua 19:13]*.

Gath-Rimmon   (winepress of the pomegranate) This priestly city, located 3 kms. **S** of Joppa, belonged to the tribe of Dan in the plain of Philistia *[Joshua 19:45; 21:24; I Chronicles 6:69]*. The site is not easily identifiable today.

Gaulini'tis   (from the Golan, unclear translation) This Roman province was ruled by Herod the Great's son, Herod Antipas, located just **E** of the Sea of Galilee and was one of the cities of refuge from the Israelite period *[Joshua 20:8; 21:27; Deut. 4:43]*. The area on the eastern side of the Sea of Galilee extending to the Golan Heights. See map at the end of this book.

Gaza   (azzah, stronghold) Philistine city. Located on the southern coastal plain on the Mediterranean coast. Before Abraham, this was a border Canaanite city *[Genesis 10:19]*. It became the capital of the Philistines and was inherited by the children of Judah *[Joshua 15:47]*. It is most famous for the story of Samson, his encounter with a harlot and his death and victory over the Philistines *[Judges 16:1-16,30]*. Both Prophets, Jeremiah and Amos spoke out against Gaza *[Jeremiah 47:5; Amos 1:6-7]* Philip witnessed to the Ethiopian treasurer on the road to Gaza *[Acts 8:26]*. See Ein Yael.

Geba   (hill) Situated 11 kms. **N** of Jerusalem, this was the Levitical city of Benjamin *[Joshua 21:17; I Kings 15:22; I Samuel 13:3, 16]*. David struck down the Philistines here, the conquest of Philistia *[II Samuel 5:25]*. It is identified with Jeba today, near Michmash.

Ge'bim   (cisterns) This Benjaminite city is located near Anathoth and Nob and is mentioned only by the Prophet Isaiah, who foretells that the inhabitants will flee and seek refuge from this place *[Isaiah 10:31]*. It is identified as Khirbet el-Battash, located 4 kms. **NE** from Jerusalem.

Ged'eroth   (fortresses, to wall up) Site 18 kms. **SW** of Lod in the valley of Judah *[Joshua 15:41]*. Judah was taken and defeated under the evil King Ahaz for the Lord was angry with Judah *[II Chronicles 28:18-19]*. Possibly village of Qatra.

Gedor   (a wall) In the Judean mountains this city was the home of some of the men who joined King David in Ziklag *[I Chronicles 12:7]*. It is located 11 kms. **N** from Hebron and called Jedur. Some scholars identify it as ancient Geder.

Ge Harashim, Ge-Har'ashim   (valley of the craftsmen) This site is just **S** of the Old City near the valley of Gihon, adjacent to the industrial quarter of ancient Jerusalem in the lower city next to the ophel. "Joab was the father of Ge-harashim" *[Nehemiah 11:35; I Chronicles 4:14]*.

Gehen'na   (hell) See Hinnom Valley of *[11 Kings 23:10]*

Gennes'aret   (garden of riches) Also called Chinnereth which applies to the lake, the Sea of Galilee and the town located on the western shore of the Sea of Galilee. Site originally given to the Reubenites and the Gadites *[Deut. 3:17]*. One of the cities fortified by the Naphtalites *[Joshua 19:35]*.

During the time of Jesus, it was a small district and many came to Him here as He was on His way home to Capernaum. They begged to touch the hem of His garment and be healed of their many ailments *[Matthew 14:34-36]*.

Gerar   (to drag, drag away) Site is 20 kms. **SE** of Gaza, one of the oldest cities in the world; inhabited continually from the Chalcolithic Period through the Middle Bronze Age. It was a Philistine city during the time of Abraham when he lived here with Sarah and was tested here by God *[Genesis 20:1-2]*. Isaac also came here; the Lord appeared to him, he dug wells here at this site *[Genesis 26]*.

Ger'asa   See Gadarenes

Ger'asene   See Gadarene

Gerizim   (to cut, cut off) The mountain of blessing in the Samarian hills. Moses commanded the blessings from God from here *[Deut. 11:29; Deut. 27:11-13]*. The mountain opposite Mt. Ebal (the mountain of cursing) next to Shechem Valley. It is 858 meters (2849 ft.) above sea level and is the holy mountain of the ancient Samaritan people. It is called Jebel el-tor 4 kms. **NW** of ancient Shechem. From this summit, most of Israel can be seen. The Samaritans believe it is the mountain on which Abraham attempted to sacrifice Isaac and not Mt. Moriah in Jerusalem. This is the Samaritans' tradition and belief. They hold a yearly sacrifice here at Pesach according to Exodus 12 and many people from around the country come as invited guests. The latest archaeological findings reveal an exact replica of the Second Temple beneath a 5th C. Byzantine Church. This site is open to tourists since 1996. 62 kms. **N** from Jerusalem.

Gethsemane   (oil press) This lovely olive grove at the foot of the Mt. of Olives in Jerusalem, was the scene of the agony and 'passion' of Jesus before He was arrested. Next to the olive grove is the Catholic Church of all Nations which encompasses 'the rock of agony', believed to be the rock where Jesus knelt and prayed and "...His soul was exceedingly sorrowful even unto death," *[Matthew 26:36-46; Mark 14:32-42; Luke 22:39-46; John 18:1-11]*. One of the few eye witness reports, mentioned in all four gospels. This is considered a very holy site to all Christian faiths, Catholics main line Orthodox and Protestants. See Grotto of Gethsemane.

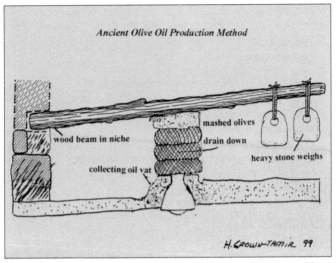

Ancient Olive Oil Production Method

wood beam in niche

mashed olives

drain down

heavy stone weighs

collecting oil vat

H. CROWN-TAMIR 99

The ancient beam oil-press used by the ancient farmers. Remnants of these structures have been found near the Garden of Gethsemane (oil press). The olive oil always played an important role in the Temples. Jesus, the Temple of the Holy Ghost, was pressed here, with the weight of what He was about to accomplish, in Gethsemane, the place of the oil press. Like the olive, He was crushed, His sweat like blood and he surrendered all.

Gezer (portion) Tel Jezer. This ancient city above the Maritime Plain is 7.5 km **SE** of Ramla, 28-30 kms. **SE** of Jaffa and was of great strategic importance since this city guarded the road from Jaffa to Jerusalem. David drove back the Philistines *[II Samuel 5:25]*. It became one of Solomon's Chariot Cities which was given to him as a dowry when he married Pharaoh's daughter *[I Kings 9:15-17]*. A modern Kibbutz is on the site. See Gezer High Place below.

Gezer's High Place (portion on higher ground) In the open air stands monumental configurations of long, high stones. There are ten stones, ranging from 5 to 11 ft. Dated from 1600 BC, these stones are symbolic witnesses to ancient covenants made on this site. *[Joshua 10:33; Judges 1:29; I Chronicles 14:16]*. See Gezer above.

Gib'bethon (mound) The Kohathites were assigned this Philistine city which was in the area, assigned to the tribe of Dan *[Joshua 19:44;21:23]*. King Nadab was killed here *[I Kings 15:27;16:15-16]* It is 5 kms. **E** of Gezer and identified as Tel el-Melat.

Gib'eath of Benjamin   (hill of Benjamin) Site near Gilgal, also known as Gib'eath of Saul where Saul sinned in numbering the people. *[Judges 19:14; I Samuel 13:15]*. It was the residence of Saul and continued to be his home after he became King. *[I Samuel 10:26; 11:4]*. Here was the site of the atrocious crime of the Benjaminites for which they almost lost their inheritance. *[Judges 19:12-30]*. Modern tel el-ful "hill of beans" now on site. 2 kms. **SE** of Jericho, 38 kms. from Jerusalem.

Gib'eah of Judah   (hill) Located 12 kms. **SW** of Bethlehem in the tribe of Judah. *[Joshua 15:57]*. It is a tradition that the prophet, Habakkuk, is buried here. Presently Jeba, a small village.

Gib'eath-Haar'aloth   (hill of the foreskins) Near Adam on the W side of the Jordan River, where the children of Israel crossed over to the Promised Land. The Lord commanded that the men be circumcised on this hill *[Joshua 5:2-4]*. The foreskins of the nation of Israelites were buried here. The exact location is unknown.

Gibeath-Haelohim   (hill of God) The Philistines' garrison stood here on this site near Gilgal *[I Samuel 10:5]*. The exact location is unknown.

Gib'eon   (hill city) Site is 12 kms. **NE** of Jerusalem on the ancient road to Jaffa. The Hivites deceived Joshua and agreed to a pact with him here *[Joshua 9:3-17]*. It became part of Benjamin, a Levitical town *[Joshua 18:25;21:17]*. See Ayyalon Valley *[Joshua 10:12]*. Solomon came here to sacrifice and the Lord appeared to him at Gibeon *[I Kings 3:4-5; 9:2]*. Hananiah, the prophet was born and lived here *[Jeremiah 28:1]*. Presently el-Jib, excavations have uncovered a pool and a very large water system complex dating from 11th Century BC *[Jeremiah 41:12]*.

Gideon Springs   (spring of Gideon) See Harod, Spring of

Gidom   (cutting, desolation) This site is just E of Gibeath, near the wilderness of Bethel, where the Benjaminites fled to escape to the Rock of Rimmon *[Judges 20:45]* 12 kms. **SW** of Bethlehem.

Gi'hon Springs   (gushing fountain, spring) This natural spring was Jerusalem's most ancient water supply from earliest times. It is in the Kidron Valley just below the eastern hill (aphelia) of the city. Solomon was brought here and anointed King *[I Kings 1:33,45]*. Here is the site of Hezekiah's tunnel which he had hewn out of the rock (701 BC), similar to the tunnels Solomon made at Megiddo and Gezer, which conducted these Gihon waters to a reservoir inside the city of Jerusalem *[II Chronicles 32:30]*. Manasseh, Hezekiah's son, built a wall as far as the Gihon *[II Chronicles 33:14]*. Now, we can see Hezekiah's tunnel and Warren's Shaft on this site. See Hezekiah's Tunnel and Pool of Siloam.

Gilbo'a (translation unclear) A mountain in northern Israel, 2 kms. **E** of Jez'reel. Its name probably comes from the spring nearby. Here Saul and his sons were slain by the Philistines *[I Samuel 28:4; 31:1,8; I Chronicles 10:1]*. King David wrote and sang a beautiful ode to Saul and his sons who were slain on Gilbo'a. He lamented the deaths, "The beauty of Israel is slain on high places," *[II Samuel 1:19-27]*. See Harod.

Gil'ead (to be rough, to lay bare) This mountain region **E** of the Jordan River extends from the Sea of Galilee to the northern end of the Dead Sea. Here, Jacob fled from Laban where he was overtaken "in the hill country of Gil'ead," *[Genesis 31:23]* The Ishmaelites took Joseph to Egypt from here *[Genesis 37:25]*. 10,000 of Gideon's warriors remained with him on this mountain before the battle against the Midianites *[Judges 7:3]*. The father of Jepthah, the judge lived here *[Judges 11:1-2]*. Hosea, the prophet, expressed his thoughts that the whole land was full of evildoers and was a place of rendezvous for wicked men *[Hosea 6:8-9]*. The Prophet, Jeremiah, asks, "Is there no balm in Gilead, is there no physician there?" *[Jeremiah 8:22]*. Presently it is tel-Ramith, 72 kms. **E** from Jerusalem extending into the country of Jordan.

Gil'gal (rolling) This site in the Jordan Valley 2 kms. **SE** of Jericho is also called Geliloth, the first encampment of the children of Israel after they crossed the Jordan River into the Promised Land *[Joshua 4:19-20]*. They kept the Passover here and were circumcised here *[Joshua 5:8-10]*. The angel of the Lord announced judgment here *[Judges 2:1]*. Samuel judged here *[I Samuel 7:16]*. Samuel killed Agag, king of the Amalekites at Gilgal *[I Samuel 15:33]*. Presently kibbutz Gilgal stands on the site which was formerly a nahal post but became a settlement in 1973.

Gil'gal of Elijah and Elisha This site 6 kms. from Bethel. Before Elijah was taken up to heaven, he was here with Elisha. They traveled from Gil'gal to Bethel together. *[II Kings 2:1-2]*. There was a famine in the land and Elisha made stew here and the miracle of the deadly stew is recorded *[II Kings 4:38]*.

Gi'loh (to cry out, rejoice) Site 9 kms. **NW** of Hebron in the mountains of Judah *[Joshua 15:51]*. The birthplace and the scene of the suicide of the traitor, Ahithophel *[II Samuel 15:12; 17:23]*. Now Kiryat Jala.

Git'taim (two witnesses) This place is located near Ramleh, the city where the Beerothites fled for fear of vengeance after they killed Ish-bosheth *[II Samuel 4:3]* The last city inhabited by the Benjaminites *[Nehemiah 11:33]*. The Armana letters identifies it today as Gamteti, 44 kms. **E** from Jerusalem.

Givat Moreh (hill of the teacher) The hill of Moreh is in the Valley of Jez'reel on the **N** side of the Harod Spring, where the Midianites were encamped when attacked by Gideon *[Judges 7:1]*. Presently new Jewish settlement on site, of the same name. 97 kms. **N** from Jerusalem.

Gob (a pit) The brother of Goliath from Gath was killed here by Jonathan, the son of Shimea *[II Samuel 21:18-19; I Chronicles 20:4]*. Near Gezer and 30 kms. **SE** of Jaffa.

Golan (translation unclear) One of the 3 cities of refuge (a place to flee to for protection) **E** of the Jordan River, 25 kms. **E** of the Sea of Galilee *[Deut. 4:43; Joshua 20:8, 21:27]*. After the Babylonian Captivity, Bashan was divided and Golan was in one of the provinces *[I Chronicles 6:71]*. It is identified as Sahem el-Jolan, a modern Arab village.

Golan Heights "For the Lord your God is bringing you into a good land, a land with streams and pools of water, with springs flowing in the valleys and hills; a land with wheat and barley, vines and fig trees, pomegranates, olive oil and honey,"*[Deut. 8:7]*. This is the Golan Heights. The **NE** area of Israel bordered by Mt. Hermon in the **N**, Israel's highest peak, at 2,200 meters (7084 ft.) above sea level and the Yarmouk River in the **S**, Nahal Ruqqas in the **E**, the Hula Valley and the Sea of Galilee in the **S**. This area was allotted to the tribe of Manasseh *[Deut.4:43]*. The Golan Jewish settlers revolted against Rome in the lst C. The area of 62 kms. long by 12 kms. was taken back from Syria by Israel, in June 1967 during the Six Day War. One third of Israel's water comes from the Golan Heights. Continue 175 kms. **N** from Jerusalem **NW** of the Sea of Galilee.

Golden Gate   See Eastern Gate

Gol'gatha   (place of the skull) The hill, in 2nd Temple time in Jerusalem, where Jesus was crucified, designated as the place of the skull because of the shape of the mound, or elevation for this hill of execution. "They came to the place called Gol'gatha…" *[Matthew 27:33; Mark 15:22; Luke 23:33; John 19:17]*. The shift of the city walls since the time of Jesus, makes it difficult to identify by sight; however, the Church of the Holy Sepulcher stands over the site and is honored as being authentic by most Orthodox and Roman Catholics, while Protestants and most Evangelicals prefer to think of the Garden Tomb as the site. See Garden Tomb and Holy Sepulcher Church.

Gomorrah   (submersion, overflowing) This city in the Jordan Valley, together with Sodom, became the scene of great wickedness and was overthrown by a cataclysmic explosion *[Genesis10:19; 13:10; 19:24-28]*. The circumstances of the Biblical account are in full agreement with the archaeological and geological findings. There was a beautiful, well watered, fertile valley here in 2054 BC and then, it was suddenly destroyed. The area is in the southern end of the Dead Sea, on the fault line of the Jordan Valley and the Dead Sea, half of which is in present day Jordan. Throughout history, to present day, we experience earthquakes in this area. Great geological activity was always here. The salt and the sulfur (imagine a match being lit), perhaps, being hit by lightning, together with the asphalt deposits, were blasted red-hot into the sky so that it literally rained down fire and brimstone *[Genesis 19:24-28]*. Zephaniah foretold judgment on Moab *[Zephaniah 2:9]*. Somewhere under the rising waters of the Dead Sea are the remains of these cities, perhaps, to be fully discovered in the future. 100 kms. **S** from Jerusalem. Jude, the half brother of Jesus refers to it *[Jude 7]*.

Good Samaritan Inn   In Arabic it is called Khan el-Ahmar or the Red Inn, because of the rose-colored rocks and soil in the area. On the road from Jerusalem to the Dead Sea area in the Jordan Valley, near Ma'aleh Adumim, is an old stone structure on the right side of the road, probably from the Crusader period which is the traditional site of the parable Jesus told, of the 'Good Samaritan' *[Luke 10:29-37]*. 36 kms. **S** from Jerusalem.

Grotto of Gethsemane (Gath-Shammah AR.; oil press) Next to the Garden of Gethsemane, at the foot of the Mt. of Olives on the **N** side, lies the Church of Mary's Assumption. The place where Orthodox believe Mary, the mother of Jesus was assumed (taken up) into heaven without experiencing physical death. It is a lovely unspoiled grotto and garden with remains from pre-Christian times. It is believed to be the place where Jesus often would have come with His disciples, to rest and pray, "…as was His custom," *[Luke 22:39; John 8:1]*. See Gethsemane.

Haceldama (Field of Blood) See Potter's Field

Hachi'lah, Hakilah (dark) The site of a long ridge in the wilderness of Judea near Jeshimon, which means devastation, an area covering 52 kms. from the Dead Sea Valley right up, **NW** direction, to the Mt. of Olives in Jerusalem. Characteristic are short bushes, thorns and succulent creepers in a brown and yellow barrenness of sand and limestone. This was one of 'the hiding places' of David, from King Saul *[I Samuel 23:19; 26:1,3]*. This long ridge of hills is visible today as one travels the road from Jerusalem through to the Dead Sea Valley route, there is a high ridge with a ruin called Yukin. 40 kms. **SE** from Jerusalem.

Hachi'lah, Hill of See Hachi'lah above *[I Samuel 26:1]*.

Hadad Rimmon, Hadadrim'mon (two Syrian gods) A site in the plain of Megiddo where there was a great mourning for the good king, Josiah, who lost his life in battle here. The Prophet Zechariah refers to the spiritual salvation of Judah in this context *[II Chronicles 35:22-25; Zechariah 12:11]*. Megiddo is 120 kms. **N** from Jerusalem.

Hahiroth See Pi-Hahiroth

Ha'math, Hamath-zobah (fortress) Once an ancient city state, capital of upper Syria. It was a Canaanite colony and taken by the Assyrians in the time of Hezekiah in 720 BC. It was the northern border where Solomon once held a feast. *[I Kings 8:65. II Kings 18:34]*. Ezekiel had his vision of the Promised Land concerning Hamath *[Ezekiel 47:20;*

48:1]. Presently 110 km. **S** of Aleppo, Syria in the fertile and well watered valley at the foot of Lebanon. See also Lebo-hamath.

Ham'math, Ham'moth-dor   (warm, hot springs) Hammath-Tiberias was allotted to Naphtali. The 17 hot springs have been famous since Trajan's day when a coin was minted in the springs honor *[Joshua 19:35]*. It is located 1 mile **SE** of Tiberias and it still sends up hot, sulfurous water. A modern spa is on the site. The remains of two synagogues from the first century can be seen with a well defined mosaic floor. See Tiberias.

Ham'onah   (multitude) Place of burial in the Dead Sea area in which the burial of Gog and his forces are prophesied *[Ezekiel 39:11-16]*. The exact location appears to be the northern area of the Dead Sea Valley 27 kms. **S** from Jerusalem.

Ham'on-gog Valley   See Hamonah above

Hanan'el, Tower of   (God has favored) This tower once formed part of the northern wall in Jerusalem's Old City, during Nehemiah's time and stood between the Fish Gate and the Sheep Gate. The Prophet, Zechariah, connects it with the Corner Gate on the other side of the Sheep Gate *[Nehemiah 3:1; 12:39; Zechariah 14:10; Jeremiah 31:38]*. Go to the Jewish Quarter in Jerusalem's Old City and see the Broad Wall which is the only part of the wall visible today. See Ancient Gates back.

Har Mageddon   See Armageddon and Megiddo *[Revelation 16:16]*

Ha'rod, Spring of, Mayan Harod   (spring of trembling or terror) This spring is in the Jez'reel Valley, at the foot of Mt. Gilboa, where Gideon's army was tested before the battle with the Midianites *[Judges7:1,4-7]*. Gideon's Spring is here, where the spring gushes forth from a rock-cut cave, from the ancient walls of the rock-cut pool. Beautiful recreation park, field school and camp sites located here. 15 kms. **W** of Bet Shean in the Jezreel Valley.

Hav'voth-jair, Bashan-havoth-jair   (huts or hamlets of Jair) Villages **E** of the Jordan village in the Bashan area, which the son of Manasseh captured and called by his name. Jair, the Gileadite and judge had thirty cities here. In Joshua's conquest, it was sixty cities with walls and bronze gates *[Deut 3:14; Judges10:4; Joshua 13:30; I Kings 4:13; Numbers 32:41]*. Present day city, Salkhat in Jordan.

Ha'zarad'dar　(village of Addar) A site in the southern Negev, the southern border between Kadesh-barnea and Azmon, whereas, Joshua simply called it Addar *[Numbers 34:4; Joshua 15:3]*. Now in present day Egypt's Sinai Peninsula, 6 kms. from the Negev Israeli border with Egypt, called Ain Qedis.

Haz'azon-tamar　See Ein Gedi (the ancient name) *[Genesis 14:3; II Chronicles 20:2]*

Ha'zer-hat'ticon　(middle village) The prophet Ezekiel names this site as part of the northern border of Israel near present day Damascus *[Ezekiel 47:16]*.

Haze'roth　(villages) In the Sinai desert this site was the 16th station of the children of Israel on their way to the Promised Land. The people remained here a while and Miriam and Aaron spoke against Moses and were punished. They continued to the wilderness of Paran *[Numbers 11:35; 12:16; 33:17-18]*. See all of Numbers 12. Now in the Sinai desert under Egyptian rule, some 50 kms. **SW** of Eilat.

Hazor, Hatzor　(enclosure, village) This is the largest ancient tel in Israel, in the Upper Galilee, 6 kms. **N** of Rosh Pina and 12 kms. **N** of the Sea of Galilee. It was on the ancient Via Maris (way of the sea) and was mentioned in Egyptian writings from the 19th C. BC. Jabin, King of Hazor fought against Joshua. Deborah fought here against Sisera with Barak. King Solomon made it one of his chariot cities, with Solomonic walls and gates *[Joshua 11:1-5,10; 19:36; Judges 4:2; I Samuel 12:9; I Kings 9:15]*. It is one of Israel's most beautiful national parks, near Lake Hulah.

Heap of Witness　See Galeed Genesis 31:52

He'bron　(haver, friend; community, alliance) It was one of the 'cities of refuge' called Kiryat Arba, 36 kms. **S** of Jerusalem, 1 km. to the **N** is Mamre. This city sits on the highest hill in the area, 3000 feet (950 meters) above sea level. The Canaanites and the Anakim lived here. Abraham came and bought the Cave of Machpelah. Isaac and Jacob lived here. David made it his royal residence for 7 years before he came to Jerusalem. Joshua took Hebron and Caleb resettled it *[Genesis 13:18; 23:2,17-20; Joshua 10:36-37; 12:10; 14:14-15; 15:13; II Samuel*

2:1-4; 5:5; 15:10; I Kings 2:11]. There is still a Jewish community in the center of this ancient holy city, even after 3500 years, Jews still live here. See Kir'iath-Arba.

He'bron, Valley of   Here Jacob sent his beloved son Joseph to seek his brothers in Shechem *[Genesis 37:14]*. Next to Hebron city.

Helena's Monument   See Tombs of the Kings

Hel'kath-haz'zurim   (field of sharp swords or edges) The name of the plain near Gibeon where David's men won the deadly victory over Ishbosheth and some of them were defeated *[II Samuel 2:12-17]*. Located 12 kms. **N** on the ancient road to Jaffa. See the steps leading down to the pool of Gibeon.

He'reth   (thicket) The site of a wooded mountain area in the land of Judah where David hid out from Saul *[I Samuel 22:5; II Samuel 23:14-17; I Chronicles 11:16-19]* See Adullam, 18 kms. **SW** of Jerusalem in the Judean wilderness.

Her'mon, Mt.   (sacred mountain) The mountain range in south Aram (Syria) and northern Israel. Also called Mt. Sion (Syr. Sirion) *[Deut. 4:48]*. The Amorite name is Mt. Snir *[Song Solomon 4:8]*. It is the highest of all the mountains in Israel. We see its snow-capped peaks almost year round 2,200 meters (9101 feet) above sea level. The Canaanites and Ba'als had sacred places and altars on these 'high places'. The top peak is called Abu-Ned, "father of the dew". This was the outline for the possession of the land, as given to Moses by God, and the conquest of the northern kingdom given to Joshua. David seeking after God, speaks of Hermon. How good it is for brethren to dwell together in unity... "like the dew of Hermon," *[Psalm 133:3]*. Solomon beckons his beloved to come to Hermon *[Deut. 3:9; 4:48; Joshua 11:17; 12:1,5; 13:5; Psalm 42:6; Psalm 89:12; Song of Solomon 4:8]* Many Bible scholars believe this is the 'Mountain of Transfiguration', where Jesus appeared to his disciples, as opposed to Mt. Tabor *[Matthew 17:1; Mark 9:2; Luke 9:28; II Peter 1:17-18]* Identified today as Jebel es-Sheikh 50 kms. **SW** of Damascus and 55 kms. **NE** of the Sea of Galilee. The hill of Mizar is on Mt. Hermon *[Psalm 42:6]*. See Caesarea Phillipi.

Her'od's sites   (hordus) Herod the Great was born in 37 BC and died 4 BC. He was alive when Jesus was born in the year 4 BC and died shortly afterwards. The ministry of Jesus and the Biblical sites throughout His life and ministry are connected to Herod and have been included in this compilation of Biblical sites. All the descendants of Herod the Great continued to use the family name, Herod, up to the fourth generation, as mentioned in the New Testament: Herod Archelaus, Herod Antipas, Herod Philip II, Herod Agrippa I and Herod Agrippa II. It was to Herod, the Great; the wise men came from the E and asked, "Where is He born King of the Jews…?" *[Matthew 2:2]*.

Herod's Sites in Jerusalem   See Her'od's <u>Antonio Fortress</u>

Herod's Family Tombs   Just behind the King David Hotel, in Jerusalem, off of King David Street, are remains of tombs believed to be the tombs of Herod's Family, several whom he murdered. Some rolling stones block the doors. They were identified from the descriptions by Josephus.

Herod's Gate   also called Flower Gate. See ancient Gates of the Old City, back book.

Herod's Palace   Located at the present site of the Jaffa Gate in Jerusalem, Herod built a magnificent palace and gardens for himself, with over 100 splendidly furnished guest rooms. It was also called the 'Upper Palace' because of its location in the Upper City. Josephus said, "it was a luxurious extravagance *[Wars,4.4/176-182]*. Here Herod was seated when the Magi, coming from the **E**, asked, "Where is He who has been born King of the Jews?" His jealous nature and demonic character caused him to slay all the male children who were in Bethlehem *[Matthew 2:1-8]*. The Praetorium may have been located here. See Pilate's Judgment Hall.

Herod's Temple, Second Temple   Herod's greatest building achievement was the Jewish Temple built on the Temple Mount in Jerusalem, began in 20 BC. He implemented a policy of employment through public works. The Temple itself only took 18 months to complete but the additional buildings, the courts and the decorations, took another 44 years. Josephus tells us that from a distance it appeared to be a large snow-covered mountain covered with gold *[War VI 394] In the year 26 AD, the Jews said to Jesus, "This temple took 46 years to build…" [John 2:20]*. Jesus was brought here by Mary and Joseph for His circumcision *[Luke 2:21]*. He

probably made His Bar Mitzvah here *[Luke 2:41-50]*. Here, He spoke to the leading Jewish scholars and rabbis "…and all who heard Him were astonished at His understanding and answers…" *[Luke 2:47]*. See Second Temple.

JESUS CAME TO THE TEMPLE

Jesus came here to this Temple to preach and teach throughout His ministry *[Matthew 26:55, Luke 22:53]*. He threw out the money changers in the courts *[Matthew 21:12]*. The lame came to Him in the temple *[Matthew 21:14]*. Here, He was sentenced to die and they led Him away from here *[Matthew 27:2]*. The veil of the temple was torn in two when He died *[Luke 23:45]*. The disciples returned here many times *[Acts 3:1; 5:20]*. No doubt, until the time of the Temple's destruction by Titus in 70 AD, there were disciples and followers in this Temple and its surrounding areas. The 2nd Temple Model can be seen in the Holyland West Hotel in the suburb of Beit Vegan (house and garden) in Jerusalem. See Specific Sites where Jesus walked after this section.

Herod's Sites Outside Jerusalem   See Her'od's Ashkelon.

Her'od's Caesarea   This was the most famous of his towns, begun in 22 BC and completed in 10 BC. A great semi-circular artificial harbor, a theater, amphitheater and recently excavated hippodrome, are located here in this gentile city. There was a Jewish community here, as the foundation of a synagogue from the time of Jesus was discovered. Did Jesus come here? Perhaps. Paul was kept in custody in the Roman guardhouse and Herod's grandchildren came together with Festus, to listen to Paul *[Acts 25:4-27; Acts 26]*. Josephus tells us that Pontius Pilate was vacationing here when he was summoned urgently back to Jerusalem because of a possible uprising over a young Jewish man whom the Jewish leaders wanted to crucify. The young Jewish man was Jesus of Nazareth. See also Caesarea.

Her'od's Caesarea Philippi   This site was built by Herod the Great's son, after Her'od's death. Here Jesus, came with His disciples and asked Peter, "Whom do men say that I am?" *[Mark 8:27-33; Luke 9:18]*. See Caesarea Philippi.

Her'od's Winter Palace   See Jericho

Herodion House Mansion   (house from Herod's time) A palatial mansion was discovered in the salvage work of the Upper City on the eastern slope of the Old City of Jerusalem (Jewish quarter) after 1967. Its design, size of over 600 sq. meters; the lavish appointments included seven mikvot (ritual purity baths) suggesting that it was the home of Annas or Caiaphas, before whom Jesus came. A home like this was not uncommon for the high priestly families of this Second Temple Period. There were 28 high priests from 37 BC until 70 AD. According to Josephus "…they were great procurers of money" (Ant. 20.205). There was a great deal of power and money in the hands of a few of these high priest families *[Luke 3:2; John 11:49-50]*. The priestly families had the monopoly on trade, sacrificial animals, the baking of the shew bread and the incense used in the temple. Jesus called them thieves and hypocrites *[Matthew 22:18; 23:13,15,23, 25,27,29]*. See Peter of Galicantu.

Heshbon   (reckoning) The Moabite town in which the children of Israel encamped as they arrived from Egypt, taken by Moses, became a priestly city *[Numbers 21:25; Joshua 13:21,26; 21:39]*. Solomon spoke about this city and its natural spring "…the eyes of the Shulamite are likened to the pools of Heshbon." *[Song of Solomon 7:4]*. It is located 38 kms. **E** of the Jordan river in Jordan. It has an excellent spring, desirable location, which runs into the Dead Sea. Archaeological ruins from the Roman period are still visible.

Heth'lon   (entwine, enwrap) The site of the northern border according to Ezekiel's vision for the land *[Ezekiel 47:15; 48:1]*. Also identified as a mountain pass on the northern border of Lebanon called Lebo-hamath, as directed by the Lord, to Moses. *[Numbers 34:8]*. See also Lebo-hamath and Hamath. In present day Lebanon, 110 kms. **S** of Aleppo, Syria.

Hezekiah's Tunnel   (Jehovah is our strength tunnel) Also known as Siloam Tunnel located in Jerusalem, in the deep Kidron valley, on the eastern steep slope of the Ophel (David's city). Here King Hezekiah (701 BC) took the waters of Jerusalem's most ancient water supply, the Gihon Spring and diverted them into a reservoir inside the city walls. The tunnel is 533 meters (1777ft.) long and is still navigable by foot for the adventurous who must bring flashlights and be prepared to get wet. *[II Kings 20:20; II Chronicles 32:4,30; Isaiah 36:2]*. See Gihon. Pool of Siloam and Warren's Shaft.

Hill Country of Gilead   See Gilead where Jacob pitched his tent *[Genesis 31:25]*

Hill of Moreh   (hill of the teacher) See Givat Moreh *[Judges 7:1]*

Hinnom,Valley of   (valley of the Ben-Hinnom, son of Hinnom) Here is a steep ravine, very narrow and rocky to the **S** and **W** of the Old City of Jerusalem. This valley separates Mount Zion on the **N**, to the Valley of Rephaim on the **S**. The boundary of the tribes of Judah and Benjamin *[Joshua 15:8; 18:16]*. Solomon erected high altars here to Molech *[I Kings 11:7]*. The kings committed abominable acts here and made their children pass through the fires *[II Kings 16:3; II Chronicles 28:3;33:6]*. Infant fire sacrifice was offered here and Jeremiah, the prophet, spoke out against this sin, telling the people that the Lord said "...I did not command this nor did it enter My mind (to do such a thing) *[Jeremiah 7:30-31]*. After this time, this area became the common cesspool of the city where the sewage was gathered. Solid filth was collected here and, thereby, later the Jews gave it the name "Gehenna" or "hell." Today it is also known by the Arabic name Wadi Jehennam, a clean and well-kept valley, full of beautiful trees and plants and graces the Old City walls. See Ketef Hinnom.

Holy of Holies   (apartness, sacredness; kodesh hakodashim) The Lord instructed Moses to make Him a sanctuary, a tabernacle so He could dwell among the children of Israel *[Exodus 25:8-9]*. Inside this tabernacle would be the 'most holy place', called the Holy of Holies *[II Chronicles 3:8,10]*. It was last erected and honored in the Second Temple, in which the priest went once a year, on Yom Kippur, to offer sacrifices for the people. Zechariah, the father of John, the Baptist, ministered here. *[Luke 1:9]*. On the 'Day of Atonement' the 'scapegoat' would be sent out into the wilderness and its red neck covering of wool would come back white indicating that the sins were forgiven. Tractate Yoma tells us that the last time this occurred was around 30 AD. The temple was destroyed in 70 AD by Titus and the Holy of Holies as well. Paul's gospel to the Hebrews speaks about this place *[Hebrews 9:3]*.

Holy Sepulcher Church (holy tomb church) To most Catholic and Orthodox Christians, this is the holiest site in all of Christendom. It is located on the border of the Moslem quarter and Christian quarters, in the Old City of Jerusalem. The site is believed to be where Jesus was crucified, laid in the tomb and resurrected. The first church over the site was built by the Emperor Constantine and his mother Helena, in the 4th C. *[Matthew 27:33,59; Mark 15:22,46;16:8; Luke 23:33,53; John 19:17; 20:1-18]*. See Calvary, Garden Tomb, Golgatha and Via Delorosa.

Hor, Mount (the mountain) Moses led the children of Israel here after they left Kadesh *[Numbers 20:22-23]*. It is located on the border, the edge of Edom in Jordan *[Numbers 33:37]*. Tradition calls it 'the mountain of Jebel Nebi-Harun', meaning the mountain of the Prophet Aaron, the brother of Moses. He is known to most as the High Priest. He died and was buried here *[Numbers 33:39]*. It is **E** of the Arava desert, a high and conspicuous mountain range of sandstone, just **E** of the ancient Jordanian city of Petra.

Ho'reb (dryness, desert) This is another name for Mount Sinai, (Jebel Musa AK), 'the mountain of Moses'. Some scholars believe it is the lower part of the peak of Mount Sinai and the whole mountain range was called Ho'reb *[Exodus 3:1; 17:6; 33:6; Deut. 1:2; 6, 19; I Kings 8:9; 19:8, II Chronicles 5:10; Psalm 106:19; Malachi 4:4]*. It is in Egypt, the entire area of Sinai was given to Egypt by Israel in the Camp David Accords, in Nov., 1978. See Mount Sinai and Karkom, Mt. of. Traveling due **S** from Jerusalem 315 kms. to Taba border, onto the Sinai Desert.

Hor'esh (wood, wooded area, forest) A site in the desert in the wilderness of Ziph, located 8 kms. **SE** of Hebron and preserved today as Tel Zif. David fled from Saul to this site where Jonathan, his beloved friend, met him and offered his support *[I Samuel 23:15-19]*. See Ziph.

Hor'mah (a devoted place, destruction) It was a Canaanite town **S** of Palestine and here, the Israelites, against the advice of Moses, were overcome by the Amalekites. *[Numbers 14:45;21:3]*. Joshua conquered this town and assigned it to Judah *[Joshua 15:30]*. Located 9 kms. **NE** of Beersheva in the Negev.

Horse Gate (shar'ar soos) Ancient gate in the Old City wall of Jerusalem, on the **W** end of the bridge leading from Mount Zion to the Temple Mount *[Nehemiah 3:28]*. The kings of Judah had brought horses through this gate and dedicated them to the sun god during the time of their gross idolatrous worship *[II Kings 23:11]*. The prophet, Jeremiah, speaks of a restored Judah from the Brook of Kidron to the Horse Gate *[Jeremiah 31:40]*. See Ancient Gates and map at the back.

House of Caiaphas See Herodion House and Peter of Galicantu

Hulda Gate (unclear translation) This double gate, currently closed, lies along the southern wall of the Temple Mount underneath the el-Aksa Mosque, in the Ophel excavation site and was one used to enter the Second Temple area. It is named after the prophetess, Huldah *[II Kings 22:14; II Chronicles 34:22]*. This whole complex was built by Herod, the Great. See Ophel Archaeological Garden.

Huleh, Lake of See Me'rom

Hundred, Tower of the (migdal shel mea, hundred) This tower was near the Sheep Gate on the ancient city wall in Jerusalem's Old City and was rebuilt by Nehemiah in the rebuilding of the walls *[Nehemiah 3:1; 12:39]*. See Ancient Gates and map at the back of this book.

Ib'leam (to swallow down, or swallow up) This Levitical, priestly city is also called Bileam and within the city were urban towns, making the natural border of the tribe of Asher *[Joshua 17:1l; I Chronicles 6:70]*. Today it is a city in ruins called Kiryat Belameh about 18 kms. **SE** of Megiddo.

Id'alah (unclear translation) This city was on the western border of Zebulun near Bethlehem and Shimron *[Joshua 19:15]*. Today it is Kiryat et Huwara, 10 kms. **S** from Jerusalem.

Idumea (from Edom) This is the name that the Greeks applied to the area around Hebron but during the time of Jesus it was the area of Edom. A great multitude came to Jesus from here *[Mark 3:8]*. Now in present day Jordan.

I'im   (heap of ruins) This city is in the most southern part of Judah and was also on the border of the territory of Simeon *[Joshua 15:29]*. It is Deir el-Ghawi located in present day Jordan, some 20 kms. **SE** of the southern tip of the Dead Sea.

I'jon   (a ruin) This storage city was in the hillside of Naphtali and was captured by Benhadad in the days of King Asa *[I Kings 15:20; II Chronicles 16:4]*. It is presently Tel el-Dibbon in the fertile valley and meadow of the spring called Merj Ayun just **NW** of Dan, 223 kms. **N** from Jerusalem in present day Lebanon.

Iph'tahel, Jiphthah   (God will open) The valley of Wadi el-Malik intersecting Naphtali and Asher at the northern side of Zebulun *[Joshua 19:14;27]*. Also known as the Wadi Abilin and is located 20 kms. **E** of the Carmel Mt. range and Haifa.

Ir'peel   (God will heal) The city just **W** of Jerusalem (3 kms.) in the tribe of Benjamin *[Joshua 18:27]*. The exact location is unknown.

Ir'shemesh   See Bet Shemesh

Israel, land of   See maps in back of this book, ancient and modern as well as all the allotments given to the children of Israel from God through Moses in Tribe section.

Issachar, Tribe of   See *Joshua 17:10; Joshua 19:17-23*. See Tribe section.

Iye-abarim   (ruins of Abarim) Here is a site in Moab, in present day Jordan, in the wilderness which was **E** of Moab, towards the sunrise. It was the 47th station of the children of Israel in the desert, and their stopping place as they approached the Promised Land on the border of Moab *[Numbers 21:11; 33:44]*. 22 kms. **SE** of the southern most end of the Dead Sea.

Jab'bok   (to empty, laid waste) **E** of the River Jordan this stream empties itself between the Dead Sea and the Sea of Galilee, some 73 kms. **S** of the Sea of Galilee. It runs 100 kms. with its headwaters rising on the border of Moab. It is shallow and easily navigable in most parts except when it runs over steep rocks, here Jacob, continuing his struggle against his brother, Esau, arose and took his wives and maidservants and crossed over. Here Jacob, was left alone and struggled with God.

Jacob meets Esau at this place. Today it is called River Zerka, the "blue river" located in Jordan [*Genesis 32:22; Numbers 21:24; Judges 11:13, 22*]. See Peniel.

Ja'besh-gilead   (dry, parched; Ja'besh of Gilead) The town of Gilead, region beyond the Jordan River and 'a night's journey by foot from Beth Shean', S of the Sea of Galilee [*I Samuel 11:1;3,5,9;31:11; II Samuel 2:4; Numbers 32:29,40*]. The residents were punished because they did not help their brothers against the tribe of Benjamin [*Judges 21:8-14*]. Nahash, the Ammonite, lay siege here, he wanted the inhabitants to have their right eyes pulled out. Saul rescued them and defeated the Ammonites [*I Samuel 11:1-11*]. The men of Ja'besh-gilead remembered Saul and took their slain bodies from the walls of Beth Shean and buried them and mourned 7 days for them; they sat shivah [*I Samuel 31:11-13*]. David sent his blessings to them for this mitzvah (blessing) [*II Samuel 2:5*]. Located in Jordan, 18 kms. SE of Beth Shean on twin hills on the Wadi Jabesh, called Tel Abu Kharaz.

Jab'neh   (God causes to be built) The site of the northern border of Judah near the Mediterranean Sea. The Philistines and the Danites fought here and the Philistines captured it. Afterwards King Uzziah captured it along with Gath and Ashdod [*II Chronicles 26:6*]. Josephus called it Jamnia and today the village is inhabited; called Jebuah just 1 km. from the Mediterranean Sea, 10 kms. S from Jaffa (Joppa).

Jackal's Spring   See Serpent's Spring [*Nehemiah 2:13*]

Ja'cob's Ladder   See Bethel *Genesis 28:12*

Ja'cob's Well   (the well named after Jacob) Well known story of the 'Woman at the Well' takes place here. Jesus came here and speaks kindly to a Samaritan woman [*John 4:1-26*]. The city is identified as Sychar, which is Shechem. Jacob came to Shechem and camped here and bought the land here (and the well) for 100 pieces of money [*Genesis 33:1-20*]. 59 kms. N from Jerusalem. See Shechem.

Jaffa   See Joppa

Jano'ah, Jano-hah   (quiet, restful) Located in the land of Ephraim on its northern border [*Joshua 16:6-7*]. It is just SE of Nablus, 10 kms. SE of Shechem and is the ancient city of Janoah and is now a small village by the same name, with extensive ruins of antiquity.

Jat'tir   (to remain or abound) This city in the mountains of Judah, located some 21 kms. **SW** of Hebron had pasture lands and was assigned to the priests. *[Joshua 15:48;21:14]*. David came here and sent presents to his friends, spoils which he had taken from the enemies *[I Samuel 30:27]*. There was a large Christian community here in the 4th C and it is called Kirbet Attin to this day.

Je'bus   (to tread down or trample) One of the many names of Jerusalem when Jerusalem was under the Jebusites. The Jebusites were a Hittite tribe which came from Ham and had captured Jerusalem from the Canaanites but only held it for 200 years. "And David and all Israel went to Jerusalem, which is Jebus, where the Jebusites were the inhabitants of the land and he took the stronghold of Zion." *[II Samuel 5:6-10 ; I Chronicles 11:4-8]*. See Jerusalem also Old City.

Je'busite City Wall   Located on the eastern hill **S** of the high ground where Solomon built the First Temple. See Jebus above. The site inside these walls was well fortified, a stronghold bounded by the Kidron and Tyropoeon (Cheese makers) Valleys. Recent archaeological excavations have uncovered portions of the Jebusite wall and can be seen today on the **S** end of the City of David. Go **S** from Dung Gate.

Je'busite Tunnel   See Warren's Shaft

Je'gar Sahadu'tha   (heap of witness, Aramean name) See Galeed

Jehosh'aphat, Valley of   (Jehovah judged) Also called the Valley of Decision and the Valley of Berachah, the Valley of Blessing. This is another name for the Kidron Valley located in Jerusalem between the Old City of Jerusalem and the Mount of Olives. King Jehosh'aphat overthrew the enemies of Israel here *[II Chronicles 20:26]*. There are modern Jewish graves built on this site. Joel speaks about the divine judgment of God upon His enemies *[Joel 3:2,12]*. Joel also speaks of the great judgment of the nations here before the Messiah's coming. Zechariah chapter 14 refers to this valley in more detail.

Jeremiah's Pit   This is also known as Jeremiah's Grotto or the Court of the Guard. It is located next to Damascus Gate on the northern wall. Jeremiah the Prophet was held prisoner by King Zedekiah *[Jeremiah 38:5-10]*. It is believed that it was here where he composed Lamentations on the destruction of the Temple *[Lamentations chapters 1-5]* Many believe this is where Jeremiah is buried. Go to Damascus Gate in **E** Jerusalem.

Jer'icho   (place of fragrance or moon city) One of the oldest cities in the world where the Jordan Valley broadens between the mountains of Moab on the **E** and the western hills near the Dead Sea valley. Moses went up to Mount Nebo and viewed Jericho *[Deut. 32:48,49]*. Here the children of Israel entered the Promised Land under Joshua *[Joshua 3:16]*. The children of Israel camped opposite Jericho and it was the most important city in the Jordan Valley at their time of entry *[Numbers 22:1; 31:12; 34:15; 35:1]*. The capture and sin of Achan and the curse are recorded vividly *[Joshua 6:1-7:26]*. The city will always remain a cursed city *[Joshua 6:26]*. David's men were humiliated and stayed in Jericho for a season *[II Samuel 10:5; I Chronicles 19:5]*. Jericho is also called the City of Palm Trees. *[Judges 1:16;3:13]*. Elisha healed the springs near here and Elijah went up in a whirlwind near here, across the Jordan River *[II Kings 2:1-22]*. The prophet Isaiah foretells a time of mourning, perhaps the city he speaks about is Jericho *[Isaiah 32:12-15]*. During Herod the Great's time, the precious perfume, parsimmon from the balsam trees, was sold to the Romans at a great cost. Jesus came to Jericho many times with His disciples as recorded in *[Matthew 20:29]*. He healed the two blind men here *[Mark 10:46; Luke 10:30; 18:35]*. Jesus saw Zacchaeus in the sycamore tree and went to his home *[Luke 19:1-10]*. Paul speaks about faith and refers to Jericho in his letter to the Hebrews *[Hebrews 11:30]*. Herod's Winter Palace and a Palace for his mother Cypros was built here on the Wadi Kelt, some 6 kms. **SW** of Tel es-Sultan here in Jericho. Another Hasmonean Palace and a monumental swimming pool have been partially excavated here. See the artificial mound and wing of the palace and sunken garden. Please note: Jericho is now part of the Palestinian Authority but passage to Jericho for tourists is generally unhampered.

Jeru'salem   (Yeru-Yir'eh, God will show; salem, peace) The holy city and city of peace. The city which promises peace someday, has had over one hundred names in its long history. The Rabbis claim it had 70 names which correspond with the names of God. They also say that 10 measures of beauty were given to the world but 9 fell on Jerusalem. The name appears more than 811 times in the Old and New Testaments combined. The undivided capital of the state of Israel is the "holy city" for three great religions: Judaism, Christianity, and Islam. In the Hebrew mind it is called "city of peace", while the Arabs call it El Kuds "holy town" though it is not mentioned once in the Koran. It is 23 kms. **W** of the Dead Sea and 51 kms. **E** of the Mediterranean Sea; Bethlehem is 7 kms. **S**. It is one half mile above sea level on a rocky plateau, an elevation of 825 meters (2550 ft.). The psalmist says, "…beautiful in elevation, the joy of the whole earth," *[Psalm 48:2]*. Its ancient water supply was the Gihon Spring in the Kidron Valley. Jerusalem is at the point of three valleys, the Kidron which runs **N** and **S** and lies **E** of the city, the Tyropoeon (also **NS**) is long and narrow and extends southward and the Hinnom also **NS** but curves easterly and joins the Kidron and Tyropoeon. There are the three mounts; Zion, the western hill, then Mt. Moriah in the center and the Mt. of Olives on the **E**. The Davidic-Solomonic era is from 1000-930 BC. when Jerusalem was officially declared and established, for David took the stronghold of Zion which had been held by the Jebusite *[II Samuel 5:6-10; I Chronicles 11:4-9]*. Today all of Jerusalem has a population of over a half a million residents and is spread out to forty nine communities and villages for over a total area of 109 square kms. (The total population grew from 266,300 in 1967 to 574,600 in 1995). See Jesus in Jerusalem and Jerusalem's Old City below. See map 'God's name is here.'

Jerusalem's Old City   (ear-ha-atiqua) The area of 209 acres or one third square miles which is inside the ancient walls. The heart of the entire city is the Old City. It is made up of four distinct quarters; the Armenian quarter, the Jewish quarter, the Moslem quarter and the Christian quarter. See Jerusalem above, and Old City.

CHRONOLOGICAL DATES OF JERUSALEM

Canaanite Period (1900-1400BC)

1900 BC First mentioned as a Canaanite city in Egyptian texts and the Tel el-Amarna letters

1250 BC Melchizedek, king of Salem (Jerusalem) comes to bless Abraham *[Genesis 14:18]*.

1210 BC Adoni-Zedek, king of Jerusalem, leads a coalition of five Amorite kings but Joshua defeats them *[Joshua 10:1,3,5,23; 12:10]*. Jerusalem remained a Jebusite city for 200 years until the time of David *[Judges 19:10-12; II Samuel 24:21-25]*.

1004 BC King David captures the city, makes it the holy City of David and brings the Ark to Jerusalem, making it a religious, as well as his political center *[II Samuel 5:5-14; I Kings 2:11]*.

First Temple Period (1000 BC – 586 BC)

1000 BC Solomon builds the Temple and his royal palace on the eastern hill *[I Kings 8:1;9:15,19; I Kings 11:36, 42]*.

925 BC After Solomon's death the kingdom of Israel is split in two: the northern kingdom with Samaria as its capital (see Shiloh) and the southern kingdom remains with Jerusalem their capital *[I Kings 12:18, 21, 27,28]*.

705-702 BC King Hezekiah reinforces the walls and builds the tunnel for the water supply in anticipation of the invasion of the king of Assyria *[II Kings 18:17; 20:20; II Chronicles 32:30]*.

597 BC Nebuchadnezzar, king of Babylon, seizes the kingdom of Judah and King Jehoiachin is exiled *[II Kings 24:10-16]*.

586 BC Nebuchadnezzar captures Jerusalem on the 9th day of Av, burns and destroys the Temple and city. King Zedekiah is killed and the population is dispersed throughout the world *[II Kings 25:1-4]*.

Second Temple Period (538 BC-70AD)

538 BC Cyrus, the King of Persia issued a decree allowing the Jews to return to Jerusalem and rebuild their Temple *[Ezra 1:1-3]*.

444 BC The Old City walls are rebuilt by Nehemiah *[Nehemiah 1:1-3]*. See Broad Wall and *[Nehemiah 3:8]*.

332 BC Alexander the Great conquers the city and the rule of the Egyptian Ptolemaics *[II Chronicles 12:9]*.

198 BC Antiochus Epiphanes seizes the city and sets up a pig in the Temple area, which leads to the revolt of Judah Maccabee.

167 BC Jerusalem is captured by the Maccabeans and purified and becomes the capital of the Hasmonean kingdom. (Hannucah is inaugurated) The Festival of Lights *[John 10:22,23]*.

Roman Period (63 BC-326 AD)

63 BC Roman rule begins when Jerusalem is captured. All the Jews are subject to the Roman rule and authority. *[Luke 1:5; Luke 2:1-3]*

37 BC Herod the Great transforms Jerusalem with all his mighty building projects. See Herod and sites.

4 BC Jesus is born in Bethlehem but His life and death are all connected to Jerusalem. See sites in Jerusalem by name. See Specific Sites where Jesus walked, next section.

Jesus in Jerusalem 4 BC-30 AD

During the time of Jesus, Jerusalem was designed to accommodate huge crowds, especially the Jewish pilgrims who came into the city for the Feasts *[Levitcus 23]*. Meir Ben Dov, a leading Israeli archaeologist has estimated that more than 150,000 lived in Jerusalem and an additional 100,000 arrived during the pilgrim feasts when Jesus walked these ancient streets of Jerusalem.

"Then the… Pharisees came to Jesus in J…" Matthew 15:1 "He showed His disciple He must go to J…" Matthew 16:21 "Then Jesus going up to J, took the twelve…" Matthew 20:17 "Behold we are going up to J (for betrayal)…" Matthew 20:18 "He came to J and the city was moved…" Matthew 21:10 "O J, you who kills the prophets…" Matthew 23:37 "The scribes came down to Him from J…" Mark 3:22 "The scribes came to Him from J." Mark 7:1 "They were on the road up to J…" Mark 10:32 "They came to J, near Bethphage…" Mark 11:1 "Jesus went to J, into the Temple…" Mark 11:11 "So they came to J, went into the Temple…" Mark 11:15 "…many women came up to Him to J…" Mark 15:41 "(His parents) brought Him to J…" Luke 2:22 "His parents brought Him to J…" Luke 2:41 "Jesus stayed behind in J…" Luke 2:43 "The he (devil) brought Him to J…" Luke 4:9 "…what He would accomplish in J…" Luke 9:31 "He steadfastly set His face to go to J…" Luke 9:51 "His face was set for His journey to J…" Luke 9:53 "J, you who kill the prophets…" Luke 13:34 "…as He went to J, He passed Samaria…" Luke 17:11 "…behold we are going up to J…" Luke 18:31 "…He spoke another parable near J…" Luke 19:11 "…He went ahead going up to J…" Luke 19:28 "…He went into the Temple (in J)…" Luke 19:45 "(He warned us) J surrounded by armies…" Luke 21:20 "And J will be trampled by the Gentiles…" Luke 21:24 "Daughters of J, do not weep (He said)…" Luke 23:28 "…and Jesus went up to J…" John 2:13 "Now when He was in J at the Passover…" John 2:23 "There was a feast and Jesus went up to J…" John 4:45 "and Jesus went up to J…" John 5:1 "…it was Feast of Dedication, Jesus came to J…" John 10:22 "…and Jesus was coming to J (to multitudes). John 12:12 "…be witnesses for Me in J, He said…" Acts 1:8 "…He was taken up in a cloud (in J)…" Acts 1:9

30 AD After the crucifixion of Jesus by the Romans, Jerusalem becomes a focal point of Hebrew-Judea and Christian worship. Many holy sites from Jesus' ministry are located here.

70 AD Titus, the Roman commander destroys Jerusalem and the Temple, by fire on the 9th of Av, the Jews and Christians flee;

135 AD Jerusalem remains the Roman central capital, though the Emperor Hadrian wants to raze it completely. He renames it Aelia Capitolina. Roman, pagan temples are erected. Additional Roman colonies are established here and all Jews are barred from entering the city.

132-135 AD Bar Kochba undertakes the Second Jewish Revolt.

Byzantine Period (324-638 AD)

324 AD Roman Emperor Constantine becomes a 'Christian' and legalizes Christianity, which leads to extensive building programs in Jerusalem. Remains can be seen today.

325 AD Helena, mother of Constantine, comes and secures many holy sites. She builds churches and shrines. Pilgrims from all over the world begin to come to the city renamed Jerusalem.

361 AD Julian, the Christian king lifts the ban against the Jews and they begin to return.

614 AD The Persians invade the Holyland, including Jerusalem.

Early Arab Period (640-1099 AD)

640 AD The Arabs in Jerusalem are inflamed with the new faith of Islam under Mohammed and many Christian sites are destroyed.

642 AD Jerusalem surrenders to Caliph Omar.

691 AD The Dome of the Rock is rebuilt over the small Byzantine chapel (8 sided Christian symbol) which first occupied the site over the rock of Mt. Moriah *[Genesis 22:2]*. The El-Aksa mosque is also built.

1009 AD Caliph Hakim murders the Christians and many churches are destroyed.

1071 AD The Turks capture Jerusalem and this provokes the Christians in Europe and Pope Urban calls for the Crusades.

Crusader Period (1099-1291 AD)

1099, July 15 The Crusaders led by Bernard invade the city and kill all the Jews and Moslems. Jerusalem becomes the capital of the Roman Crusader kingdom. The Dome of the Rock becomes a church. See it is 8 sided for the 8 Beatitudes.

1187 AD Saladin, the Ayyubid recaptures the city and it becomes a Muslim city for 15 years.

1250 AD The Mamlukems overthrow the Ayyubids in Egypt and as a result, Jerusalem remains part of the Mamluke kingdom.

1260 AD The Mongols try to invade but are overthrown by Mamlukems The development of many institutions in the city.

Ottomon Period (1517-1917 AD)

1517 AD The Ottomon Turks take over and replace the Mamlukems.

1520 AD Suleiman, the Magnificent (as the British called him) starts his building programs and rebuilds the walls of the Old City which we see and enjoy today. See Old City Gates and Walls.

1750 AD The Ottomon period seems to be declining which leaves Jerusalem in a state of decline and decay.

1838 Christians start to come, John Nicolayson, an evangelical Christian buys the property next to the Jaffa Gate and the Turks allow him to build and establish the British consul at Christ Church, 10 major foreign consulates follow suit.

1860 The Jews start to return and there is new growth in the ancient city. Montifiore and Rothchild come with their money and a extensive building program. The First aliyah begins and Jews begin to return to Zion.

1880 The first walls outside the city, in Yemin Moshe, are built.

1897 The state of Israel is proclaimed by Theodore Herzl at the First Zionist Conference in Basel Switzerland on Aug., 27th. He declared, "Within 50 years we shall see a Jewish state."

The British Mandate Period (1917-1948 AD)

1917 General Allenby enters Jerusalem at Jaffa Gate and declares the British Mandate on Dec. 11, 1917, lst day of Hannucah.

1929 Major Arab disturbances and riots result in an increase in aliyah as the pogroms in Europe and anti-Semitism increase.

The State of Israel 1948

1948 May 15, 1948 David Ben Gurion declares the state of Israel. The war of Independence begins and the city is divided. The Old City held by Jordan and the New City under Israel.

1949 Jerusalem is declared the official capital of the state and the Knesset is moved to Jerusalem.

1949-1967 Great development in the New City of Jerusalem. Hadassah Medical Center, Vad Vashem Holocaust Museum, the Hebrew University, Israel Museum, the Knesset and many of the western suburbs are built and developed.

The 6 Day War sees Jerusalem reunified into undivided city after almost 2000 years.

Jesh'imon   (waste, desolation) The wilderness of Judea is also called Jesh'imon which covers the area from the Dead Sea Valley, area of 72 kms. by 28 kms. to the roots and base of the Mount of Olives *[Numbers 21:20; 23:28; I Samuel 23:19]*. Hiding place of David from Saul. See Hachi'lah

Jeshurun   This is another name for Jerusalem as described by the Prophet Isaiah *[Isaiah 44:2]*.

Jezebel Springs   (Ein-Izevel) The springs which boast a therapeutic water temperature of 20 C., are located next to the ancient vineyard of Naboth, which Jezebel's husband, King Ahab, stole *[I Kings 21:1-16]* Jezebel was also killed here. *[II Kings 9:36-37]*. The spring is near the Navot junction at the foot of Tel Jezreel and the spring comes to the surface in a small pool. Located between Bet Shean and Afula, 120 kms. **NW** from Jerusalem.

Jez'reel Spring of   (Ein, spring where God sows) The spring where the Israelites camped in their attack against the Philistines *[I Samuel 29:1]*. Presently it is a very large spring issuing from the foot of Mt. Gilboa. *[I Samuel 29:1]*. 112 kms. **N** from Jerusalem.

Jez'reel, Tower of   (migdal, tower where God sows) One of the guard stations at the entrance to the city, where the guards were positioned overlooking the city and valley *[II Kings 9:17]*. 112 kms. **N** from Jerusalem.

Jez'reel, Valley of   (emek, God sows) This prophetic valley is located 95 kms. **N** from Jerusalem in a wide plain. Here the Kings of Israel had palaces *[II Samuel 2:8-9; I Kings 18:45-46; II Kings 10:11]*. Major battles were fought here as armies and men crossed this valley many times. The Midianites and the Amalekites gathered here *[Judges 6:33]*. There was also Ba'al worship here *[I Kings 16:32-33]*. The evil King Ahab had a palace here on the eastern side and Jezebel's house was on the city wall, with the windows facing **E** *[I Kings 21:1; II Kings 9:30;10:11]*. The vineyard of Naboth was here *[I Kings 21:1-16]*. Elijah the Prophet said, "...on the plot of land called Jez'reel dogs shall eat the flesh of Jezebel," *[II Kings 9:30-37]*. King Ahaziah came here to recover from the wounds he sustained at Ramah *[II Chronicles 22:6]*. The Prophet Hosea speaks of the bloodshed in this valley and the restoration of Israel will be likened to the restoration of the Jez'reel Valley *[Hosea 1:4,5,11]*. "The earth shall answer with grain, with new wine, and with oil; they shall answer Jez'reel and God shall sow" *[Hosea 2:22]*. It is also called the Plain of Esdrae'lon which is the Greek form of the name Jez'reel. See Esdrae'lon, Plain of. 6 kms. **SE** from Afula, 112 kms. **N** from Jerusalem.

Jop'pa (beauty) An old city on the Mediterranean Sea, 50 kms. **NW** of Jerusalem. Its name, meaning beauty, comes from the sunshine that it reflects against the waters. The harbor became the port of Jerusalem and it was at this port that Hiram floated the wood from Tyre, the fir trees of Lebanon for Solomon's Temple in Jerusalem *[II Chronicles 2:16]*. The rebuilding of the temple by the edict of King Cyrus brought trees here from Lebanon *[Ezra 3:7]*. Jonah left here en route to Tarshish and was swallowed up by a whale *[Jonah 1:3]*. In New Testament times Jop'pa plays an important role. Peter resides with Simon the tanner *[Acts 9:36,43]*. Here Peter has a vision which gives him the freedom to go to the gentiles. He leaves here to go to Cornelius in Caesarea *[Acts 10:8-23]*. The city now is part of the greater municipality of Tel Aviv-Jaffa and contains a wonderful walk-through museum, as well as a lovely residential neighborhood and many fine restaurants.

Jordan, Country of The ancient areas were Moab: *[Genesis 19:37]*; Edom: *[Genesis 25:25]*; Ammon: *[Genesis 19:38]* See maps at end of the book.

Jordan, River of (ha yarden; the descender) The river gets its name from the rapid descent of the streams coming all the way down from Mt. Hermon to the Sea of Galilee, totaling 48 kms. and winding its way down to the Dead Sea for another 100 kms., ending in the Dead Sea. The main river sources are the Dan, the Hizbani and the Banias. The total length is 322 kms.(195 miles). It looks like a snake as it winds its way down stream. Joshua's conquest *[Joshua 1:2; 3:16;4:1-24]*. As it is today the Jordan is a border between tribes and people *[Joshua 22:25]*. Naaman was cured of his leprosy when he washed in the Jordan River as commanded by God through the Prophet, Elisha *[II Kings 5:10]*. The miracle of the floating ax took place by the Jordan *[II Kings 6:2]*. John the Baptist used the waters of the Jordan for baptism. Jesus was baptized in the Jordan *[Matthew 3:13-17; Mark 1:9-11; Luke 3:21-23]*. See Bethabara.

Jordan, Valley of   (emek ha yarden; the descender) It is also referred to as the Arava. The Israelis call it the "Becka" which is the Hebrew for valley. It is actually a rift, part of the Great African Rift, from Syria to Africa, and runs 250 km. inside of Israel, from the Sea of Galilee to the Dead Sea. This Jordan rift is part of a geological fault that extends from Mt. Hermon in the N down to **E** Africa. Geologists claim there was a great deal of volcanic action here forcing up the two folds of limestone, running **N** and **S**, and forcing the Dead Sea to be separated from the Red Sea, thus creating a natural boundary and border between Jordan and Israel *[Genesis 32:10; Deut.3:20;27:4; Numbers 34:10-12]*. It is a military frontier both in ancient times and now *[Judges 7:24;12:5]*. Many of the most remarkable events in Biblical history happened here. Joshua leading the children of Israel into the Promised land *[Joshua 3]*. Jesus was baptized by John the Baptist and He fasted and prayed here. He was filled with the Holy Spirit *[Matthew 4:1; Mark 1:10-13; Luke 4:1-14]*. See Jordan River.

Judah, Tribe of   See Joshua 15:1-12 and Tribes at back of this book.

Jude'a, land of   (of the Jews) The name assigned to the area by the Romans. It was their division of Palestine which encompassed the maritime plain and the desert, and no more than 1350 square miles (3915 square kms.) It is 95 kms. long from Bethlehem to Beersheva and 50 kms. wide. On the **E**, we see the Jordan Valley and on the **W** the desert and then the "hill country", to the "shephelah" or the lower hills, then to the Maritime plain bordering the sea. Amos the Prophet was born in Tekoa here in Judea *[Amos 1:1]*. Jeremiah the Prophet was born in Anathoth *[Jeremiah1:1]*. Jesus was born in Bethlehem of Judea *[Matthew 2:1,5]*. Jesus rose up and came to the regions of Judea on the other side of the Jordan *[Mark 10:1]*. Herod proclaimed himself King of Judea *[Luke 1:5]*. Pontius Pilate was Governor of Judea *[Luke 3:1]*. Jesus taught in the synagogues of Judea *[Luke 4:44]*. He traveled throughout all Judea *[Luke7:17]*. After the resurrection the church prospered throughout Judea *[Acts. 9:31]*. The disciples and gospel writers refer to the saints in Judea *[Acts 28:21; II Corinthians 1:16; Galatians 1:22]*. See maps of the times of the Romans and Jesus' time.

Julias   (GK feminine name) In 30 AD Herod Philip, Herod's son, renamed Bethsaida to Julias, in honor of Tiberias' mother. The city was then elevated to a Greek polis (city state). There are extensive excavations going on presently on the site. See Bethsaida.

Ka'desh, Ka'desh-Barnea   (consecrated) This site is rich in Biblical references as the first place Abraham encountered King Chedorlaomer of Elam *[Genesis 14:1-7]*. The name was changed to En-Mishpat (fountain of judgment) when the tabernacle rested here *[Genesis 14:7]*. Hagar in her distress rested here on her way to Shur *[Genesis 16:7,14]*. Abraham moved from Hebron and lived here *[Genesis 20:1]*. In the rebellion of Korah, "the earth opened, swallowed them up" *[Numbers 16:1-32]*. Miriam died here and Moses struck the rock on this site *[Numbers 20:1;2-11]*. Moses sent messengers to the king of Edom asking that they might pass through his country on their way to the Promised Land *[Numbers 20:14-21]*. The children of Israel encamped on this site twice on their way to the Promised Land *[Deut. 1:2,19,46;2:14]*. Joshua sent the twelve to spy out the land from this place *[Deut 1:23-24; Joshua 14:7;15:3]*. It is located in the Sinai of Egypt S of Beersheva called 'Ain Kadesi'. It is a well watered oasis with a natural spring. A fortress from the 10th century BC has been discovered. Moshav Kadesh-Barnea, which is on the Israeli side, was established on the site in 1977 and was literally moved just over the border after the Camp David Accords were signed, giving the Sinai to Egypt. It is also called tel Ain el Qudeirat, 90 kms. S of Beersheva in the NE of the Sinai.

Ka'mon   (to arise, stand up) Located on the plain of Jez'reel or Esdraelon and Josephus tells us it is 6 Roman miles N of Legio, a city of Gilead (Ant. 5.7.6.) Jair the judge is buried here *[Judges 10:5]*. The exact location is not identifiable.

Ka'nah   (place of reeds) This is a small brook that empties into the Mediterranean Sea between Caesarea and Joppa. It served as the border between Ephraim and Manasseh *[Joshua 16:8;17:9]*. Today it is called the River Aujeh. See modern map.

Karantal, Quarantal   See Mount of Temptation

Karkom, Mt. of   (from the ground) This mountain, located **S** of Mt. Sinai in the Sinai Desert is believed to be the real Mt. Sinai by several renowned archaeologists. Mt. Karkom was a major cultic center (pagan and idol worship) for 1000 years before the Exodus, dated 1250 BC. Scholars believe something special drew ancient man to this spot overlooking the Paran Desert. Moses would have been quite familiar with it since at that time, he was a shepherd in this area *[Exodus 3:1]*. See Mt. Horeb.

Kar'kor   (soft level, ground) A site **E** of the Jordan River where the 300 men of Gideon's army lay weary, yet pursuing Zebah and Zalmunna *[Judges 8:4,12]*. Today it is Wadi Sirhan, 200 kms. **SE** of the capital of Jordan, Amman.

Kar'tan   (town, city) The site is **N** just across the Israel/Lebanon border, one of the cities of refuge belonging to the tribe of Naphtali *[Joshua 21:32]*. Also called Kiriathaim *[I Chronicles 6:76]*. Today it is in southern Lebanon and known as Kiryat el-Kureiyeh, 22 kms. **S** of Tyre.

Kaubab   (translation unclear) This small village is 2 kms. **N** of Zippori (Sipporis), 4 kms. **NW** from Nazareth. We have writings from Jules, a pilgrim from Africa who came here in 250 AD which confirm that the blood relatives of Jesus still lived here in the 3rd century. See Zippori.

Ked'emoth   (eastern places) A city in the tribe of Reuben with pasture lands for the Levites (priests) *[Joshua 13:18; 21:37; I Chronicles 6:79]*. Moses sent a delegation from here to the King of the Amorites, for permission to pass through the land. *[Deut. 2:26]*. Located in Jordan, 15 kms. due **E** of the Dead Sea near Arnon River.

Ke'desh   same as Ka'desh Barnea

Ketef Hinnom   (the shoulder of the Hinnom Valley) This hill, or ridge, was a watershed between two valleys, the Hinnom and the Reph'aim and rises 80 meters (262 ft.) above the Hinnom Valley. This ridge forms the border between the tribes of Judah and Benjamin [Joshua 15:8;18:16]. This hill is now at the junction of Bethlehem and Hebron roads. Most of the burial caves here show continual use from the time of the First Temple Period. The discovery of the Priestly blessing on several small silver plaques called 'Silver Scroll Amulet' which were hung around the neck, has provided us with absolute proof of these blessings given by the priests in the First Temple Period, as directed by God to Moses [Numbers 6:24-26]. They are the earliest witnesses to the text of the Bible. See Scottish Church in Jerusalem.

Kei'lah   (stench, or stinking weeds) The inhabitants were false brethren and sought to deliver David up to Saul when David hid out from him [I Samuel 23:1-13]. The site is Kiryat Qila 14 kms. **NW** of Hebron. Two men from here were sent to Nehemiah to help repair the walls of Jerusalem's Old City [Nehemiah 3:17,18].

Kib'roth-Hatta'vah   (the graves of lust) Here was the Wadi Murrah, one of the encampments of the children of Israel but it was the scene of their murmuring and discontent which was followed by their punishment from God [Numbers 11:34-35; 33:16-17; Deut. 9:22]. They did not enter the Promised Land. In the Sinai, 50 kms. **NE** of Mt. Sinai.

Kid'ron, Valley of, Brook of,   (dark, turbid, dusty, gloomy) In Jerusalem **SE** corner from the walls of the Old City; this brook runs in the valley of Jehoshaphat. The historian Smith tells us, "To the **N** of Jerusalem begins the torrent-bed of the Kidron. It sweeps past the Temple Mount, past what was afterward Calvary and Gethsemane. It leaves the Mount of Olives and Bethany to the left, Bethlehem far to the right. It plunges down among the bare terraces, precipices, and crags of the wilderness of Judea-the wilderness of the scapegoat. So barren, so blistered, so furnace-like does it become as it drops below the level of the sea, that it takes the name Wadi-en Nar, or the Fire Wadi. Its dreary course brings it to the precipices of the Dead Sea, into which it shoots its scanty winter waters; but all summer it is dry." The valley itself is only 38 kms. long but has a descent of 1178 meters (3912 ft). It enters the Jordan river at a narrow gorge. David crossed here when he fled from his rebellious son, Absalom [II Samuel 15:23]. Solomon fixed it as off limits to Shimei [I Kings 2:37]. It became a receptacle for the abominations and impurities that had been put in the Temple by the idol worshippers *[II Kings 23:4; II Chronicles 29:16;30:14]*. In the time of King Josiah this was the common cemetery of Jerusalem *[II Kings 23:6; Jeremiah 31:40]*. Jesus went across here many times from the Mt. of Olives *[John 18:1]*. It was still a cemetery in the Ist C.

King's Garden　The meeting area, irrigated by the Pool of Siloam where the Kidron and Hinnom Valleys meet. It is an area of fertile land where Zedekiah escaped and fled from the city by night *[Jeremiah 39:4]*. Follow the road **S** from Dung Gate to the village of Silwan in Jerusalem.

King's Highway　Ancient roads and paths were formed by caravans passing through from one point to another and, eventually regular paths were made on top, by adding stones and gravel and smooth earth. The king's highway was the public road which was built and paid for by the kings for the use of their armies and perhaps they accepted a toll for its use. Moses asked for permission to use this road *[Numbers 20:17;21:22]*. Perhaps many of the modern roads which we travel on today were once those 'ancient paths'. See map of ancient roads in the back of this book.

King's Pool　See Siloam, Pool of

King's Tomb　See Tombs of the Kings

King's Valley　See Shaveh, Valley of

Kinneret　See Sea of Galilee

Kir'har'eseth　(city of pottery) "Kir-heres" It was a strongly fortified city of Moab, also known as Kerak, located 90 kms. **E** of Jerusalem in Jordan. King Joram of Israel took the city and destroyed all but the walls *[II Kings 3:25]*. Isaiah, the Prophet, speaks about the mourning that will take place here in this troubled site. *[Isaiah 16:7,11]*.

Kir'iath-arba, Kiryat Arba　(city of Arba) The city in the mountains of Judah named after Arba, the Anakite. This Jewish settlement is next to the town of Hebron. Sarah died here and Abraham mourned for her *[Genesis 23:2]*. The name of Hebron and this site of Kir'iath-arba are sacred and synonymous to most Orthodox Jews *[Joshua 14:15; 15:54; 20:7; Judges 1:10; Nehemiah 11:25]*. See Hebron.

Kir'iath-je'arim   (city of forests) It is also called Baalah or Kiriath-baal, a Gibeonite town first assigned to Judah *[Joshua 9:17; 15:60]*. It was then assigned to the tribe of Benjamin *[Joshua 18:28]*. It is located 12 kms. **N** of Jerusalem, just **W** of Abu Ghosh. David brought the ark here and it rested for 20 years until he brought it to Jerusalem *[II Chronicles 8:6; II Samuel 6:2-3]*. David speaks of his desire for the ark and a resting place for it in his *Psalm 132*. See Abu Ghosh.

Kir'iath-sepher, Kir'iath-san'nah   (city of books) or Debir. This southern Judah highland site was fully conquered by Joshua *[Joshua 10:38-40]*. It is 20 kms. **WSW** from Hebron and when the site was excavated, they discovered strata from 2200 BC until 586 BC when Nebuchadnezzar came and destroyed it. Othniel took the site and received Caleb's daughter as a reward *[Joshua 15:7;15,16]*. The city was given to the priests *[Joshua 21:15]*. See Debir. Today it is Tel Mirsim.

Ki'shon   (ending, winding) Also known as the "waters of Megiddo" *[Judges 5:19]*. It is a winter stream when it runs from the hills of Mount Tabor and Gilboa. in a **NE** direction through the plains of Jez'reel (Esdraelon) and Akko. Then it empties itself into the Mediterranean at the foot of Mount Carmel. In summer the whole riverbed is dry but after a heavy rain in the Winter it is impassable. The name today is Nahr el Mukatta, "the river of slaughter" *[I Kings 18:40]*. The song of Deborah speaks of this river *[Judges 5:21]*. Here at Megiddo, Sisera was defeated and while the battle raged, a violent windstorm arose, together with heavy rains and this riverbed became a marshy, foaming torrent *[Judges 5:20-21]*. Here, Elijah had the prophets of Ba'al killed at the foot of Mount Carmel *[I Kings 18:40]*. The psalmist pleas with God to destroy Israel's enemies here on this site *[Psalm 83:9]*. See Muhraka.

Kora'zin   See Chorazin

Kursi   See Gadarenes

Laban   (white) See Libnah *[Numbers 33:20]*

La'chish   (faithful, trustworthy) This was a large Canaanite city and one of their chief fortresses. It is an 80 dunam (22 acres) mound known as Tel ed-Duweir, 25 kms. **W** of Hebron, on the ancient road through Palestine from the highland to the Nile River in Egypt. The city was occupied several thousand years before Abraham and when Joshua came here, King Japhia formed a confederacy against him but Joshua won the battle *[Joshua 10:3,5,31-35]*. Lachish was fortified by Solomon's son, Rehoboam *[II Chronicles 11:9]*. Amaziah, the son of Joash, king of Judah, was killed here *[II Kings 14:19]*. The city was destroyed twice, once by Nebuchadnezzar in 598 BC and 589 BC *[II Kings 24]*. The most important archaeological find here is called the "Lachish Letters" attesting to its aforementioned importance.

La'ish   See Dan

Lake Gennesert   See Galilee, Sea of, one of its known names.

Lake Huleh   See Me'rom

Land of Israel   (Eretz Israel) The whole land of Israel. See map of Ezekiel's vision.

Last Supper Site   See Upper Room

Lazarus' Tomb   (abridged form of HB. Eleazar) Lazarus and his two sisters, Mary and Martha, lived in Bethany and they were good friends of Jesus. This site located on the eastern slope of the Mt. of Olives, 2 kms. from Jerusalem's Old City, is called El-Eizariyya meaning 'the place of Lazarus' in Arabic. Lazarus was sick and died and Jesus raised him from the dead *[Matthew 21:17; John 11:1-44]*. He came to the house of Simon, the leper *[Mark 14:3]*. He rebukes Martha *[Luke 10:38-42]*. See the tomb next to the Greek Orthodox Church. See Bethany.

Le'bo Ha'math   See Ha'math "entrance to Hamath"

Lebo'nah   (frankincense) Also called Lubbam, here the young men of the tribe of Benjamin were directed to capture the maidens from Shilo. There is a festival in Israel celebrating this occasion every year *[Judges 21:19]* 6 kms. **NW** from Shiloh, 66 kms. **N** from Jerusalem. See Shiloh.

Le'hi   (cheek or jawbone) The site in Judah where Samson killed the Philistines with the jawbone *[Judges 15:9,14-17]*. Samson renamed the place Ramath Lehi. "God split the hollow place that was in Lehi and water came out…" *[Judges 15:19]* 20 kms. W from Jerusalem. See En-hakkore.

Levi, Tribe of   The sacrifices of the Lord, the Levitical tribe of Israel is the inheritance of the tribe of the Lord. The Lord Himself is their inheritance *[Joshua 13:14]*. See Tribes of Israel.

Lib'nah   (whiteness) The Canaanite city near Lachish captured by Joshua. Josiah's queen, Hamutal, was born here *[Joshua 10:29-32;12:15; II Kings 23:31]*. It is presently Tel es-Safi, 9 kms. **N** of Lachish and 34 kms. **W** from Hebron.

Lithostrotos   (pavement LT.) This large stone pavement is found in the convent of the Sisters of Zion at the Church of the Flagellation and the Church of the Condemnation of Jesus, located at the lst and 2nd stations of the cross on the Via Delorosa, in Jerusalem's Old City. On these pavement stones, game boards were inscribed on the stones and used by the idle and bored soldiers of the Roman army, to while their time away. There are parallel grooves in the stones to prevent the horses from slipping. Christian tradition has placed this site as the place where Jesus was brought before they led Him away to be crucified. Some scholars believe these stones are only from Hadrians time (2nd C). One Bible pilgrim stated, "Some things are defined by faith and not by history' *[Matthew 27:26-31; Mark 15:15-17; Luke 23:24,25; John 19:16]*. See Ecco Homo and Struthion Pools.

Lod   See Lydda *[I Chronicles 8:12; Ezra 2:33; Acts 9:32]*.

Lord's Prayer Site   It is called "the church of the Pater Noster" in Latin meaning the site where Jesus taught His disciples the 'Our Father Prayer'. Here on the Mt. of Olives, this church belongs to the Carmelite Sisters and is built over the grotto where Jesus stood with His disciples *[Luke 11:1-4]*. The present day church was built in 1875. It is famous for the mosaic plaques which line the walls on which the Lord's Prayer is inscribed in 70 different languages. On the Mt. of Olives **E** of the Old City in Jerusalem.

Luz   (almond tree) See Beth'el

Lyd'da   (unclear translation) This site was called Lod in the Old Testament *[I Chronicles 8:12]* and today, in Israel, we still call it Lod. Ben Gurion airport is located on the site. It is a rich and fertile plain and was the most westerly Jewish settlement after the Exile of 586 BC and the return of the Jews. It is also described as the "Valley of Ge-haharashim", the valley of the smiths and craftsmen. Here Peter healed the paralytic and there were many people who came to the faith in this area *[Acts 9:32,35,38]*.

Ma'ale Adummim   (the red earth ascent) This 'ascent', 15 kms. **E** from Jerusalem is approached from the French Hill turn off. It is off the Jerusalem-Jericho road and was part of the tribe of Benjamin. These limestone hills are reddish in color and give off an additional reddish glow at sunset *[Joshua 18:17]*. This is next to the site of the 'Good Samaritan Inn' and Roman ruins have been discovered here. A large modern Jewish community stands atop the mountain and bears the same name. See Good Samaritan Inn.

Ma'ale Akrabbim   (scorpion's ascent, way) Here 35 kms. **SE** of Dimona, in the Negev desert, just **SW** of the Maktesh Ha Katan (the small crater). This was the 'old road' to Eilat and the southern side of the border as directed by God to Moses *[Numbers 34:4; Joshua 15:3]*. Here is the former boundary of the Amorite tribe. *[Judges 1:36]*. Some scholars believe it was part of Moab, next to the Dead Sea. The ascent is still a thrilling drive in either direction, since it was cleared by the Israeli Corp of Army Engineers in 1950 and made more passable.

Ma'arath   (desolation) In the mountains of Judah, 11 kms. **N** of Hebron lies one of the cities assigned by Joshua *[Joshua 15:59]*. It is identified as Bet Ummar.

Machpe'lah   (double) In Hebron, the synagogue/mosque that is also called the 'Cave of the Patriarchs'. Here was the field containing the cave that Abraham bought as a burial cave for his family. He is buried here together with Sarah, Isaac, Jacob, Rebecca and Leah *[Genesis 23:9,17; 25:8-9; 49:30-31; 50:13]*. The building is built over ruins from the 2nd Temple period, Herod's time. It is one of the holiest sites in Judaism and Islam and is loved and honored by Jews and Moslems around the world. See Hebron, Kiryat Arba. 31 kms. **S** from Jerusalem.

Madaba   See Medeba

Madman'nah   (dunghill) This town was first assigned to Judah and then to Simeon. *[Joshua 15:31]* Shaaph, the son of Maacah lived here *[I Chronicles 2:49]*. It is located several kms. **S** of Gaza.

Madme'nah   (dunghill, manure pile) Just **N** of Jerusalem on the route of the invaders from Assyria (700 BC) between Nob and Gibeah. The exact location is uncertain.

Ma'don   (strife) The Canaanite king, Jobab ruled here. He and the city were captured by Joshua *[Joshua 11;1;12:19]*. Located on the **W** side of the Sea of Galilee just near the Hills of Hittin, presently called Madin. 175 kms. **N** from Jerusalem.

Mag'adan, Mag'dala   (tower) This small town on the western shore of the Sea of Galilee is between Capernaum and Tiberias and was the birthplace of Mary Magdalene, the great woman disciple of Jesus, from whom He cast out seven demons. Also called the region of Dalmanutha *[Matthew 15:39; Mark 8:9-10; John 19:25; 20:1,18]*. Presently called el-Mejdel, 5 kms. **NW** of Tiberias.

Mag'dala   See Mag'adan above.

Mahana'im   (double camp or camps) A site just **N** of the Jabbok River where the angels came and met with Jacob *[Genesis 32:1-2]*. Here, Ish-bosheth reigned and was assassinated *[II Samuel 2:8,12; 4:5-8]*. David came here and was entertained by the people of Ammon with food and beds for the troops who were weary, after their pursuit against Absalom. The battle between David and Absalom was fought on this site *[II Samuel 17:24, 27; I Kings 2:8; II Samuel 18]*. One of Solomon's governors came here *[I Kings 4:14]*. Presently, the site is called Maneh, 5 kms. **N** of Ajlun, **N** of the Jabbok River in present day Jordan.

Ma'haneh-dan   (camp of Dan) See Dan.

Makke'dah   (herdsmen place) This site was a royal Canaanite city located to the **SW** of Ekron. Here, Joshua put to death the five kings who had fought against Israel *[Joshua 10:10-29; Joshua 12:16]*. It was later assigned to Judah *[Joshua 15:41]*. It is called el-Mughar, meaning the caves. 48 kms. **W** of Jerusalem.

Mam're   (earnestly pray) Abraham dwelt here, next to Hebron and he entertained the 3 angels here. See Machpelah, which lies just to the **E**. *[Genesis 23:17;19; 35:27]*. Isaac was promised here *[Genesis 18:1,10,14]*. Herod the Great built a wall around the well of Abraham which enclosed an area of about 66 meters (200 ft.) In 68 AD, Vespasian, the father of Titus who destroyed Jerusalem, destroyed this well and wall. It was

Constantine who built a church here, whose ruins can be seen today. See Oaks of Mamre, Hebron and Machpelah.

Manasseh, Tribe of (causing to forget) *[Joshua 17:1-18]* See Tribes of Israel.

Maon See Wilderness of Maon

Mar Elias Monastery (Elijah the Prophet LT.) Here on the southern outskirt of Jerusalem, some 5 kms. just **N** of Bethlehem, lies a Greek Orthodox Monastery on the isolated hilltop. This is the site traditionally believed to be the place where Elijah, the Prophet, fled from Jezebel on his way **S** to Beersheva *[I Kings 19:1-3]*. The stone inside the church is believed to be where Elijah rested.

Ma'rah (bitterness) The 6th place the children of Israel encamped in Egypt on their way to the Promised Land. Here, the waters were miraculously sweetened when Moses cast a tree in the bitter waters. The Lord made a great promise here, that none of the diseases which befell the Egyptians would fall on the children of Israel *[Exodus 15:22-27]*. Today, it is identified as Ain Hawarah in Sinai desert, Egypt.

Mare'shah, Marisa (summit) In the Greek period it was known as Marisa. This was a town of Judah, rebuilt by Laadah and fortified by Rehoboam *[Joshua 15:44; I Chronicles 4:21; II Chronicles 11:8]*. Eliezer, the Prophet, lived here and he prophesied against King Jehoshaphat *[II Chronicles 20:35-37]*. Today, it is identified as Tel Sandahannah 2 kms. **S** of Beit Guvrin and 30 km. ESE of Ashkelon.

Ma'roth (bitterness) A town just **W** of Judah on the route of the invading Assyrian army (701 BC) as they came from Lachish. Micah, the Prophet, spoke about the 'disaster that would come from the Lord,' *[Micah 1:12]*.

Mary's Well, Mary's Fountain See En Kerem and Nazareth

Masada (Mezada, fortress) This large fortress, built by Herod the Great, of the time of Jesus, is 17 kms. **S** from Ein Gedi, 67 kms. **SE** from Jerusalem in the Dead Sea Valley; built on the summit of a steep cliff some 450 meters (135 ft.) above sea level. It occupies just 80 dunam or 20 acres. It was originally built by the Maccabees but it was Herod who rebuilt it, fortified it and made it the strongest fortress in Judea. This fortress attests to

Herod the Great's fears and paranoia. When the wise men came looking for Jesus whom they called the King of the Jews, Herod had all the children slaughtered. He wanted to be the only King *[Matthew 2:1-3,16]*. Herod knew he was hated for these and other acts so he built himself many fortresses throughout the land like Masada. One of the top National Parks in Israel today.

Massah   See Mer'ibah

Mayan Harod   See Ha'rod

Med'aba, Madaba   (waters of quiet) This site, about 29 kms. **E** of the Dead Sea in Jordan, has great significance for us today. It was a city of great antiquity in Moab *[Numbers 21:30]*. David's enemies encamped here *[I Chronicles 19:7]*. In the days of Ahaz, it was a sanctuary for the Moabites and Isaiah, the Prophet, named it in his prophesies against Moab *[Isaiah 15]*. Recent archaeological excavations revealed a 6th C. mosaic map from the Byzantine period which was virtually intact showing Jerusalem's Old City, the oldest surviving map of the Holy Land. The map is incorporated into the church on the site governed by the Greek Orthodox Church and a replica of this Medeba Mosaic Map can be seen in Jerusalem's Old City Jewish quarter, in the **N** side of the Cardo under the tunnel. Jerusalem lies at the center of the map because it was thought to be the center of the world *[Ezekiel 5:5]*. See Medaba Map.

Megid'do   (place of troops) Also called Armeggedon (Har Megiddo, the mountain of Megiddo) This was a royal city of the Canaanite tribe, first assigned to Issachar then to Manasseh *[Joshua 12:21;17:11; Judges 1:27]*. It was fully occupied by the Israelites. When Solomon erected houses and walls, it was one of his 'chariot cities' and administrative centers. See Solomon's city gate *[I Kings 4:12;9:15]*. The valley of Megiddo was part of the plain of Esdraelon and was the battlefield where Barak gained a victory over the King of Hazor and his troops *[Judges 4:15]*. King Ahaziah fled and died here *[II Kings 9:27]*. King Josiah endeavored to stop Pharoah Neco, of Egypt, from advancing in battle but Josiah was killed on this site *[II Kings 23:29; II Chronicles 35:20-24; Zechariah 12:11]*. Today it is one of the most important archaeological sites in the center of Israel and called Tel Mutesellim and has been extensively excavated showing the great water system dating to King Ahab's time and over 20 strata of civilization have been identified. 110 kms. **NW** from Jerusalem.

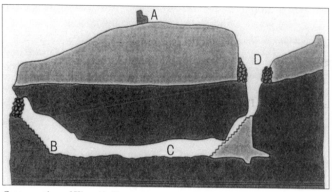

Cross section of King Ahab's water system at Megiddo [I Kings 16:28-29]. A) the city wall B) the natural spring C) the tunnel (accessible) D) the shaft

Mer'ibah, Massah   (quarrel, strife) There are two sites by this name. It is the name Moses gave to the fountain that came forth from the rock he struck after the complaints of the people *[Exodus 17:1-7]*. It is near Rephidim in the wilderness of the Wadi Feiran, on the western gulf of the Red Sea. In the Sinai Desert, some 80 kms. SW of Eilat.

Mer'ibah, waters of   (quarrel, strife) This site is near Kadesh-barnea and also called 'waters of strife' or 'waters of provocation' where Moses struck the rock and offended God by his impatience. Here, he stood at the close of his 40 years of desert wanderings and his outburst of anger attributed to the reason of Moses' failure to enter the Promised Land *[Deut. 32:51; Deut. 34; Numbers 20:10-13; Psalms 81:7; Psalm 95:8; 106:32]*. 90 kms. **S** from Beersheva in Egypt, Sinai Desert.

Me'rom   (height or upper waters) Lake Huleh, this triangular-shaped body of water which is presently owned and cared for by the JNF (Jewish National Fund, Keren Kayemet) is in the northern part of Israel, on a level plain in the foothills of Naphtali, touching the roots of Mr. Hermon. Most of the water in the Huleh valley had been drained in order to prevent the continued breeding of diseases and for productive farmland purposes but recently, it was reflooded in order to balance the ecology in the area. The Jordan River passes through it and here, Joshua won a great victory over the Canaanites *[Joshua 11:5-8]*.

103 kms. **N** from Jerusalem and 23 kms. **N** from the Sea of Galilee.

Me'roz   (from root, cedar) This site in northern Israel is the place where Deborah laid a curse on the people by her song *[Judges 5:23]*. The people should have helped in the battle against Sisera but they failed to do so. It is Khirbet Marus today, some 20 kms. **S** of Kadesh of Naphtali. 50 kms. **N** from the northern tip of the Sea of Galilee. The exact site is not identifiable.

Mich'mas, Mich'mash, Mic'mash   (something hidden) Here was the great battle between Saul and the Philistines. Saul positioned 2000 men here and the other 1000 at Gibeah with his son, Jonathan. They had 30,000 foot soldiers and 6,000 horsemen encamped on this site *[ISamuel 13:2,5,11,16,23,14:5,31]*. Saul had to retreat down to the valley near Jericho but Jonathan remained and God gave him the great victory *[I Samuel 14:1-14]*. Here is the place where the exiles returned from captivity. *[Ezra 2:27; Nehemiah 7:31;11:31]*. Presently, it is a small village in ruins, called Mukhmas on Wadi Suweinit, 20 kms. **NE** of Jerusalem.

Mig'dal-el   (tower of God) Belonging to the tribe of Naphtali, this fortified city is now Mujeidil some 20 kms. **NW** of Kadesh, some 70 kms. **N** from the northern tip of the Sea of Galilee.

Mig'dol   (watchtower in Canaanite language) This may have been a Canaanite military outpost and was the encampment of the children of Israel near the Red Sea. *[Exodus 15:4,22; Deut. 11:4]*. The Lord commanded them to make camp here before Pi-Hahiroth which is by the sea *[Exodus 14:1-2, Numbers 33:7]*. Presently in Egypt called Tel el Heir, on the Mediterranean Sea near El Arish. A second occupation of the children of Israel occurs here after the destruction of Jerusalem in 586 BC and is referred to by both *[Jeremiah 44:1; 46:14 and Ezekiel 29:10; 30:6]*.

Mig'ron   (precipice, steep cliff) A site in Benjamin on the route of the invading Assyrian army *[Isaiah 10:28]*. Saul was stationed here "under the pomegranate tree which is in Migron," *[I Samuel 14:2]*. It is Tel el-ful at Gibeah, "hill of beans" located 6 kms. **N** of Jerusalem.

Millo   (the filling) The Millo, the filled in area, in Jerusalem was a fortification built by the Jebusites. "And David built all around from the Millo (and terraces) and inward…"*[II Samuel 5:9; IChronicles 11:8]*. Also Solomon rebuilt this area around the Millo *[I Kings 9:15; 11:27]*. Hezekiah used it in preparing against the approaching Assyrians *[II Chronicles 32:5]*. Joash was killed and it was called Beth-Millo or the "house of Millo"*[II Kings 12 20-21]*. Ruins from the Jebusites, Davidic and Solomonic periods have been explored on the **N** end of the City of David and can be seen today. It is also referred to as the Ophel. See Beth Millo located at Shechem. See Ophel. Enter the Old City of Jerusalem through Dung gate.

Mis'rephoth-ma'im   (hot springs, burning of waters) Some Rabbis and Christian commentators render the meaning to be "salt pits, smelting huts or glass huts." It is a place between Sidon and the Valley of Mizpeh where Joshua battled the Canaanites *[Joshua 11:8; 13:6]*. Today as Kiryat el-Musheirifeh, 20 kms. **N** of Akko.

Miz'peh   (watchtower, view, site to view) There are several sites named Mizpah. The site where Jacob made a covenant with his father-in-law, Laban, and both called it a "heap of witness." They promised not to pass beyond this spot or to harm one another *[Genesis 31:49]*. The site is Gilead, **E** of the Jordan River in Jordan.

Miz'peh of Benjamin   (observation point in the tribe of Benjamin) This site is listed as part of the allotment between Beeroth and Chephirah *[Joshua 18:26]*. It was a place fortified by King Asa against the attacks of the kings of northern Israel *[I Kings 15:22; II Chronicles 16:6; Jeremiah 41:10]*. After the destruction of Jerusalem, in 586 BC, it became the residence of the officer in charge who was appointed by the Babylonians *[Jeremiah 40:6-15]*. It is the hill of Nebi Samuel, 15 kms. **NW** of Jerusalem where the tomb of the Prophet Samuel is honored. See Nebi Samuel.

Miz'peh Elon Moreh   (lookout point by the oak of the teacher) Abraham came here to this point, God showed him the land and Abraham built an altar here in honor of God *[Genesis 12:6; Deut. 27:4]*. Abraham's well can still be seen here today and there is always water in it. 64kms. **N** from Jerusalem. See Elon Moreh.

Miz'peh of Gilead   (watchtower, observation area of Gilead) This is the site where Jephthah lived and where the Israelites assembled under him against the Ammonites *[Judges 10:17;11:11,34]*. The site is Ramath-mizpeh of Gad *[Joshua 13:26]* **E** of the Jordan River in Jordan.

Miz'peh, land of   (area of the lookout points) The district of the Hivites in Gilead below Hasbeya *[Joshua 11:3]*. This is presently a Druse village at the foot of Mt. Hermon called Mutelleh. The area is a high hill overlooking the Huleh basin in the **N**. 60 kms. **NE** of the Sea of Galilee.

Moab, land of   (from the father) The destruction of Sodom was in the year 2055 BC. Lot, Abraham's nephew, had an incestuous relationship with his daughters and named one son Moab, who founded the Moabite tribe and calling the region Moab *[Genesis 19:30-37]*. The land of Moab included three distinct areas. Ruth came from Moab *[Ruth 1:1-2]*. Its site had natural fortifications with the Arnon River in the **N**, on the **W** were the cliffs of the Dead Sea and the Plains of Moab were those in the tropical depths of the Jordan Valley in the **S** *[Numbers 22:1]*. Before Moses came into the area, the king of the Amorites took from the "former king of Moab", all the land "from the Arnon (River) to the Jabbok," *[Numbers 21:26]*. The children of Israel approached Israel, the 'Land of Promise', led by Moses through the desert facing Moab outside the bordering circles of hills on the **SE**. The Lord forbade them to harm the Moabites and they asked for permission to pass through. Being refused, they went around her borders *[Deut. 2:9-11]*. God gave the covenant to Moses here *[Deut. 29:1]*. Balaam is sought by Balak, king of Moab, to curse the Israelites *[Numbers 22 through chapter 25]*. Israel committed sins with the daughters of Moab *[Numbers 25]*. Moses took his last view of the Promised land from here and the Lord said to Moses, "I will give it (the land of Israel) to your descendants, I have caused you to see it with your own eyes, but you shall not cross over there." Moses died and is buried in the land of Moab, *[Deut. 34:1-6]*. In Jeremiah 48, the prophet utters a curse against Moab. We can view Moab in Jordan approaching the Dead Sea from **N** and **S**.

Monastery of the Cross   See Valley of the Monastery of the Cross

Monastery of St. George   Here on the northern bank of Wadi Kelt, 5 kms. **W** of Jericho and 30 kms. **SE** from Jerusalem lies this monastery built on a steep slope, named after the Greek monk, Georgias, who spent most of his life here. It is built on the site where tradition honors Elijah, the Prophet, being fed by the ravens *[I Kings 17:1-3]*. Wadi Kelt is identified as the ancient Brook of Cherith.

Monument of Absalom   See Absalom's Pillar

Mo'reh   (teacher, teaching) Abraham came here as he entered the Promised Land and the Lord appeared to him so he built an altar *[Genesis 12:6]*. Moses addressed the Israelites concerning this site even before they entered the Promised Land. *[Deut. 11:30]*. This site is 3 kms. **N** from Shechem. See Oaks of Moreh.

Mo'reh, hill of   (the hill of the teacher) In the valley of Jez'reel on the **N** side of the Harod spring, where the Midianites were encamped when attacked by Gideon *[Judges 7:1]*. Presently Jebel Dahy 12 kms. **NW** of Mt. Gilboa.

Mo'resheth-gath   (possession of gath) The birthplace and the home of the Prophet Micah *[Jeremiah 26:18, Micah 1:1,14]*. Presently Tel ej-Judeideh,8 kms. **W** of Gath.

Mori'ah, land of, mount of   (a prim. root to utter) Abraham came here, journeying from Beersheva in the **S**. He came here in obedience, to this hill in Jerusalem called Moriah to offer his only son Isaac *[Genesis 22:2]*. This is the hill where Solomon built the Ist Temple on the threshing floor which David his father bought from the Jebusites *[II Samuel 24:24; II Chronicles 3:1]*. The Jews believe that the altar of 'burnt offering', in both the Ist and 2nd Temples stood on this very site where Abraham attempted to offer Isaac. The Samaritans believe that Moriah is Mt. Gerizim and honor that site. Today Moriah, is called the Temple Mount (Har Ha bay'it) and it is the site of the Dome of the Rock and El Aksa Mosque, ruled by the Moslem Wakf. Orthodox Jews are forbidden to enter this site for fear of stepping on what was the Holy of Holies which once lay beneath these stones. Jesus walked here many times. See Jesus in Jerusalem. It is highly controversial, for all the 3 major religions claim it. See Temple Mount. Enter the Temple Mount area from the Jewish or Moslem quarters of the Old City of Jerusalem.

Mortar Maktesh (hollowed place) A place somewhere in ancient Jerusalem where the prophet, Zephaniah, cries out that its inhabitants will be cut off *[Zephaniah 1:11]*

Mountain of God See Sinai *[Exodus 24:13]*.

Mountain of the Pieces (Brit Bein ha-Betarim) On the slopes of Mt. Hermon, 1270 meters (4000 ft.) above sea level is the site where God confirmed His covenant with Abraham. He passed between the pieces of the animals that Abraham had sacrificed. During the ceremony Abraham was promised the land, "…from the river of Egypt to the Euphrates," *[Genesis 15:9-18]* 60 kms. **NE** from the northern border of the Sea of Galilee.

Mount of Ascension (to go up, ascend) See Mount of Olives and Mt. Olivet

Mount of Beatitudes (sermon, discourse) The greatest sermon that was ever preached was preached here. "…and seeing the multitudes, He went up on the mountain… He opened His mouth and taught them," *Matthew 5 through chapter 7.* This is the site where Jesus went up to pray before He delivered the Sermon on the Mount *[Luke 6:12].* On the **W** of the Sea of Galilee, part of the mountain range of the Horns of Hittin near His home town of Capernaum (Kfar Nahum, village of comfort). Jesus came here. It was centrally located for the peasants of the hills and the fishermen to come, a natural resort site, pleasant and calm as it is today. His disciples retired from the shores of the Sea of Galilee for solitude and came to this site. The multitudes assembled here. They came from Jerusalem, from the Decapolis, from Judea and from 'beyond the Jordan' to hear the words of "The Man from Galilee." This mountain stood alone as it merged into the Sea and is a lovely 'gathering place'. A lovely hospice and small Italian Franciscan 8 sided church representing the 8 Beatitudes, sits on the site. Every pilgrim should come here and savor the landscape that so influenced the thoughts of a man who influenced the thoughts of the world. 160 kms. **N** from Jerusalem.

Mount Berniki, Bernice (bear, bring forth GK) This impressive mountain, just off the eastern shore of the Sea of Galilee is named after Bernice, the granddaughter of Herod the Great and the daughter of Herod

Agrippa I. According to Josephus, she was a raving beauty but was having an incestuous relationship with her brother, King Agippa and even the Romans were offended by their indecent conduct. Paul appeared before them *[Acts 25:13, 23; 26:30]*.

Mount Carmel   See Carmel, Muhraka

Mount of Abraham   Called Armon Hanatziv (castle of the representatives) in Hebrew. **S** of the Old City of Jerusalem stands a high mount 820 meters (2722 ft.) above sea level. The buildings here were once occupied by the British High Commissioner and now houses the offices of the United Nations. Here is the traditional site where "…Abraham lifted up his eyes, and saw the place (Mt. Moriah) afar off *[Genesis 22:4-5]*. It is on the road approached through Abu Tor past the Sherover Promenade. See Mount of Evil Counsel.

Mount of Ebal   See Ebal *[Deut. 11:29]*

Mount of Evil Counsel   Located in Jerusalem near the Abu Tor neighborhood, S of David's City on the eastern hill, next to the headquarters of the United Nations. Traditionally, the site where the High Priest, Caiaphas, might have lived. It was he who made the decision for Jesus to be put to death. He said, "It is better that one man should die for the people and not that the whole nation should perish *[John 11:45-51]*. The name may also come from the belief and tradition that this is the mountain where Solomon erected an altar for his foreign wives in order for them to burn incense to their gods, thus its name. Solomon received evil counsel from his wives *[I Kings 11 7-8]*. See Abu Tor and Mount of Abraham.

Mount of Ga'ash   See Ga'ash *[Joshua 24:29-30]*

Mount Gerizim   See Gerizim *[Deut. 11:29]*

Mount Gilbo'a   See Gilbo'a *[I Samuel 28:4]*

Mountain of God   See Moriah and Sinai *[Dan. 9:20]*

Mount Hermon   See Hermon

Mount Hor   See Hor

Mount Horeb   See Mt. Sinai and Karkom, Mt. of

Mount Kabir   See Ga'ash

Mount Mizar   See Hermon

Mount Mori'ah   See Moriah above

Mount Nebo   (a prim. root to hollow out) Moses stood here, viewed the Promised Land and is buried here in a ravine *[Deut. 32:49, 50; 34:1,6]*. Nebo was the head of the summit of Mt. Pisgah and a part of the mountain range of Abarim. Josephus tells us that "it is a very high mountain, situated over against Jericho, one that affords a view of much of the excellent land of Canaan." *[Ant.4.8.48]*. Nebo is in present day Jordan, in the land of Moab. See Moab and Mount Pisgah.

Mount of Olives   (Har Ha Zatim) The olive trees that stand in silence along the hills of time. Today, we still see the many olive trees on this ancient, holy site. The ridge of hills **E** of Jerusalem is a limestone ridge, 2 kms. in length and covers the whole eastern side of the city of Jerusalem. David fled from his son, Absalom, weeping as he ascended this mount *[II Samuel 15:30]*. Zechariah the Prophet foretells the day when the Mt. of Olives will be split in two and there will be a tremendous earthquake. It is on a natural fault line *[Zechariah 14:4]*. The Jews believe that the Messiah will come here according to the prophecy of Zechariah. It was the custom of Jesus to come to this site many times *[Luke 22:39]*. Jesus traveled this route from the Temple through the Mt. of Olives to Bethany and to the homes of His friends, Lazarus, Mary and Martha *[Matthew 21:1; Mark 11:1;13:3,14:26; John 8:1]*. Jesus' farewell message was pronounced here and is called "The Olivet Discourse." He outlined the future of the nation and what was about to take place, He predicted the fall of the Temple and Jerusalem. He sat on the Mount of Olives with His disciples many times *[Matthew 24, Mark 13, Luke 21]*. See Mount Olivet below. See Gethsemane (Olive Press).

Mount Olivet   (little olive hill) This site is a little hill on the Mount of Olives in Bethany and also called the Mount of Ascension. Here Jesus took His disciples after His resurrection. He lifted up His hands and blessed them and He parted from them, ascending into heaven *[Luke 24:50; Mark 16:19; Acts 1:9,12]*. The angel spoke to them and promised that He would return here to this same site in the same manner in which He left *[Acts 1:8-12]*. Today, there are two churches on this site, one is the Russian Church of the Ascension, built on the ruins from the 4th C. and the other, also called the Church of the

Ascension, is located next to the Church of Pater Noster (Lord's Prayer site). It was in Moslem hands from the time of Saladin and has never been rebuilt. See Mount of Olives.

Mount Pera'zim (possessor of breaches, master of breakthroughs) Also called Ba'al-pera'zim. Here David fought the Philistines *[II Samuel 5:20; I Chronicles 14:11]*. Isaiah the Prophet speaks of this site. "The Lord will raise up as at Mount Perazim," *[Isaiah 28:21]*. In the Valley of Rephaim, **S** of Jerusalem, 2 kms. **N** of Bethlehem. The exact location is unknown.

Mount Pis'gah (cleft or to pass between) In Moab, the headland of the summit of the mountain range of Abarim. It is slightly **NW** of Mt. Nebo. Here from Nebo, from Pisgah, God commanded and Moses took a long look at the Promised Land *[Numbers 21:20; 23:14; Deut. 3:27; 34:1]*. It appears to be one of the ancient 'high places of Moab' where sacrifices took place. Balaam offered sacrifices here *[Numbers 23:14; 33:52]*. In Jordan, now identified as Jebel Siyaghah.

Mount of Scandal (Mt. of Offense) The small mount rising on the southern side of the village of Silwan adjacent to the Old City of Jerusalem, down its southern slope from the Dung Gate. So named for here, Solomon built homes and palaces for his foreign wives *[I Kings 11:4-8]*. See Mount of Evil Counsel.

Mount Scopus See Nob

Mount Se'ir (rough, hairy) There are three Biblical references to this site in the Bible. One site is the range of mountains running from the Dead Sea, **E** of the Arava. The earliest reference is at the time of Abraham, during the Chedorlaomer campaign *[Genesis 14:6]*. After Jacob struggled with the angel, he sent messengers to his brother, Esau in the land of Seir *[Genesis 32:3; 33:14,16]*. Esau dwelt here on Mount Seir *[Genesis 36:8]*. Jehovah gave this region to the sons of Esau as an inheritance, so the Israelites were forbidden to enter *[Deut. 2:5]*. The area of Seir, at the foot of the mountain, appears to be dry and arid and, indeed, it is in accordance to what Isaac said to his son Esau, "Behold, away from the fertility of the earth shall be your dwelling…" *[Genesis 27:39]*. The land of Seir, where Esau was a dweller, in the country of Edom is in present day Jordan.

Mount Sinai (prim. root thorny) The mountains that the children of Israel reached three months after leaving Egypt *[Exodus 19:1]*. They stand 2642 (8700 ft.) meters above sea level. It is composed of various kinds of volcanic rocks. The landscape is wild and windy and always gets snow in Winter. The view from the summit is breathtaking and encompasses all of the Sinai itself. It might have gotten its name from the moon god, Sin, whose cult had made its way in this area. Moses went up to this mountain for forty days and received the ten commandments from God *[Exodus 19:2,11,18 20,23]*. He ascended a second time and was acquainted with the details, the rites and ceremonies in the Pentateuch (first 5 books of Moses) *[Exodus 31:18; chap.34; Leviticus 7:37-38]*. They continued to set out from Sinai in the presence of the Lord. Moses requested the Lord, "If Your Presence does not go with us, do not bring us up from here...except You go with us..." *[Exodus 33:15-16]*. It is also called Horeb and today is in the Sinai, referred to as Jebel Musa, the mountain of Moses. A monastery today, called St. Catherine's run by Greek monks, stands at its foot with a guest house nearby. See Sinai, land of. See Horeb, some scholars believe Horeb is a completely different mountain next to Sinai, there are differences of opinion. Several sources believe Horeb is Mt. Karkom, **S** of Sinai. See Horeb and Karkom, Mt. of.

Mount Sion See Hermon

Mount Tabor (Tavor), Mt. of Transfiguration (prim. root, to bear new fruit) Also called the Mount of Transfiguration (transforms the figure, outline) It almost looks like a tel from the distance, with its dome-shaped form. Josephus said it had the shape of a woman's breast, conical and symmetrical in shape; it is a mound of limestone on the plain of Esdraelon in the Jez'reel Valley. It was the mountain of an important city called Tabor in ancient times, being on the Via Maris (the way of the sea) the route between Egypt and Damascus. The northern slope is covered with oak trees and stands about 588 meters (1952 ft.) above the Mediterranean Sea. Here, Barak at the command of Deborah, gathered his forces *[Judges 4:6,12,14]*. Here the brothers of Gideon were slain *[Judges 8:18-19]*. During Jesus' time the city had a town on its summit and the ruins can be seen today *[I Chronicles 6:77]*. The psalmist speaks about the Lord's joy concerning Tabor *[Psalm 89:12]*. Jeremiah, the Prophet speaks of the 'certainty' of this mountain *[Jeremiah 46:18]*. The main claim today for its holiness is the tradition that this is the site where Jesus took His disciples and was transfigured before them. "And after six days He took (them)…to a high mountain set apart…"*[Matthew 17:1-2; Mark 9:2-13; Luke 9:28-36; II Peter 1:17-18]*. This site has been honored since the 4th C. It has one of the more beautiful churches in all of Israel on its summit, run by the Franciscans. Private cars and taxis take you up the narrow road as tour busses are forbidden. Some scholars believe that Mt. Hermon is the site of the transfiguration because it is also seen as a mountain that stands alone. See Hermon.

Mount of Temptation (Mons Quarantana LT.) The mountain of '40 days', also called Mount Karantal or Quarantal, meaning of the forty days, just above Jericho. A footpath leads to a Greek Monastery honored as the site where Jesus spent 40 days fasting and praying, being tempted by the devil. He then started His public ministry *[Matthew 4:1-5; Luke 4:1-13]*. The peak is 341 meters (1135 ft.) above sea level. Travel to Jericho 27 kms. **N** from Jerusalem. See Jericho.

Mustard Seed site One of the more well-known plants of the Holyland is the mustard seed. Jesus refers to this mustard seed in the city and countryside, comparing its size to faith. The term mustard tree is exaggerated in contrast to its tiny seed to be explained by the parable "but when it is full grown, it is larger than the garden plants, and becomes a tree" *[Matthew 13:32]*. After He left the Mt. of Transfiguration with the disciples, He makes reference to their faith "…if you have faith as a mustard seed, you can say to that mountain (Mt. Tabor perhaps) "Move from here to there and it will move; and nothing will be impossible for you." *[Matthew 17:20; Luke 17:6]*. The Israeli mustard seed trees sometimes grow to a height of 3 meters (10 ft.) and in the Spring, many pilgrims love to take a leaf or seed or two. In the Spring you may find them throughout the land.

Mount Zion (dryness, drought) The entire western ridge of early Jerusalem. The term, Zion, is sometimes used to include the entire city of Jerusalem but by the 4th C. the term was adapted to mean the southern portion of the western hill. It is bounded by steep slopes on the **E, S** and **W**, which gives it the appearance of a separate mountain. On the **N** it gently slopes to the flat ground where the Armenian quarter inside the Old City is built. Before the Turkish period, the entire Old City wall encompassed all of Mt. Zion. The psalmist makes mention of

Zion 38 times. "The Lord dwelt on Mt. Zion" *[Psalm 74:2;78:68]*. "Those who trust in the Lord are like Mount Zion" *[Psalm 125:1]*. "When the Lord brought back the captivity of Zion, we were like those who dream" *[Psalm 126:1]* "For the Lord has chosen Zion, He has desired it for His habitation"*[Psalm 132:13]*. Mt. Zion was a natural, formidable fortress for the Jebusites before David took over the city *[II Samuel 5:7]*. David took the stronghold of Zion *[IChronicles 11:5]*. "...Solomon brought up the ark of the Lord to the City of David, which is Zion," *[I Kings 8:1]*. See Jebus. From the Crusader times, the tradition is that David is buried here. See Tomb of David. Isaiah tells us for Zion's sake he will not keep silent *[Isaiah 62:1]*.

Jesus on Mt. Zion

Jesus came here many times with His disciples. He brought them to the Upper Room on Mt. Zion and instituted communion *[Matthew 26:26-35; Mark 14:15-25; Luke 22:14-38; John chapters 13,14,15]*. He prayed for unity for His disciples here *[John 17]*. Jesus comes to the pinnacle of the Temple here, on the **SE** corner of Mt. Zion *[Luke 4:9-12]*. He appeared to them after the Resurrection *[John 20:19-29]*. They came together in the Upper Room and waited for the Holy Spirit, who came and filled them with power and authority *[Acts 1:12-26; Acts 2:1-4]*. The High Priest, Caiaphas, probably lived here, and Jesus was detained in his house after His arrest *[Mark 14:53-72; John 18:24]*. See Peter of Galicantu. One of the earliest churches in Christendom stood here, called Church of Mary or the Church of Mount Zion, built in the 4th C, now called Church of the Dormition where Mary the mother of Jesus 'fell asleep' or is buried. The Catholic Benedictine monks live in the monastery and run the church. The Cathedral of St. James is here *[Acts 12:1-2]*. See Cathedral of St. James and Church of St. Mark.

Muhraka (scorching AK) The scorching of God, El Muhraka. Also referred to as the Horn of Carmel because on this summit of the Carmel mountain range, 482 meters (1600 ft.) above sea level stands a small Carmelite monastery built over the site where Elijah challenged the prophets of Ba'al *[I Kings 18:19-40]*. The fire that came down from heaven was 'scorching' and ate up the sacrifice. The top of the monastery offers a magnificent view of the surrounding Jezreel Valley and area.

145 kms. from Jerusalem going **N**, heading toward Haifa onto Carmel. See Carmel and Kishon.

Na'arah, Na'arath, Naaran   (a girl, a youth) In the tribe of Ephraim, this was the southern border between Beth-el and Jericho *[Joshua 16:7; I Chronicles 7:28;11:37]*. It is in the Jordan Valley just **N** of Jericho and is identified as Tel el-Jisr.

Nacon's Threshing Floor   (even place belonging to Nacon; 'to be firm') The even place where the wheat was sifted belonging to Nacon; Uzzah one of David's men took hold of the ark and he died *[II Samuel 6:6-8; I Chronicles 13:9]*. Located in Perez-Uzzah I km. **N** of Jerusalem called Khirbet el-Uz today.

Nacon   See Perez-uzzah

Nahal David   See Ein Gedi

Na'halal, Nahalol   (pasture) Here on the border of Zebulun this site was inhabited by the Canaanites but was given to the Levites because of these good pasture lands *[Joshua 19:15; 21:35; Judges 1:30]*. It is just **S** of Akko called Tel en-Nahl. 173 kms. **N** from Jerusalem.

Naha'liel   (wadi, torrent or valley of God) **N** of the Arnon River. The children of Israel encamped here between Mattanah and Bamoth *[Numbers 21:19]*. It was near the slopes of Pisgah on the eastern side of the Jordan River, about 19 kms. **SE** of Jericho but the exact location is unknown.

Na'in   (pleasantness, beauty) Here Jesus raised up the weeping widow's son who had died *[Luke 7:11-15]*. The site 10 kms. **SW** of Nazareth stands on a bleak, rocky slope on the northern descending slope of "the hill of Moreh (Givat Moreh)" which is in the Jez'reel Valley. See Givat Moreh.

Na'ioth, Na'ioth in Ramah   (dwellings) Samuel and David took refuge here after their escape from Saul *[I Samuel 19:18]*. Saul followed David and Samuel and he came, took off his clothes and prophesied day and night *[I Samuel 19:20-24]*. This is believed to be a site where there was a common dwelling for the prophets. In the neighborhood of Ramah, **N** of Jerusalem, 6 kms. **N** of Gibeath.

Naph'tali, tribe of   (my wrestling) When the children of Israel were marching through the wilderness, the district of Naphtali occupied a position on the **N** of the sacred tent of Dan and Asher *[Numbers 2:25-50; Joshua 19:32-39]*. In the land this site is the northern angle of Israel and was enclosed by Zebulun in the **S**, Asher in **W** and Manasseh in the **E**. Jesus spoke about this land, quoting from the Prophet Isaiah *[Matthew 4:15]*. See tribe map in back of book.

Naph'tali, Hill Country of   The mountain region that forms the northern area of the territory of Naphtali. The land is similar to the hill country of Ephraim and Judah *[Joshua 20:7]*. See tribes map in back of book.

Nativity Site   See Bethlehem

Naz'areth   (root unclear, En Nasira AK.) The home of Jesus, Mary and Joseph and the place where Jesus grew up and was subject to His parents *[Luke 2:51]*. "And Nathanael asked, "can anything good come out of Nazareth…?" *[John 1:46]*. Archaeological evidence indicates that it was a Jewish city during the time of Jesus and even after the destruction of the Temple, Jews remained and lived here. The city itself is located on the most southern range of mountains of lower Galilee, about 20 kms. **N** from the Esdraelon plain in the Jez'reel Valley. Nazareth actually lies in a basin and you cannot see Nazareth from afar until you climb the edge of the basin. Today it is a bustling, busy city with a large Arab Christian population. The Jewish communities, called Nof Ha Emek and Nazareth Elite are on the hill overlooking the city. The church of the Annunciation, Roman Catholic, which was built in 1966, is the traditional site of Mary's home. "…the angel Gabriel was sent by God to a city of Galilee named Nazareth" *[Luke 1:26]*. Mary's well in the center of the city still provides water as it did in the time of Jesus. See scriptures below.

Jesus in Nazareth

"And He resided in a city called Nazareth…" *[Matthew 2:23]* "And leaving Nazareth He came and settled in Capernaum…" *[Matthew 4:13]* "…this is Jesus, the Prophet from Nazareth in Galilee." *[Matthew 21:11]* "And it came to pass that Jesus came from Nazareth…" *[Mark 1:9]*

"They performed all things according to the law of the Lord, they (Joseph, Mary and the infant baby Jesus) returned to their own city Nazareth." *[Luke 2:39]* "Then He went down with them and came to Nazareth." *[Luke 2:51]*

Jesus in the Nazareth Synagogue / and on the Brow of the Hill

"So He came to Nazareth where He was brought up, and as His custom was He entered the synagogue on the Sabbath day and He stood up to read," *[Luke 4:16; Mark 6:1-6]*. See church of the synagogue.

"And when all those in the synagogue heard Him they were filled with rage and rose up and led Him to the brow of the hill so as to throw Him over" *[Luke 4:28-29]*.

NAZARETH POEM

When I am tempted to repine
That such a lowly lot is mine
There comes to me a voice which sayeth
Mine were the streets of Nazareth
So mean, so common, so confined
And He the Monarch of mankind
Yet patiently He traveled
These narrow streets of Nazareth
It may be I shall never rise
To place or fame beneath these skies
But walk in common walks til death
Narrow as these streets of Nazareth
But if through honor's arch I tread
And there forget to bend my head
Ah! Let me hear the voice which sayeth
Mine were the streets of Nazareth!

Nettie Rooker

Nebi Samuel (prophet Shmuel, ha Nebi; Nabi Samwil AK) The Prophet Samuel's tomb is on a high, conspicuous hill 912 meters (3,027 ft.) above sea level) just above the town of

Gibeon in Ramah, on the road to Jerusalem from the **W**, some 7 kms. He was buried here in his home town in 1017 BC and there was a great mourning made for Samuel by all the Israelites *[I Samuel 25:1]*. The building today is used as a mosque on one side and a synagogue on the other. Archaeological work is still proceeding. A great deal of Crusader remains can be seen.

Nebo, city of   (root Gk. to stir up or in AK. 'to be high') Its name could have been for the worship of Nebo, a Babylonian god. The city is on Mt. Nebo, **E** of the Jordan River and situated on a fertile country area which was taken by Reuben, next to Mt. Nebo *[Numbers 32:38]*. It was rebuilt by the Reubenites but the city reverted back to Moab *[Numbers 32:38; 33:47; I Chronicles 5:8]*. In the country of Jordan.

Nebo, mountain of   (Jebel Nabba, to be high AK) The Lord said to Moses, "You shall see the land before you, but you shall not go there…" *[Deut. 32:52]*. From here Moses viewed the Promised Land and here is where he is buried, though we don't know the exact location *[Deut. 32:49,50; 34:1-8]*. Nebo is the head of the summit of Mt. Pisgah. Just to the **E** of the Kings Highway, Mt. Nebo is 20 kms. from the Israeli border on the **E**, in the land of Jordan, opposite Jericho.

Necropolis   (cluster of tombs GK) The largest and most magnificent of tombs in the ancient City of David. Go to the southern area around Hezekiah's tunnel in City of Silwan, Jerusalem, close to the first eastern wall where there are many caves. Scholars believe this may be the site of the tomb of David and the other kings. This area is yet to be fully explored and excavated. See Tombs in the City of David for all the scripture references.

Nephto'ah, Springs of   (an opening) From these waters, springs were the boundaries that separated the tribes of Judah and Benjamin *[Joshua 15:9;18:15]*. It is 1 km. **NW** of Jerusalem and is today identified as Ein Lifta near the village of Ein Kerem.

Neto'phah   (distilling, dripping) Just **S** of Jerusalem, about 7 kms. near Bethlehem is this city of Judah whose inhabitants returned with Zerubbabel from their exile *[Ezra 2:2; Nehemiah 7:26]*. David's guards lived here *[II Samuel 23:28-29; I Chronicles 27:13,15]*. The exact location is not known.

Nib'shan (smooth) On the shores of the Dead Sea in the area of En Gedi which was one of the cities of Judah *[Joshua 15:62]*. 51 kms. **SE** from Jerusalem.

Nob (root, to abandon) The priestly town of Benjamin situated on a hill overlooking the Old City of Jerusalem *[Isaiah 10:28-32]*. It was on a road coming from the **N** and here, David asked for bread from Abimelech after he fled from Saul and he received the shewbread *[I Samuel 21:1-6]*. The ark was here just before coming to Jerusalem *[II Samuel 6:1-2]*. A company of Benjaminites settled here after they returned from exile *[Nehemiah 11:32]*. Saul killed those who stood with David and it was a great massacre *[I Samuel 22:17-19]*. The site is on Mt. Scopus and known as Ras Umm et-Tala just on the **E** on the Mt. of Olives range. 2 kms. from Old City.

Oaks of Mamre (terebinth) Abraham came and moved his tent settling by the oak trees near Hebron and he built an altar to the Lord *[Genesis 13:18]*. The report came to Abraham of Lot's abduction while he was sitting by these oaks *[Genesis 14:13]*. The Lord appeared to him by these oaks and he saw the three angels, he ate with them under these trees *[Genesis 18:1-8]*. Here, he heard that Sarah would bear the promised son of his old age as he sat underneath these oaks *[Genesis 18:9-10]*. The angels asked, "Is anything too hard for the Lord…?" *[Genesis 18:14]*. The site is next to Hebron, 37 kms. **S** of Jerusalem.

Oaks of Moreh (the teaching oaks) Here, Abraham came to Shechem as far as these oaks *[Genesis 12:6]*. See Moreh.

Oboth (water skins) Here the children of Israel encamped in their 47th encampment on their way to the Promised Land *[Numbers 21:10-11;33:43-44]*. It is today the oasis of el-Weiba in Edom, in Jordan.

Old City of Jerusalem (ear-ha atique) The famous and most wonderful city, the city within the city, the Old City of Jerusalem, the land located within the Old City walls, encompasses 1005 dunam or 209 acres, one third square mile and has 4 distinct quarters. The Jewish quarter is **SE** inside the city walls, the Armenian is **SW**, the Moslem is **NE** and the Christian is **NW**. There are 8 gates to this Old City and one new one next to Dung Gate, built for pedestrians. The Old City is one of the most ancient cities in the world, founded 5000 years ago, next to the Gihon Springs in the Kidron Valley. Here David conquered the city from the Jebusites. *[II Samuel 5:6-10; I Chronicles 11:5-9]*. Here the First and Second Temples stood. See Jebus, Jerusalem and Jesus in Jerusalem.

Old City Gates See Gates at end of the book

Old City Walls Present and ancient, see maps at the back of this book.

Olives, Mount of See Mount of Olives

Ono (strong) The city in the tribe of Benjamin which was restored by Shemed. *[I Chronicles 8:12]*. Some of the exiles returned here and resettled after the captivity *[Ezra 2:33; Nehemiah 7:37]*. It is located in what is called 'the plain of Ono' *[Nehemiah 6:2]*, also called the 'valley of the craftsman,' *[Nehemiah 11:35]*. It is identified as Kefr Ana, just **SE** of the city of Joppa **S**, of Tel Aviv.

Ophel (mound or tower) This site was the original City of David occupied by the Jebusites when David captured it and made it the capital of the Hebrew kingdom *[I Chronicles 11:5-9; II Samuel 5:6-10]*. King Jotham built the upper gate and extended the Ophel *[II Chronicles 27:3]*. King Manasseh also rebuilt this wall and enclosed the Ophel *[II Chronicles 33:14]*. This Ophel is a ridge extending **S** of the Temple Mount between the Kidron Valley in the **E** and the Tyropoeon Valley on the **W**. After the return of the exiled Jews from the Babylonian Captivity, Nehemiah rebuilt the wall around the Ophel *[Nehemiah 3:26,27]*. The temple servants lived here *[Nehemiah 11:21]*. The mount is clearly visible and can be walked on today and there is still room for much excavation. Go **E** from Dung Gate down the valley. See Ancient Gates at the end of this book.

Ophel Archaeological Garden (garden mound, tower) Also called 'Western Wall Excavations' along the southern wall of the Old City in the Jewish quarter, Jerusalem, just **N** of Dung Gate is an exposed area revealing the administrative complex of Solomon's First Temple *[I Kings 6]*. There are paved streets from the Second Temple period, Jewish ritual baths (mikvot) and sections of Robinson's Arch. Presently archaeological dig in progress. See Robinson's Arch.

Oph'rah   (fawn, hind) This town was the hometown and birthplace of Gideon. His father was an Abiezrite, the family name for 'helper' and here, Gideon was threshing wheat in the wine press when he received a call on his life from the angel of the Lord *[Judges 6:11-23]*. Gideon built an altar and named it 'The-Lord-Shalom' (the Lord is my peace) *[Judges 6:24]*. Gideon ruled from here and was buried on this site *[Judges 8:27,32]*. Abimelech came here and killed his brothers *[Judges 9:5]*. The site is 10 kms. **SW** of Shechem.

O'reb, rock of   (raven's crag, steep cliff) The site where Gideon slew Oreb, one of the princes of the Midianites *[Judges 7:25]*. Isaiah, the Prophet speaks about the Lord stirring up a scourge like at Oreb *[Isaiah 10:26]*. It is **W** of the Jordan River near Beth Barah but the exact location is uncertain.

Ornan's Threshing Floor   See Araunah's Threshing Floor

Outer Valley   See Tyropoeon Valley

Palm Sunday Path   The first Sunday in the week before the Christian holiday of Easter (Resurrection Day) is called Palm Sunday, celebrating the Sunday or first day of the week, when Jesus rose from the grave. All the major Christian denominations celebrate it on a different Sunday but it is generally in the Spring and coincides with the Jewish holyday of Pesach (Passover). The beginning of the path extends from the top of the Mount of Olives on the **E** and has a steep to mild slope which winds around past the Dominus Flavius Church (Tear Drop Church) on the right, continuing onto the Russian Church of Mary Magdalene, with the Jewish cemetery on the Mount of Olives on your left. You arrive at the Church of All Nations and the Garden of Gethsemane. The path ends here. It is very significant to all Christian pilgrims, for this is the path that Jesus walked down when He made His triumphal entry into Jerusalem. People cut palm branches and laid them on the pavement as Jesus went by. The traditional belief is that this happened one week before He was crucified. It is still the ancient path from the 2nd Temple period, that led from the Mt. of Olives to the Temple and the Temple Mount inside the Old City of Jerusalem *[Mark 11:1-10; Luke 19:29-38; John 12:12-15]*.

Palm Tree, City of   See Jericho

Pa'ran (from root, bough or branches) A wilderness area on the eastern side of the Sinai Peninsula, bordered by the Arava southern desert and the Gulf of Eilat, A'qaba on the **E** and taking in the wilderness of Zin, Kadesh-barnea. The kings of the **E** had an expedition here *[Genesis 14:6]*. Ishmael dwelt here *[Genesis 21:21]*. The children of Israel camped here after they left the Sinai *[Numbers 10:12;12:16]*. The spies were sent out from Paran to the Land of Promise *[Numbers 13:3]*. They returned here to this wilderness *[Numbers 13:26]*. Moses gave his preamble to the covenant here *[Deut. 1:1]*. After the death of Samuel, David arose and came here to this wilderness *[I Samuel 25:1]*. Hada, the Edomite revolted against Solomon and went to Egypt by way of Paran *[I Kings 11:18]*. Now located in Egypt, Sinai desert, travel **S** from Taba border, Eilat.

Paran, Mount of Only two references are made to this mountain. Moses blesses the children of Israel, and reminds them that the Lord came down on them from Mt. Paran *[Deut. 33:2]*. Habakkuk, the Prophet also refers to the glory of the person of God, 'The Holy One from Mount Paran,' *[Habakkuk 3:3]*. See Paran above.

Par'bar (suburb) A part, precinct or suburb of the ancient cities of Jerusalem in the Temple periods. It could also refer to a court extending **W** of the Ist Temple. The rabbis refer to it as the "outside place," *[I Chronicles 26:18]*. Josephus refers to this area called Parbar, as he describes Herod's Temple in 2nd Temple time, as the area lying in the deep valley that separated the **W** wall of the Temple from the city opposite it, or the southern end of the Tyropoeon Valley. See maps at back of the book.

Pasture Lands (migrash, suburbs) These lands were most important in ancient times for the cattle had to graze. There were many open fields, places for this purpose especially around the Levite cities. The priests would need the animals for sacrifice *[Numbers 35:2; Joshua 21:11; I Chronicles 6:55-60]*. See Common lands.

Pater Noster See Lord's Prayer Site

Patriarch's Cave of See Machpelah, Cave of *[Genesis 23:9,17]*.

Peni'el, Penuel (face of God) The site where Jacob struggled and wrestled with God *[Genesis 32:30,31]*. The people of Penuel treated Gideon with disrespect when he passed through pursuing the Midianites across the Jordan River and he tore down their tower *[Judges 8:8,9,17]*. The tower was rebuilt by Jeroboam *[I Kings 12:25]*. The site is just **E** of the Jordan River and **N** of the Jabbok River. In present day Jordan about 15 kms. **E** of Jordan River, opposite Bet Shean.

Pe'or, mountain of   (opening, cleft) Balak led the Prophet Balaam to the top of this mountain so Balaam could see and curse the children of Israel *[Numbers 23:28]*. It is written that Peor overlooks the wastelands which is the wilderness on either side of the Dead Sea. Mt. Peor was one peak of the northern part of the mountains of Abarim, by the town of Beth-peor and opposite, where Israel encamped in the steppes of Moab *[Deut. 3:29; 4:46]*. Presently, in Moab in Jordan, opposite the Dead Sea and the city of Jericho, some 20 kms. **E** of the border of the Jordan River.

Pera'zim   See Ba'ale-perazim *[Isaiah 28:21]*.

Pe'rez-uz'zah, Pe'rez-uzza   (the breach of Uzzah) This site is also called Nacon and Chidon *[II Samuel 6:6; I Chronicles 13:9]*. Here, Uzzah died because he reached out his hand and touched the Ark of God *[II Samuel 6:6-8]*. It is on the road to Jerusalem about 1 km. from Kiriath-jearim and called Khirbet el-Uz today.

Peter of Galicantu   (the denial of Peter site, the cock crowed, LT.) This site on Mt. Zion is built on the ruins of the house of the High Priest Caiaphas. Under the church, some two floors down is a very impressive dungeon/ cave which is believed to be the place where Jesus would have remained the night before His crucifixion. Pilgrims recite *Psalm 88* here. The first church here was Byzantine, destroyed by the Persians in 614 AD. Jesus predicted that Peter would deny Him 3 times before the rooster crowed *[Matthew 26:34; Mark 14:26-31; Luke 22:34; John 13:37,38]*. They led Jesus away to the house of Caiaphas and Peter followed *[Matthew 26:57]*. Peter denied the Lord 3 times here in the courtyard by the open fire *[Matthew 26:69-74; Mark 14:66-72; Luke 22:55-62; John 18:1-18; 25-27]*. The present site is a modern church built in 1931 and run by the Catholic Assumptionist order. The area on the ground to the **N** is not fully excavated but stone steps from the 2nd Temple period are visible and there appears to be mikvot (ritual baths), rooms and other remains indicating the Jewishness of this ancient site. Read *Psalm 88* here in the 'Pit site'. See Mt. Zion.

Peter's House (bite shel Kefer, Petros GK.) This site is in Capernaum on the **NW** shore of the Sea of Galilee and boasts conclusive history, from the Ist C, identified as the house of Peter where he dwelt with his wife and mother-in-law. It was very near the synagogue. It is next to an 'insular' which was common in those days. Many rooms for the extended family, many generations living under one roof and sharing a common kitchen. Many modern day scholars and archaeologists suggest that Peter was really a wealthy fisherman and had a thriving business here on the shores of the Sea of Galilee. This is evidenced from his home and its privileged position next to the synagogue. The site is owned and run by the Catholic order of Franciscans and is well kept, an impressive site. See Roman Via Maris stone in the garden *[Matthew 8:14,15; Mark 1:29-31; Luke 4:38,39]*. See Capernaum.

Pe'tra, Sela (rock GK; sela HB) The ancient capital of the Nabateans in Edom. It is in Jordan, some 90 kms. **S** of the Dead Sea. This rock-cut city was a pagan center, a fortress and a stronghold. The boundary of the Amorites was from Sela and upward *[Judges 1:36]*. Amaziah, the King of Judah killed 10,000 Edomites in the Dead Sea Valley and took the city of Sela *[II King 14:7-10; II Chronicles 25:11-12]*. Isaiah, the Prophet, speaks of Sela in the wilderness *[Isaiah 16:1]*. Obadiah, the Prophet predicted God's judgment on this fortress. *Obadiah* (all 21 verses) The site is 1 mile long and one half mile wide and here, we see excellent examples of "high places" to pagan gods. Petra is in ruins but its color of dark red sandstone and the buildings cut into the rock cliff, makes this site quite outstanding. Present day Jordan, easily accessible from Israel both by tour and private car and now air travel.

Pharaoh's Daughter's House Solomon made a treaty with Pharaoh, king of Egypt and married his daughter *[I Kings 3:1]*. He built a house for her which was then part of the City of David *[I Kings 7:8; II Chronicles 8:11]*. The outline of her house can be seen in one of the 'cave dwellings' in Silwan, overlooking the City of David from the Observation Platform at Peter of Galicantu. It is still to be fully excavated.

Pi-Hahiroth (root GK., shapeless) The children of Israel turned and camped here with Moses, **E** of the Red Sea, near Migdol and the sea, opposite Baal Zephon, by the sea of Reeds *[Exodus 14:1-2;9; Numbers 33:7]*. While they were encamped here, the Lord put it in Pharaoh's heart to pursue them. It is in Egypt just **E** of El Arish and the Lake of Shihor.

Pilate's Judgment Seat, Praetorium (headquarters LT.) This seat was named after Pontius Pilate who was the Roman procurator, or governor of Judea. He was appointed to this post in 26 AD. It was the custom for the procurators to reside in Jerusalem and Pilate came here from Caesarea in order to judge the uproar arising in Jerusalem over a man called Jesus, whom the Jews wanted to crucify. Pilate came to the judgment hall in the former palace of Herod the Great and took his seat here to assess the charges against Jesus. Pilate's name is mentioned 54 times in the NT in all 4 gospel accounts. They led Him to Pilate *[Matthew 27:2,13,17,22,24; Mark 15:1-44; Luke 3:1; 23:1]*. It is evident from the gospel accounts that Pilate did not want to condemn Jesus to death and Pilate's wife, according to Josephus (Appendix 3) was healed by Jesus. "While he was sitting on the judgment seat, his wife sent to him saying, "have nothing to do with this just Man, for I have suffered many things today in a dream because of Him," *[Matthew 27:19]*. Pilate gave permission and Jesus was taken away. "...You take Him and crucify Him, for I find no fault in Him" *[John 19:1-16]*. Its location is at the Jaffa Gate and some remains of the towers that were built by Herod, next to his palace, can still be seen in the Old City, Jerusalem, at the right of the Jaffa Gate area. See Ecco Homo.

Pinnacle of the Temple (wing, any pointed extremity GK.) This is the "highest point" or the corner of the highest or extreme point. Jesus was brought by the devil into the holy city and suffered temptation *[Matthew 4:5, Luke 4:9]*. It is probable that the reference is to the **SE** corner of the Herodion wall which has presently been preserved up to 10 meters (33 ft). The exact spot on the wall where Jesus might have stood is not identifiable. See Mt. Zion.

Pir'athon (height, summit) Abdon, who was a judge for 8 years, lived and died here *[Judge 12:13-15]*. Located in the land of Ephraim on the mountains of the Amalekites 20 km. **W** of Shechem.

Pis'gah (root, to pass between; cleft) Mt. Nebo is the head of the summit of this ridge of mountains, together with the Abarim range, located in Jordan. Pisgah skirts the **NE** end of the Dead Sea opposite Jericho. From this mountain, Moses took his survey of the Promised Land *[Numbers 21:20; 23:14; Deut. 3:27; 34:1]*. See Nebo.

Place of the Skull   See Golgotha

Plains of Jericho   (wide expanse of land in Jericho) Joshua brought the children of Israel over the Jordan River into the Land of Promise and 40,000 men prepared for war here *[Joshua 4:13]*. The children of Israel were circumcised here in Gilgal on the plains of Jericho, and they celebrated their first Passover in the Promised Land on this plain *[Joshua 5:10]*. The Chaldeans pursued King Zedekiah and overtook him on these plains and his army scattered *[II Kings 25:5; Jeremiah 39:5; 52:8]*. This site is **W** of the Jordan River, next to Jericho, 36 kms. **NE** from Jerusalem.

Plains of Moab   (wide expanse of land in Moab) The children of Israel encamped here on their way to the Promised Land and Moses spoke to them here by the Jordan River across from Jericho *[Numbers 22:1;26:3,63]*. The spoils from the Midianites were brought to them here *[Numbers 31:12; 33:48-50; 35:1; 36:13]*. From these plains Moses departed from them and went up to Mt. Nebo to die and be with God *[Deut. 34:1,8]*. This site is in Jordan across from Jericho, and 20 kms. **E** of the Jordan River. See Moab, land of.

Plains of Ono   See Ono

Pool of Bethesda   See Bethes'da *[John 5:1-9]*

Pool of Gibeon   See Gibeon

Pool of Hezekiah   (Yahweh has strengthened pool) King Hezekiah in 701 BC opened up a basin in the city and fed it by a water course that came from the Gihon springs. He directed the waters to the **W** part of the City of David by a subterranean channel. The Arabs call it Birkat el-Hammam, located outside and just **E** of the Dung Gate down the sloping hill about 1 km. *[II Kings 20:20; II Chronicles 32:30]*. See Hezekiah's Tunnel, Pool of Siloam and Warren's Shaft.

Pool of the Kings   This ancient pool is also called "The Fountain of the Virgin Mary" **E** of the Ophel in the ancient city of Jerusalem. Nehemiah came to inspect the broken walls and came here to this pool *[Nehemiah 2:14]*. See

Ophel. Go **SE** from Dung Gate though remains are not easily identifiable. See Ancient Gates map.

Pool of Siloam, Pool of Shelah, (sent) This is actually a
Pool of Silwan, Waters of Shiloah large reservoir next to the tunnel of
Hezekiah, also called 'Artificial Pool'. In Nehemiah's time, stairs went down to this pool from the City of David on the **S** hill of the city of Jerusalem, from the Temple Mount *[Nehemiah 3:15;12:37]*. The King's garden was close by. The pool was the termination of the Valley of Tyropoeon (cheese makers valley). It is the present site of Birkat Silwan (Pool of Silwan) in the city of Silwan and is fed by a conduit that is fed and starts at the so-called Virgin Spring (see En Rogel) as this spring is the only fresh water source in this area. Hezekiah completed a tunnel here in 701 BC which completely covered this ancient spring and diverted it through a conduit 533 meters (1777 ft). It was amazingly hewn out of solid rock *[II Chronicles 32:30; II Kings 20:20]*. Jesus sent His disciples out to meet a man carrying a jar of water (perhaps from this pool) *[Mark 14:13-14]*. A blind man was sent by Jesus to wash in this pool. "And Jesus said to him, Go, wash in the pool of Silwan, (which is translated, sent). So he went and washed, and came back seeing," *[John 9:7]*. See Hezekiah's Tunnel and Warren's Shaft.

Pool of Shelah (Bre-ha shel Aquaduct) See Pool of Silwan above, although some scholars believe it is a different pool which may have been called the King's Pool *[Nehemiah 2:14]*.

Pools of Solomon See Solomon's Pools

Porch of Solomon See Portico of Solomon below.

Portico of Solomon, (ulam shel Shlomo) The entrance hall of
Solomon's Porch the Temple, the pillar hall or the verandah and here, it is applied to the vestibule of the Temple, both the lst (Solomon's) and 2nd Temples (Herod's) in Jerusalem *[I Kings 7:6; II Chronicles 15:8]*. In Solomon's Temple, it was open at the front and at its sides; it was capable of being enclosed with awnings or curtains. It was also called a colonnade. In Herod's 2nd Temple, a covered portico ran on three sides with 2 rows of Corinthian columns spanned by cedar beams carrying a flat roof. The colonnade along the eastern side was known as Solomon's Portico. The area of the

Temple which was adjacent to the portico, known as the Court of the Gentiles because it was open to the general public, Jews and Gentiles. This area was usually crowded with people. Jesus came here with His disciples. He came and cast out the money changers. He made a whip and cast them out in His anger *[John 2:13-17]*. During the Feast of Hannucah (Dedication) Jesus walked in the Temple in Solomon's porch *[John 10:22-23]*. John and Peter were together with the multitudes and a lame man was healed *[Acts 3:11]*. The apostles did many signs and wonders here after the Resurrection and they were all in one accord *[Acts 5:12]*.

Potsherd Gate, Valley Gate   (dung, garbage gate) The gate from the Ist Temple period. Jeremiah, the Prophet, was admonished by God here at this gate, to speak to the people about the coming catastrophe *[Jeremiah 19:1-3]*. It is also called the Valley Gate and the Refuse Gate (Dung Gate in Ist C) which led down to the Hinnom Valley *[Nehemiah 2:13;3:13-14;12:31]*. Potters worked here in this vicinity and many potsherds (pottery pieces) were discarded, thus the name, Potsherd Gate. See map of Ist Temple period at the back. See Hinnom, Valley of.

Potter's Field, Field of Blood   (Acel'dama) This field was the burial site for the Jews who were not belonging to the city of Jerusalem or strangers *[Matthew 27:7]*. Judas betrayed Jesus for 30 pieces of silver. He repented and brought the 30 pieces of silver back to the priests, and throwing them at their feet *[Matthew 26:15;27:9]*. Here, Judas hung himself and was buried in this field of blood, Potters Field *[Matthew 27:8]*. This site is the southern end of the Hinnom Valley and its entry was from the Potsherd Gate. See Potsherd Gate and Aceldama. Many pieces of old pottery were discarded here and Jeremiah preached here *[Jeremiah 18:1-3]*. A Greek Orthodox Monastery stands on the site, which can be viewed from the Observation Platform at Peter of Galicantu's Church. Current excavations suggest that valuable King's tombs are located here, perhaps the real tombs of the kings.

Praetorium   (judgment hall, palace guard house) The headquarters in the Roman camp and also the palace where the Roman governor resided. In Jerusalem, it was located in the magnificent palace Herod the Great built for himself and when the governors came to Jerusalem, they resided here. In Caesarea Maritima, it was the governor's office and residence *[Acts 23:35]*. In the time of Jesus' judgment and trial, Pilate probably lived here and heard the case against Jesus *[Matthew 27:27; Mark 15:16; John 18:28;33]*. Paul was imprisoned in one *[Philippians 1:13]*. See Pilate's Judgment Hall. The site is located **E** of the Jaffa Gate in Jerusalem's Old City but not visible today except for the bottom stones of the outside wall.

Primacy of Peter, Mensa Peter   (recognition of Peter's primacy 'authority' and the table (mensa LT.) of the Lord) A lovely, small, contemporary church, built by the Franciscans in 1934, stands on this site also the site of Tabgha, noted for the multiplication of the loaves and fishes by Jesus *[Matthew14:13-21; Mark6:30-44; John 6:1-14]*. Here in the last chapter of the last gospel *[John 21]* Jesus appears to the disciples and invites them to come and dine. This site is located on the northern shore of the Sea of Galilee. See Tabgha.

Ptolemais   (hot sands) See Akko

Quarantal   (of the forty days) See Mount of Temptation

Qumran, Kiryat   (two moons AK.) The village of Qumran was named after the wadi of Qumran which runs along the mountainside. The name comes from the Arabic legend that when the moon is full, on a still night one can see two moons, one in the heavens and one reflected on the sea, hence its name. The community of the Essenes who called themselves 'Messengers of righteousness' (mesad hassidim) lived here in this northern outpost next to the Dead Sea. They were an ascetic group of devoted Jews who rebelled against the abuses of the Second Temple in Jerusalem. Scholars believe that John the Baptist may have been associated with them because of his lifestyle and the close proximity of John's waters of baptism, which was located just a few kms. away. Perhaps he came here for refreshment and fellowship. *[Matthew 3:1-12; Mark 1:2-8; Luke 3:1-6; John 1:19-28; 10:40]* Jeremiah speaks of finding grace here. *[Jeremiah 31:2]* The Dead Sea Scrolls were discovered here in 1947 and a broad consensus of opinion confirms the Essenes as the authors. 36 kms. **E** from Jerusalem from French Hill junction. Contineu to Dead Sea.

Rab'bah   (great) This was the chief city of the Ammonites and it is called Rabbah of the sons of Ammon *[Deut. 3:11; II Samuel 12:26; 17:27]*. Jeremiah prophesied against Ammon *[Jeremiah 49:2]*. Og, the giant king of Bashan, had his iron bed here *[Deut. 3:11]*. This city was not included in the territories of the tribes of Israel E of the Jordan, for the border of Gad stopped at "Aroer which is before Rabbah," *[Joshua 13:25]*. Abishai led his forces here while holding the Ammonites in check *[II Samuel 10:10,14]*. It appears that the city was not totally demolished during David's time, when Joab overthrew the city *[I Chronicles 20:1]*. In the time of Amos, the Prophet, this city had a wall and citadel and was still a sanctuary to the god Molech *[Amos 1:14-15]*. Ptolemy, the Roman named it Philadelphia in 285 BC and it became one of the important cities of the Decapolis. Today, it is the modern city of Amman, the capital of Jordan, 65 kms. **NE** of Jerusalem. Many ancient remains are still visible in the city itself.

Ra'chel's Tomb   (female ewe, caver shel Rahel) This site located 7 kms. **S** of Jerusalem, just **N** of Bethlehem on the Jerusalem / Bethlehem road is the authentic site of the burial of our matriarch, Rachel. It is one of the holiest sites in Judaism. Rachel's own father foretold her death *[Genesis 31:32]*. "So Rachel died and she was buried on the way to Ephrath (that is Bethlehem)" *[Genesis 35:16-19]*. Saul's donkeys were lost and found near here *[I Samuel 9:3]*. The Prophet, Jeremiah, speaks as from the Lord, concerning Rachel weeping for her children *[Jeremiah 31:15]*. Christians see this scripture fulfilled insofar as the Jewish children were slain under Herod the Great when Jesus was born *[Matthew 2:18]*. A special new road leads to the site. See Bethlehem.

Ra'mah   (height) In Biblical times, several places were called Ramah, because they were conspicuous and were located on the tops of hills for the sake of safety. They are listed below in the order of importance.

Ra'mah of Asher   (high place of Asher, the 'happy one') The boundary of the tribe of Asher *[Joshua 19:29]*. Located on the Mediterranean seacoast, just 2 kms. **E** of Tyre in present day Lebanon.

Ra'mah of Samuel, Ramathaim-zophim   (the high place of Samuel; double high view) Here is the birthplace and home of the Prophet, Samuel *[I Samuel 1:19; 2:11]*. The Prophetess, Deborah, sat under the palm trees here and the Israelites came up to her for judgment *[Judges 4:5]*. Both sites are located on the **N** side of Mt. Gaash, the whole tableland of Judah, 9 kms. **S** of Shechem, in the hill country of Ephraim. It is not easily identifiable today.

Ra'mah of Gilead, Ramoth-gilead (the heights of Gilead) One of the chief cities of the tribe of Gad and it was allotted as a city of refuge where men could flee. *[I Kings 4:13;22:3; II Kings 8:28; I Chronicles 6:80]*. Solomon made it the residence of one of his 12 deputies *[I Kings 4:13]*. It is located in the mountain region of Gilead, just E of the Jordan River. Today it is Tel Ramith in **N** Trans Jordan in the country of Jordan. Perhaps this is where Jeremiah, the Prophet, was held and bound in chains after Nebuzaradan invaded Jerusalem *[Jeremiah 40:1]*.

Ra'mah of Naphtali (heights of Naphtali) One of the fortified cities of the tribe of Naphtali located between Adamah and Hazor, in the mountainous country **NW** of the Sea of Galilee *[Joshua 19:36]*. Today it is a village inhabited by Christians and Drusim, surrounded by extensive olive trees and an ancient well. It is **SW** of Safed on the slopes of the beautiful plain of Safed 188 kms. **N** from Jerusalem.

Ramat Rachel See Beth-HaKerem

Ramatha'im-zophim See Ra'mah of Samuel

Ra'moth-gilead See Ramah of Gilead

Ra'moth of the Negev (the heights of the Negev, southern country) David sent portions of the spoils from the Amalekites to the brethren here *[I Samuel 30:27]*. It is on the southern border of the tribe of Simeon and simply called Baal, perhaps the same as Bealoth *[Joshua 15:24]*. Located on the **SE** edge of the Negev desert, **SE** of Arad in southern Israel, 100 kms. **S** from Jerusalem.

Ramparts (fortress, wall) The best way to view the ancient city of Jerusalem is to walk on her walls, 'Ramparts Walk'. Most ancient cities were enclosed by walls, or ramparts, for defense *[II Samuel 20:15; Isaiah 26:1; Habakkuk 2:1]*. The psalmist tells us to consider them *[Psalm 48:12-13]*. These present 2 miles of walls, were rebuilt during the 16th C by Suleiman the Magnificent, the ruler of the Ottoman Turks. Enter through the Jaffa, Damascus or Herod's Gate in the Old City of Jerusalem. See Gates of Jerusalem at the back of this book.

Red Sea (yam suf "sea of reeds") The first mention of this sea is when the Lord caused a violent west wind to take up one of the plagues of locusts and send them into the Red Sea *[Exodus 10:19]*. It would seem that a large body of water, large enough to drown the millions of locusts, had to be the Red Sea not the Sea of Reeds. After the great Exodus from Egypt, the children of Israel left with Moses, led by the Lord, by way of the wilderness toward the Red Sea *[Exodus 13:18]*. The most famous episode is the drowning of the army of Pharoah *[Exodus 14:1-30;15:1-4]*. The news of their marvelous victory spread throughout the lands *[Joshua 2:10; Psalm 106:7,9,22; 136:13,15]*. Jews throughout the world celebrate the Exodus from Egypt and the crossing of the children of Israel in the Red Sea, every Passover eve, in a meal called the Seder. Today the topography of this region has been altered considerably since the digging of the Suez Canal. Some scholars argue the exact location was not the Red Sea but the Sea of Reeds but the NT also recalls the Red Sea *[Acts 7:36]*. Paul's letters to the Hebrews also calls it by its proper name *[Hebrews 11:29]*. It is 1,350 miles (2200 kms.) long from the Indian Ocean to the Gulf of Suez. The Arabian Peninsula borders it on the **E** and Egypt on the **W**.

Refuge, Cities of (place of protection, sanctuary) On the plains of Moab, the Lord commanded Moses to appoint six cities of protection *[Numbers 35:6]*. Kadesh in Naphtali; Shechem near Mt. Ephraim; Hebron in Judah; Golan in Bashan; Ramoth in Gilead and Bezer in the tribe of Reuben *[Numbers 35:9-34]* See separate entries.

Refuse Gate (ash heap, dung hill) Nehemiah (comfort of Yahweh) the prophet, had found favor in the courts of the King of Persia, as the cupbearer to the King. His great concern for the welfare of his people and the broken walls in Jerusalem allowed him to take a bold step and ask to return to Jerusalem in order to rebuild the walls. In 426 BC, he returned to inspect and rebuild against great opposition *[Nehemiah 2:13; 3:13-14; 12:31]* See Nehemiah walls and gates at end of this book.

Re'hob, Beth-rehob (wide street, open space) A city on the northern border in the tribe of Naphtali. It was the border for the exploration of the spies sent out by Joshua *[Numbers 13:21; II Samuel 10:8; Judges 18:28]*. It is presently modern Tel el-Kadhy, in northern Israel on the border with Lebanon.

Reho'both   (broad places) Isaac dug a series of wells here *[Genesis 26:22]*. It is presently Wadi Ruhaibeh. It contains many ruins and a large well lying 26 kms. **S** from Beersheva.

Reph'aim, Valley of   (emek of the giants) Joshua describes it as the northern border of Judah and it was the scene of the conflict between the Philistines and David. *[Joshua 15:8; II Samuel 5:17-22; 23:13-17; I Chronicles 14:9-11]*. Close to Bethlehem, a valley known for its crops and grains *[I Chronicles 11:15-16]*. It is 5 kms. in length, lying **SW** of Jerusalem and extends to Bethlehem. It is called Baqa in Arabic and also known as Wadi Al-ward or Valley of Roses. It is believed that rose water was processed here in the 19th C for the local churches. Just to the **S** is Nahal Rephaim. Go to Givat Masua next to Kiryat Menahem, see the landscape and the surrounding deep wadis overlooking this site.

Reph'idim   (prim. root to spread, refresh) In the wilderness of Zin enroute to Mt. Sinai, the children of Israel murmured against the Lord and Moses because of the lack of water *[Exodus 17:1-7; 19:2]*. The Amelekites fought against them here but Aaron and Hur supported the hand of Moses for the great victory *[Exodus 17:8-16]*. It is presently Wadi Rufaid and is 20 kms. **N** of Mt. Sinai in the Sinai desert Egypt.

Resting Places of the Ark   The Ark of the Covenant was one of the holiest pieces of furniture in Judaism because it symbolized God's presence. It was 4 ft. long by 2.5 ft. high and 2.5 ft. wide, made of acacia wood and overlaid with gold, both inside and out *[Exodus 25:10-22]*. Only the priests were allowed to move it and the cloud of the presence of God was over the mercy seat *[Leviticus 16:2; I Samuel 4:4]*. It rested at Gilgal, Shechem, Bethel and Shiloh. The Philistines captured it at Ebenezer and held it for seven months. They took it to Aphek, Ashdod, Gath and Ekron. From Ekron, it went to Beth Shemesh and then to Kiryat-jearim. David moved it to Jerusalem when he became king *[II Chronicles 1:4]*. Solomon moved it to the Ist Temple *[I Kings 8:6,21; II Chronicles 5:2-14]*. After the destruction of Jerusalem, in 586 BC there is no more mention of the ark, except in the NT *[Revelation 11:19]*. Many scholars believe it is still under the Temple Mount, in a secret chamber which was built by King Solomon. This remains to be seen. See the Arc of the Covenant back of book.

Reuben, Tribe of   (root to see, behold a son!) *[Joshua 13:15-23]* See tribes at back.

River of Egypt   See Brook of Egypt

River Jordan   See Jordan River

Roads up to Jerusalem   (ancient paths) "Stand in the ways and see, and ask for the ancient paths, where the good way is, and walk in it…" *[Jeremiah 6:16]*. Jeremiah spoke about the roads to Zion which were in mourning for no one was coming to the feasts *[Lamentations 1:4]*. "Now they were going on the road up to Jerusalem and Jesus was going before them…" *[Mark 10:32]*. The main roads during Jesus' time were from Jericho in the **NE** and Ashdod in **W** and the roads from the Dead Sea in the **S**. *[Matthew 21:8; Mark 10:32,46,52; Luke 9:57; Luke 24:32]*. See King's Highway and Via Maris.

Robinson's Arch   (keshet shel Robinson) The American scholar Edward Robinson, in 1838, identified this 'arch' which is really the vestige (sign) of a protruding stone, indicating that there was a bridge here joining the Temple Mount to the Upper City. The arch is actually the overpass which rests over a larger arch over the street. The paved Herodion street which passed underneath from **NS**, has also been discovered and can be seen in the Ophel Archaeological Garden. Here, on one of the lower stones near the arch, is an inscription from the prophet, *[Isaiah 66:14]*. See Ophel, Ophel Archaeological Garden.

Rock of the Agony   See Gethsemane

Rock of Etam   See Etam

Rock of Escape   (even, cliff of divisions) This rock is in the wilderness of Maon, the scene of David's most remarkable escapes from Saul *[I Samuel 23:25]*. It is 11 kms. **S** of Hebron, presently Tel Main, a heap of ruins.

Rock of Foundation   (even pinah) Here is the mountain of Moriah where Abraham attempted to offer Isaac *[Genesis 22:2-18]*. Both Jewish and Moslem tradition sees this rock as the rock from which God created the entire universe, thus, its name 'foundation rock'. All agree that both

Jewish Temples stood on this rock and it is now the center of the Dome of the Rock on the Temple Mount in Jerusalem.

Rock of Rimmon   (even shel pomegranate) The cliff, mountain pass where the Benjaminites fled after the slaughter in Gibeah. Here, 600 men maintained themselves for 4 months *[Judges 20:45,47;21:13]*. It is adjacent to the wilderness, in the desert next to Jericho and runs to the mountains of Bethel *[Joshua 16:1]*. It is presently the village of Rammun, 22 kms. **N** of Jerusalem on a limestone hill.

Rock of Oreb   See Oreb

Rocks of the Wild Goats   (mountain goats, ibex) David was hiding out from Saul here at Ein Gedi, in the wilderness of Ein Gedi. Saul and his men of 3000 camped out against David here on these rocks of the wild goats with their many natural caves, next to Ein Gedi *[I Samuel 24:2]*. Located on the eastern shore of the Dead Sea. See Ein Gedi. Ibex can be seen today all throughout this area.

Sabbath Pavilion   (musak ha'shabbat) In the court of the Temples, this was a covered place, or hall, used by the kings whenever they visited the Temple on the Sabbath and the Feast days. King Ahaz removed it because of fear of the invading army of the Assyrians *[II Kings 16:18; II Chronicles 28:24]*. See the model of the Second Temple at the Holyland Hotel in West Jerusalem.

Sal'ecah   (lattice) This city is in Bashan, district of Jordan and one of the capitals of Og's kingdom *[Deut. 3:10; Joshua 13:11;12:5]*. It is located on the **E** of both the tribe of Manasseh and Gad *[I Chronicles 5:11]*. It is today Salkhad, **E** of the Jordan River in the mountains in Jordan, 60 kms. **SE** from Amman.

Salim   (peaceful) Melchizedek, the King came here, perhaps it is Jerusalem, the city of Peace, as many Bible scholars tend to believe *[Genesis 14:18; Hebrews 7:1-2]*. The psalmist tells us that the Lord's name is great in Israel and Salem, is His dwelling place in Zion *[Psalm 76:1-2]*. The other area is **E** of the border of the Jordan River where John the Baptist was baptizing, which would make it Bethabara or Bethany, beyond the Jordan *[John 1:28; John 3:23]*. See Bethabara, 38 kms. **E** from Jerusalem.

Salt, City of   (ear ha-melech) In the wilderness of Judea at the **SW** extremity of the Dead Sea where the hills are pure salt *[Joshua 15:62]*. Har Sodom, the Mt. of Salt is just past the Zohar Hot Springs which contain sulfur, iron, aluminum, magnesium and other chemicals with a high salt content. Mt. Sodom is a mountain of rock salt, 11 km. long by 1/2 km. wide, the salt content is up to 470 meters (160 ft.) thick. This mountain was once part of the Dead Sea and the infamous twin cities of Sodom and Gomorrah, together with Admah and Zoar *[Genesis 14:2-3; Deut 29:23]*. See Salt, Valley of, 110 kms. **S** from Jerusalem taking the Dead Sea Road.

Salt Sea   (yam ha-melech) This is the Dead Sea, named the Dead Sea from the 2nd C. but formerly, called the Sea of Salt or Eastern Sea. It is called the Salt Sea throughout scripture. Also known as the Sea of the Aravah (desert) and the Asphalt Sea *[Genesis 14:3; Numbers 34:12; Deut. 3:17; 4:49; Ezekiel 47:18; Joel 2:20; Zechariah 14:8]*. It lies at the southern end of the Jordan Valley, 85 kms. long and 430 meters below sea level. The level, size and shape of this sea varies from year to year depending on the rainfall. It is fed by the Jordan River and various small streams pour millions of tons of fresh water into it each day but because there is no outlet, a high salt and chemical content, plus the strong sun rays, the waters are evaporated and form a very heavy vapor. This intense evaporation causes the bitterness of the sea. There are hot springs at the sea's bottom and the sea itself appears to be covered with "sea salts." The waters and air have proven to be healthy for the entire body. Many tourists and Israelis come from all over the world to bathe and float in these "oily and buoyant" waters. The Prophet, Ezekiel, foresaw a time when the waters from the Temple in Jerusalem would flow into the Dead Sea *[Ezekiel 47]*. 42 kms. **SE** from Jerusalem begins its northern coast.

Salt, Valley of   (emek ha-melech) This valley is on the border between Judah and Edom, **S** of the Dead Sea and was the scene of some major battles of the kings *[II Samuel 8:13; II Kings 14:7; I Chronicles 18:12; II Chronicles 25:11]*. Lot, the son of Haran and nephew of Abraham, settled here and once called it "the garden of the Lord." *[Genesis 13:10-11]*. There was great destruction here in this valley. See all of *[Genesis 19]*. Archaeological research confirms an unusual cataclysmic explosion in this area where once a fertile valley stood. See Salt Sea, Sodom, Salt, city of, Dead Sea and Zoar.

Samaria, City of   (shomron, city of the watcher of mountains)
After the division of the kingdom and King Solomon's death, this area in central Israel became the capital of the northern kingdom. It is a large valley from Shechem to the Mediterranean coast about 20 by 50 kms. On the central hill next to Shechem is Shemer the former name of the city *[I Kings 16:24]*. Ahab built a temple to Ba'al. *[I Kings 16:32-33]*. It was always a place of idol worship *[Isaiah 9:9; Jeremiah 23:13; Ezekiel 16:46-55]*. Both Elijah and Elisha had their ministry here in the midst of the idolatry *[I Kings18:1-3; II Kings 10:36]*. Herod, the Great rebuilt the city and renamed it Sebaste, "the illustrious" in honor of Augustus. Jesus speaks to the woman at the well *[John 4:3-26]*. Philip went down to the city *[Acts 8:5]*. 60 kms. N from Jerusalem. See Jacob's Well.

Samaritan Inn   See Good Samaritan Inn

Sanctuary, Oracle   (heichal) Here was the inner part in the Temples, the rectangular structure which was entered through the porch and at its far end stood the Holy of Holies *[I Kings 6:3,5,16,17; II Chronicles 3:16;4:20]*. A cry of David, *[Psalm 28:1-2]* See Temples, First and Herod's Second Temple.

Scorpion's Way   See Akrabbim

Scottish Church in Jerusalem   (church of Scotland) On the Ben Hinnom ridge, past Yemin Moshe, on Remez Street due **E** of Mt. Zion, is the church compound; the Scottish church called St. Andrews. The church itself was built in 1927 and upon its building, an archaeological excavation began revealing finds from the First Temple Period. A silver talisman with the Jewish priestly blessing was discovered with the text from *[Numbers 6:24,25]*. There are Jewish graves from the First Temple period, quite visible today. See Ketef Hinnom.

Scythopolis   See Beth-Shean

Sea of Aravah   See Salt Sea

Sea of the Desert   See Salt Sea

Sea of Galilee   See Galilee, Sea of

Sea of Tiberias   See Galilee, Sea of

SEA OF GALILEE POEM

The tax was due, the Master's and disciple's
And to the sea, the Master strangely sent:
A fish would yield the needful piece of silver
Strange bank indeed, from which to pay the rent!

J. Danson Smith

Sebaste   See Samaria

Second Temple   (bay'it ha sha-ne) The magnificent Temple that Herod the Great built was begun in 20 BC and was still being built when Herod died in 4 BC. It is called the Second Temple, as opposed to the First Temple which Solomon built. Both Temples were destroyed on the 9th of Av. The first in 586 BC, by the Babylonians and the Second by the Romans, in 70 AD, by Titus. Josephus tells us that Herod's Temple looked like a piece of gold on a snowy day and like a large snow covered mountain covered with gold (War VI 394). Herod had a passion for architecture and he wanted to control and appease the Jews but, secretly, he wanted to be the King of the Jews so he called himself "King of Judea", for this reason. He was angry when the wise men came to him, he felt threatened *[Matthew 2:1-3]*. The building was 46 yrs in building *[John 2:20]*. Most Evangelical Christians believe that Jesus and His Temple (body) eliminated the need for God to dwell in a house and a 'new covenant was established' *[Jeremiah 31:31-34; All Hebrews 8,9,10]*. See the model of this Temple at the Holyland Hotel in West Jerusalem. See Herod's Temple.

Jesus in the Second Temple of Herod's

Jesus entered the Temple and cast out the moneychangers *[Matthew 21:12]*. The lame came to Him here *[Matthew 21:14]*. The priests confronted Him here *[Matthew 21:23]*. He came out and went to the Mt. of Olives *[Matthew 24:1]*. The veil of the Temple was torn in two when He was crucified *[Matthew 27:51]*. He went into the Temple to look around *[Mark 11:11]*. The chief priests, scribes and elders came to Him here *[Mark 11:27]*. He answered questions and taught *[Mark 12:35]*. They brought Him here to the Temple *[Luke 2:22]*. After 3 days

His parents found Him here *[Luke 2:46]*. He taught daily in the Temple *[Luke 19:45,47]*. He taught the people in the day and early morning here *[Luke 21:37,38]*. In the middle of Feast of Tabernacles He came here *[John 7:14]*. All the people came to Him here and He taught them *[John 8:2,20]*. He said nothing in secret in the Temple *[John 18:20]*.

Second Quarter   (rova of repetition, district) The prophetess Hulda lived here in this area in the Old City of Jerusalem, near Solomon's Temple *[II Kings 22:14]*. Zephaniah foretells of the mourning that will take place some day in this quarter *[Zephaniah 1:10]*. Scholars believe it is the present Jewish quarter in the Old City of Jerusalem.

Seir   See Edom

Seir, Land of   (hair, hairy) The land and hill country where Esau, Jacob's twin brother dwelt *[Genesis 32:3; 36:8]*. **S** and **E** of Beersheva and also called the land of Edom. See Edom. 81 kms. **S** from Jerusalem in Jordan today.

Seir, Mountain of   (har shel hair, hairy) This is the mountain range from the Dead Sea, running southward to the Aravah desert, to the Gulf of Eilat, about 40 kms. in length. The Horite tribe came here during Abraham's time *[Genesis 14:6]*. The Lord gave the land and mountains to Esau as a possession and the Israelites were forbidden to enter here *[Deut. 2:5,8]*. It is in present day Jordan and can be viewed from the western coast of the Dead Sea at its most southern border.

Sei'rah   (woody district, shaggy) The site is on the tribe of Benjamin's border, in the Ephraim mountains, where Ehud ran for shelter after killing Eglon at Jericho *[Judges 3:26]*. 15 kms. **S** from Shechem. Exact site is unknown.

Sela   (rock, GK) See Petra

Senir   See Hermon

Sephoris   See Zippori

Serpents' Pool   (bre'ha nahesh) Josephus said it was called the Pool of the Snake (Wars 5. 3.2/108). Now this pool is called Sultans' Pool (bre'ha Sultan) named after the

Sultan Suleiman, the Magnificent who repaired and strengthened this water conduit in 1538. The rock excavated from this pool was used in the construction of the wall of Mt. Zion and Herod the Great's palace as well as the three towers of Hippicus Phasael and Mariamme, adjacent to his palace. This pool was part of the great aquaduct which Herod, the Great constructed during the Second Temple period *[Matthew 2:1]*. It is located at the northern end of the Ben Hinnom Valley in front of Yemin Moshe. Today it is used for numerous outdoor concerts and events. See Hinnom, Valley of.

Sha'alim, Shu'al Land of   (eretz shel jackals or foxes) Before Saul was anointed king by Samuel, he lost his donkeys and passed through this land *[I Samuel 9:4]*. The Philistines passed through here *[I Samuel 13:17]*. Located 10 kms. **NE** of Bethel or 25 kms. **NE** from Jerusalem. Exact site is not identifiable.

Shali'shah   See Ba'ale Shalisha

Shamir of Judah   (dill shel Yehuda) In the Judean mountains this town was part of the allotment of Judah *[Joshua 15:48]*. The tel and ruins of Somerah are found here, 20 kms. **SW** of Hebron next to town of El Birch.

Shamir of Ephraim   (dill shel Ephraim) The Judge, Tola, arose after King Abimelech to save Israel. He lived, died and is buried here *[Judges 10:1-2]*. The exact location is unknown.

Shar'on   (plain) The Mediterranean coast of Israel from Jaffa (Joppa) to the hills of Carmel, 80-100 kms., with a width of from 10 to 20 kms. It has always been a very fertile plain and like a well watered garden area *[I Chronicles 27:29; Isaiah 35:2; Song of Solomon 2:1]*. It was part of the route of the Via Maris by the way of the sea of the ancient travelers. Today, we still see much vegetation, well watered fields, citrus groves and more. Go **N** from Tel Aviv / Jaffa on route 2.

Sha'veh, Valley of   (emek of the plain, emek of seven) This valley in East Jerusalem is opposite Gethsemane, in the Kidron Valley, also called the King's Valley and the Valley of Jehoshaphat. Here, Abraham met with the King of Sodom and other kings were with him, perhaps seven. Melchizedek, king of Salem blessed Abraham here. *[Genesis 14:17-20; Joel 3:2,12]*. Absalom, King David's rebellious son, erected a monument to himself which can still be seen today *[II Samuel 18:18]*. See Jehoshaphat, Valley of and Beracah, Valley of. See Absalom's Monument.

She'chem (shoulder, ridge) In the hill country of Ephraim, under the mountains of Gerizim and Ephraim, lies this city. Abraham came here on his way to possess the land and the Lord appeared to him *[Genesis 12;6-7]*. Jacob came and pitched his tent and bought the land of this place *[Genesis 33:18-20]*. The city was named after the son of Hamor, a Hivite. Shechem lay with Dinah, Jacob's daughter and defiled her here causing a big problem *[Genesis 34]*. In the NT, Stephen makes mention of this city *[Acts 7:16]*. Ancient Shechem today is Tel Balatah and remains indicate that it was once a very prosperous city. 60 kms. **N** from Jerusalem. Currently under Palestinian control.

Sheep Gate (sha'ar ca-ves) This gate was also called the Benjamin Gate (son of my joy gate) The prophet Jeremiah was put in stocks here in the 'high gate of Benjamin' *[Jeremiah 20:2]*. This gate was next to the sheep market in the Old City of Jerusalem and was rebuilt by Nehemiah *[Nehemiah 3:1,32;12:39]*. It had an upper room and a guard house. Today one can go to the courtyard of St. Ann's Church, next to the Pool of Bethesda from St. Stephen's/Lion's Gate and see the ruins from the pool of Bethesda and what remains of the sheep gate. Jesus healed the man who was sick for 38 years *[John 5:1-9]*. See Bethesda and Ancient Gates at the back of this book.

Shephe'lah, The (lowland) The region **S** of the Sharon plain, an area of low hills between the Mediterranean sea and the high central plain, 65 kms. from **S** to **N** from Ashkelon to Ramla, on the modern map, 12 kms. wide. The Biblical defense cities of Lachish, Debir, Libnah and Beth-shemesh are within its borders.

Shepherd's Field (s'de ro-im; field of one who tends) The western hills flowing down from Manger Square in Bethlehem and continuing to the eastern suburb. Here, shepherds were out in the field keeping watch over their flocks by night, when an angel of the Lord appeared to them and told them of the birth of Jesus *[Luke 2:8-20]*. The Christian Arab village of Beth-Sahur has a Greek Orthodox Church and Byzantine remains which indicate that this site has been honored for ages as the site of this miracle. Go 7 kms. **S** to

Bethlehem from Jerusalem and continue 2 kms. **SE** to Beth-Sahur. Currently under Palestinian control.

Shi'bah   (seven, an oath) The city of Beersheva (the well of seven) was named from this well dug by Isaac *[Genesis 26:32,33]* First Abraham had made an oath here with Abimelech, the Philistine *[Genesis 21:30]*. Go to Tel Beersheva, 81 kms. **S** from Jerusalem.

Shi'hor   (black, dirty) This is the Brook of Egypt, El Arish. Joshua admonishes the children of Israel that there is still much land to be possessed "…from Shihor as far as the border to Ekron," *[Joshua 13:3]*. King David brought the people together from here to celebrate the moving of the ark *[I Chronicles 13:5]*. See Brook of Egypt. In Egypt on the Mediterranean border.

Shiloah, Waters of   See Siloam, Pool of

Shiloh   (root, he whose it is) The Israelites came here during the time of Joshua and the Judges, assembled here due to its central location *[Joshua 18:1,8,9,10]*. Joshua stood before the Lord and divided the land *[Joshua 19:51]*. It was the home of the Ark of the Covenant for over 369 years. Hannah was told she would conceive *[I Samuel 1:17]*. The maidens danced in the vineyards *[Judges 21:19-25]*. The Lord directs Jeremiah to go there *[Jeremiah 7:12,14]*. The archaeologist, Robinson, found 1000 pieces of pottery here, indicating that many people came and made a feast in this place as they celebrated before the Lord. There is a new, modern village on the ancient site, also called Kiryat Sailun and is located just **E** of the Jerusalem/Shechem road some 60 kms. **N** from Jerusalem.

Shit'tim   (acacia trees) A desolate valley above the Dead Sea in Jordan where the children of Israel encamped before their entrance into the Promised Land under Joshua *[Numbers 25:1]*. The acacia tree grows in dry and barren soil. The spies were sent forth from here *[Joshua 2:1]*. The prophet Joel speaks of its lushness *[Joel 3:18]*. Presently Tel el-Hammam 15 kms. **E** of the Jordan River border, northern tip of the Dead Sea in Jordan. See Abel-Shittim.

Shu'al   (jackal, fox) The Philistines invaded the land *[I Samuel 13:17]*. In the area of Benjamin, 10 kms. **NE** of Beth-el but exact location is not identified.

Shu'nem   (translation unclear) In the beautiful Jez'reel Valley on the Esdraelon Plain lies this village where the Philistines encamped before the last struggle with Saul. *[Joshua 19:18; I Samuel 28:4]*. Elisha restored life to the dead son of the notable woman who prepared an upper room for him in this site *[II Kings 4:8-37]*. It is identified as Sulam 6 kms. **N** of the heart of Jezreel, at the foot of Mt. Tabor.

Shur   (wall, fortification) This was a wilderness area also called the 'wilderness of Etham' and appeared to be a barrier, or a border of some kind, separating the lands of Egypt *[Numbers 33:8]*. Here, Hagar fled from Sarah and was found by the angel *[Genesis 16:7]*. Both Abraham and Isaac settled here *[Genesis 20:1;25:18]*. After the Israelites crossed the Red Sea, they camped here *[Exodus 15:22]*. Saul attacked the Amalekites *[I Samuel 15:7]*. The desert of Shur today is a vast desert, separating western from eastern Egypt. See maps at the end of this book.

Sid'dim, Valley of   (emek of the fields) Before the Lord destroyed Sodom and Gomorrah we know this area was a well watered fertile field *[Genesis 13:10]*. After the cataclysmic explosion of the salt flats 'pits' in this area appeared *[Genesis 19]*. The Salt Sea, Dead Sea area *[Genesis 14:3]*. The region begins at the southern end of the Dead Sea near Ein Boqeq which is called 'the tongue of the Dead Sea' and much archaeological evidence affirms this site. 100 kms. **S** from Jerusalem, past Masada on the Dead Sea road. See Dead Sea, Gomorrah and Sodom.

Silo'am, Pool of   (sent) There are several names to this pool in the village of Silwan just **E** of Jerusalem's Jewish Quarter of the Old City. It is most famous for the miracle of the blind man receiving his sight, after Jesus anointed his eyes *[John 9:1-7]*. It is also called the Kings Pool and the Pool of Shelah *[Nehemiah 2:14; 3:15]*. Isaiah, the prophet, refers to the gentle flowing water *[Isaiah 8:6]*. During the Davidic Kingdom, there were stairs that led down to the waters. Josephus called it the 'Bikat Silwan' on the other side of the Kidron. The natural spring of Gihon, through the Virgin's Spring fed these waters. The pool itself today is an oblong tank hewn out of rock and can be reached by going **SE** from the Dung Gate down to the village of Silwan, less than 1 km.

Silo'am Tower   See Siloam, Pool of and Silwan

Silwan (reservoir) This village is **E** of the Kidron Valley in Jerusalem and contains the pool of Siloam. See above. This area was part of the original City of David. Scholars believe it was here that the 'Tower of Siloam' fell, mentioned by Jesus *[Luke 13:4]*. Speculation sees this tower which killed 18, falling when the construction of the aquaduct by Pilate was initiated in this area. Go **SE** from Dung Gate to village. See Siloam above.

Simeon, Tribe of area See Tribes at back of this book

Simon, the Tanner's House Simon, whose house was by the sea in Jaffa (Joppa) provided lodging for Peter *[Acts 10:6]*. Here, Peter received his message and commission that he, though a kosher Jew, would be sent to the gentiles with the good news of salvation *[Acts 10:19-48]*. In Jaffa's Old City, you go to Simon-the-tanner St. and come to an inconspicuous 19th C dwelling. Ring the bell, for a small fee one may enter. The hospitable owner will show you the ancient well, the rooftop and remains. Jaffa is 58 kms. **E** from Jerusalem on Mediterranean coast.

Sin, Wilderness of See Zin, Wilderness of

Sion, Mount See Hermon

Siph'moth (unclear translation) David wandered here in this site in the **S** of Judah. *[I Samuel 30:28]*. The exact location is not identifiable.

Sirion See Hermon

Sit'nah (strife) The root word is the same as Satan and denotes opposition and contention. Isaac dug two wells and he fought with the Philistines here, near this place *[Genesis 26:21]*. Tel Shutneh near Beersheva 82 kms. **S** from Jerusalem.

Skull, Place of See Golgotha

So'coh (brushwood, branch) In the Judean lowlands *[Joshua 15:35]*. It is Wadi el-Khalil 15 kms. **SW** of Hebron.

Sodom (translation unclear) This Canaanite city, together with Gomorrah was noted for its wickedness especially the homosexual activity. It was once part of the well watered fertile valley in the plain of the Jordan, the southern part of the Dead Sea *[Genesis 13:11-12]*. The cities were destroyed *[Genesis 19]*. Zephaniah refers to the destruction on Moab like Sodom

[Zephaniah 2:9]. Jesus refers to its destruction *[Matthew 10:15; 11:23; Luke 17:29]*. Paul also refers to these cities *[Roman 9:29; Revelation 11:8]*. Sufficient archaeological evidence confirms these cities now to be under the waters of the Dead Sea at its most southern end. Jude, the half brother of Jesus, also refers to them *[Jude 7]*. 100 kms. **S** from Jerusalem. See Gomorrah and Siddim, Valley of.

Solomon's Gates   King Solomon built many chariot cities and we can see remnants of the 'Solomonic Gate' which describes his particular choice of architecture for the gates of the cities of Megiddo, Gezer, Hazor and both Upper and Lower Beth Horon. Hazor, Megiddo and Gezer were his important administration centers as well. He chose Phoenician design, pre-Greek *[I Kings 9:15-19]*. Megiddo has a particularly rich complex of imposing public structures with the Solomonic Gate style. They can be seen built of ashlar masonry and decorated with ornate capitals. See Megiddo, 110 kms. **NW** from Jerusalem. See Hazor.

Solomon's Pools   (birkat shel Shlomo) Three large pools have been carved out of the rock, 4 kms. **S** from Bethlehem, alongside the main Jerusalem-Hebron road. These pools store rain water and spring water from underground springs. They were built in the Second Temple period by Herod, the Great, to improve Jerusalem's water supply and by means of gravitation, the water came to Jerusalem through the aqueductsbuilt by Herod *[Matthew 2:1]*. The names of several Roman army commanders can be seen on the stones today. They have no connection with King Solomon, name only. Today the water is used only by the local residents.

Solomon's Porch   (merepeset shel Shlomo) This area was the outer court of Solomon's First Temple which he completed in 950 BCE and it was also called the 'Porch of Judgment' or the 'Hall of the Throne' *[I Kings 6:1-38; 7:6-7]*. The porch, or portico, was also named after Solomon and rebuilt in Herod's 2nd Temple. Jesus walked and taught here *[John 10:23; Acts 3:11;5:12]*. See the model of the Second Temple at the Holyland Hotel in West Jerusalem.

Solomon's Quarries   This excavation, or pit, from which the stone was cut for Solomon's Temple, is located below the Old City wall just **E** of Damascus Gate in Jerusalem *[I Kings 5:17-18]*. The quarried (cut) rock is clearly visible and there is a cave known as Zedekiah's Cave (1000 meters in circumference) named for King Zedekiah as the place where he escaped during the pursuit from the Chaldeans *[Jeremiah 39:4]*. See Solomon's Temple below.

Solomon's Temple, (bay 'it ha rishon) Solomon built
First Temple magnificent royal buildings and the
Temple on the property that his father, David, purchased from Araunah, the Jebusite *[II Samuel 24:21-24; I Chronicles 21:22-28]*. It was the site of Moriah where Abraham was tested *[Genesis 22:2]*. It is on the Temple Mount in Jerusalem's Old City, occupied now by the Dome of the Rock. Solomon's purpose and accomplishment was to build this First Temple to the Lord *[I Kings 5:5,12-18; II Chronicles 2:1]*. He ruled from 965-926 BC and this Temple was completed in 950 BC, seven years in the building and then the Lord dwelt in the tabernacle *[I Kings 6; II Chronicles 3-5]*. It was destroyed by Nebuchadnezzar, on the 9th of Av, 586 BC. No visible remnant can be seen today of the Temple itself but the Broad Wall can be seen in the Jewish Quarter. The Jebusite Wall, on the right of the Gihon Spring in the city of Silwan can be seen. The remnants of the First Temple Period's burial caves can be seen at the Scottish Church. See Broad Wall, Moriah, Mt. of, Scottish Church and Ketef Hinnom.

Sorek, Valley of (emek shel excellent vine) Samson loved
Delilah from the Valley of Sorek *[Judges 16:4]*. The ark of the covenant was taken by the Israelites to Beth Shemesh through here *[I Samuel 6:10-12]*. Today, it is identified as Wadi es Surar. The Sorek Cave, in the Avshalom Nature Reserve. The stalactite and stalagmite rock formations are the most outstanding geological remnants of this kind found in Israel. Go to En-Kerem Junction 6 kms. **SW** of Jerusalem, then 4 kms. **E** to the Nature Reserve.

Spring of Ha'rod See Ha'rod, Spring of

St. George's Monastery A most impressive Greek
Orthodox monastery is built on the slope of the hill on the northern bank of the Wadi Kelt, also called the Brook of Cherith. It is 3 kms. **W** of Jericho and can be reached by using the Old Jericho/Jerusalem road. The building itself was only built in 480 AD and was named after the monk George of Cosiba who spent his life here. It was built over the

cave where Elijah, the Prophet, was fed by the ravens *[I Kings 17:3-6]*. See Cherith, Brook of.

St. Mark's Church   In the Armenian section of Jerusalem, near Jaffa Gate, on St. Marks Rd., is a Syrian Orthodox Church and Convent built on Byzantine ruins to mark the site of the home of Mary, the mother of John Mark *[Acts 12:12]*.

St. Peter's Church   On the summit of the tel (hill) of ancient Jaffa, sits this large, impressive Franciscan church built over Byzantine remains above the site where Peter raised Tabitha from the dead *[Acts 9:36-42]* She was a Hellenistic Jewess (Greek) as was known as Dorcas. 58 kms. **E** from Jerusalem. See Jaffa.

Stations of the Cross   See Via Delorosa

Stream of Egypt   See Brook of Egypt

Stronghold of Ein Gedi   (fortress, inaccessible place) King David, although he was anointed King by Samuel, still remained a fugitive and had to flee from Saul who was seeking his life *[I Samuel 22:1-5]*. He fled with his men to the strongholds of En-Gedi, 50 kms. **SE** from Jerusalem *[I Samuel 24:1-22; Psalm 62:6]*. See Adul'lam 18 kms. SW of Jerusalem.

Stronghold of Zion   See Ophel and City of David

Struthion Pools   (sparrow GK.) Herod, the Great, built the Antonio Fortress **N** of the Temple Mount digging a deep moat **N** of this fortress and thus, dug into the Hasmonean water system. Herod corrected the flow of water by making this pool 150 ft. long by 50 ft. wide. This pool was open and uncovered in Jesus' time and the Lithostrotos (the pavement) is above it *[John 19:13]*. Rainwater was collected about 1000 ft. **N** of the Old City and brought inside by the Hasmonean channel which Herod utilized. According to Josephus (War V,4.2/467) it appears that during the siege of 70 AD by Titus, this pool was still an open reservoir for Titus who built a ramp through it in order to gain access to the Antonio. He gives its exact location. The site is in the basement of the Sisters of Zion convent in the Old City of Jerusalem. See Ecco Homo and Lithostrotos. See 2nd station of the Cross.

Suc'coth   (booths) After Jacob fled from Esau, he built a house and shelters, or booths, for his livestock *[Genesis 33:17]*. The border of the tribe of Gad *[Joshua13:27]*. Solomon had the bronze work for the Temple made here in a foundry *[I Kings 7:46; II Chronicles 4:17]*. The Midianites opposed Gideon here *[Judges 8:5,8,14-16]*. The psalmist speaks of God's holiness here *[Psalm 60:6]*. The site is Tel-Ahsas in Jordan just **N** of the Jabbok River 47 kms. **NE** from Jerusalem, near the Adam Bridge.

Sultans' Pool   See Serpents' Pool

Suph   (reeds) This is an abbreviation of 'Yam suph' which is 'Red Sea' in Hebrew. Moses spoke to the children of Israel opposite this sea *[Deut. 1:1]*. See Red Sea.

Sy'char   See Shechem

Synagogue   (bet knesset, gathering of the people, place of prayer) The word synagogue itself is only mentioned in the NT. Jesus healed the man with the withered hand here *[Matthew 12:10; Mark 3:1; Luke 6:6]*. Jesus taught in the synagogue in Nazareth *[Matthew 13:54; Luke 4:16,28]*. He came to Capernaum, His hometown *[John 6:59]*. See Capernaum and Nazareth. The synagogue is the Bet Knesset. This term is used today throughout Israel and Jewish communities as opposed to the term "Temple" because the term Temple today refers to the First and Second Temples respectively.

Synagogue of the Freedmen   The synagogue of the Jews from Alexandria, Egypt who conspired against Stephen *[Acts 6:9]*. The foundations of this site have been located in the lower hill of the Ophel in the City of David. Go **SE** from Dung Gate to the village of Silwan.

Ta'anath-Shi'loh   (approach to Shiloh) Many large cisterns were found here on the northern boundary of the tribe of Ephraim *[Joshua 16:6]*. It is presently Khirbet Ta'na which remains a heap of ruins just **SE** of Shechem, 59 kms. **N** from Jerusalem.

Tab'bath   See Abel Meholah

Tab'erah   (burning) The fire of the Lord came down and consumed some of the complainers in the camp of Israel *[Numbers 11:3; Deut. 9:22]*. It is located in the wilderness of

Paran which is now in the Sinai Peninsula of the Sinai Desert in Egypt. The exact location within the Sinai is not identifiable.

Tabernacles of Israel (dwelling, resting place) Both Temples were modeled and designed after the plan of the Tabernacle which was given to Moses in the wilderness *[Hebrews 8:5]* See *[Exodus chapters 25-28]*. See Herod's Temple, Second Temple and Solomon's Temple entries.

Tabgha (heptapegon GK. "seven springs") Jesus performed two great miracles here next to these seven natural springs which run into the Sea of Galilee. He fed the multitudes *[Matthew 14:13-21; Mark 6:30-44; John 6:1-14]*. The millstone in the front courtyard exemplifies a point *[Luke 17:2]*. A typical Byzantine basilica can be seen inside the 'Church of the Multiplication of the Loaves and Fishes' and the mosaic floors are most exceptional and well preserved. As early as 385 AD a pilgrim named Aetheria mentions that "the stone on which the Lord put the bread" was made into an altar. The Benedictine Monks are the guardians here. Go to the Sea of Galilee, **NW** shore, 157 kms. **N** from Jerusalem. See Primacy of Peter entry.

Tab'itha's House and Tomb See St. Peter's Church

Tabor, Tavor See Mt. Tabor

Tadmor (palm tree) The city of palm trees in the land of Judah. Solomon was a most enterprising builder. This was one of the cities he built in the wilderness and settled the sons of Israel there *[I Kings 9:18; II Chronicles 8:1-4]*. 12 kms. **N** from Jerusalem, exact location is unknown. Some scholars believe this site is actually Hammath-Zobah in Syria.

Tear Drop Church See Dominus Flevit Church (The Lord wept)

Teko'a (trumpet, clang) Jehoshaphat, king of Judah, exhorted the people to rely on the Lord for their help here in the wilderness *[II Chronicles 20:20-21]*. Joab, David's commander commanded a 'wise woman' to come to the king, to effect a reconciliation between him and his rebellious son, Absalom *[II Samuel 14:2,4,9]*. The people helped Nehemiah rebuild the walls of Jerusalem *[Nehemiah 3:5,27]*. Amos, the farmer/prophet was born here *[Amos 1:1]*. Located 11 kms. **S** of Bethlehem on the hills which extend from Hebron to the Dead Sea.

Tel   (hill) A tel is a man made mound, a hill; the word comes from the Arabic which denotes an artificial mound that has been developed by many layers of civilization. There are many tels in Israel but the most famous are Tel Jericho, Tel Megiddo and Tel Bet Shean. See separate entries.

Tel Dan   See Dan

Tel Megiddo   See Megiddo

Tel Shiloh   See Shiloh

Tel Tamar   (hill of the palm tree) This site is also called Thamara off the main road to Eilat, 30 kms. **S** from Sedom, the southern point of the Dead Sea. This city was built up by Solomon in the wilderness *[I Kings 9:18]*. The southern boundary of the land according to Ezekiel's vision *[Ezekiel 47:19;48:28]*. It was a way station for the Nabateans and was again built up during the Roman period. Presently called Hazava, next to a modern moshav by same name and kibbutz Ir Ovot. The oldest tree in the country, the jubjub, is believed to be on site. Active archaeological dig.

Temple   See Herod's Temple, Second Temple, Solomon's Temple and Zerubbabel's See Temple Gates, maps and descriptions at end.

Temple Mount, Mount Moriah   (Har Ha-bayit) This site refers specifically to the flat open area, or the rectangular esplanade, in the southeastern corner of the Old City, on the top of Mount Moriah, which is 731 meters (2428 ft.) above sea level. It covers 144,000 sq. meters or 35 acres (140 dunam). The first and second temples were built here. The Dome of the Rock is built over the Foundation Stone on Mount Moriah and is outstanding with its golden dome. Many Christian scholars (premillennialists) see this area in Muslim hands being the 'Abomination of Desolation' which Daniel speaks about in the holy place *[Daniel 9:27; 11:31;12:11; Matthew 24:15]*. David purchased the threshing floor of Ornan (Araunah) the Jebusite *[II Samuel 24:24-25; I Chronicles 21:15,25,26]*. See Moriah. Enter through the Jewish or Moslem quarters in the Old City of Jerusalem. See second Temple.

Temptation, Mount of   See Mount of Temptation

Tent of Meeting   (mifgash mahane) The place where the Lord met with Moses is mentioned 164 times from Exodus through all of Chronicles. It was located outside the veil which was before the 'Altar of Testimony' *[Exodus 27:21]*. The instructions were given by God to Moses in the desert *[Exodus 25:9]*. This holy meeting place was used in the desert wanderings and no remnant can be found of it today. See Tent of Testimony.

Tent of Testimony   Also called the Tent of Witness. The place where the Priests would go *[Exodus 31:7]*. It was used by the Levite priests for service *[Exodus 38:21]*. They also carried it and all its furnishings *[Numbers 1:50]*. They stood before it and served *[Numbers 18:2]*. It was used in the desert wanderings. No remnant can be found of it today. See Tent of Meeting above.

Threshing Floor of Araunah   See Arau'nah's Threshing Floor

Threshing Floor of Nacon   See Nacon's Threshing Floor

Tiberias   (translation unclear) The city built by Herod Antipas, son of Herod, the Great, in honor of the Roman Caesar Tiberias, who ruled from 14-37 AD. Jesus probably did not come here for it was a pagan city built over a cemetery and was noted for its hot baths for the sensual Romans. These baths are still the attraction today. Orthodox Jews avoided the place. The inhabitants were mostly Greeks and Romans. It became the capital of Galilee under King Herod Agrippa. It is one of the names for the sea of Galilee *[John 6:1,23; John 21:1]*. In 150 AD, it became the seat of the Sanhedrin and is now one of Israel's four holy cities together with Jerusalem, Hebron and Zefat. 152 kms. **N** from Jerusalem. A very popular vacation spot for Israelis. See Ham'math.

Tim'nah   (an allotted portion) In Judah on the **N** but belonging to the tribe of Dan. *[Joshua 15:10; 19:43]*. Tamar tricked her father-in-law here *[Genesis 38:12-14]*. Samson went down here and married a Philistine woman, Delilah *[Judges 14:1,2,5]*. The Philistines took this city *[II Chronicles 28:18]*. The modern name of this village is Tibnah, located 1 km. **W** of Beth Shemesh, 28 kms. **W** from Jerusalem.

Timnah-Heres   (portion of the sun) See Timnah-Serah

Timnah-Serah   (double portion) Mount Gaash is on the **N** of this site, in the area of Ephraim, where Joshua is buried in the hill country of his inheritance. *[Judges 2:9; Joshua 19:50; 24:30]*. It is Kefar Cheres, located 11 kms. **S** of Shechem, 48 kms. **N** from Jerusalem. The exact location is not identifiable.

Tirzah Valley   (delightful, pleasant) This ancient Canaanite city was captured by Joshua after he crossed the Jordan *[Joshua 12:24]*. It became the capital city of the Kings of Israel *[I Kings 15:21, 33; 16:6,8]*. Solomon compared it with the beauty of Jerusalem *[Songs of Solomon 6:4]*. It is 10 kms. **NE** of Shechem and excavated as Tel el-Farah which means "mound of the elevated ridge." Archaeological finds from 3000 BC with walls and towers can be seen. The end of the city came after the Assyrian invasion in 725 BC. 71 kms. **N** from Jerusalem.

Tomb of Abraham   See Machpelah

Tomb of David   See Mt. Zion, Necropolis and Tombs in City of David

Tomb of Jehoshaphat   (caver of he whom Jehovah judged) In the Kidron Valley, the Valley of Jehoshaphat area next to Absalom's Monument, is this highly decorated stone structure believed to be built over the original tomb of King Jehoshaphat. *[II Chronicles 21:1]*. Go to Kidron Valley between the Mt. of Olives and the Old City of Jerusalem.

Tomb of Mary   See Grotto of Gethsemane

Tomb of Patriarchs   See Machpelah

Tomb of Rachel   See Rachels' Tomb

Tomb of Samuel   See Nebi Samuel

Tomb of Zechariah   (root. to remember), Zacharias (like an east wind GK) In the Kidron Valley, Valley of Jehoshaphat area towards the **N**, is this massive monument which was carved from one piece of rock with a pyramid and pillars on its sides. It appears to be the authentic tomb of either the prophet Zechariah or Zacharias, the father of John the Baptist *[Zechariah1:1,7;7:1,8; Luke 1:5,12,13,18; Matthew 23:35]*. Scholars cannot agree on the remains. Go to Kidron Valley in front of the Garden of Gethsemane. See Jehoshaphat, Valley of.

Tombs in the City of David (heaped up, "a remembrance" GK.) The ancient Jewish tombs were hewn from the rock, they were sepulchers and had an antechamber for the mournful to sit, mourn and pray. The bodies were deposited in the inner or lower cave. Many tombs had as many as 13 bodies and the entrance was guarded by a large rolling stone as the one that can be seen in the Garden Tomb, Jerusalem, outside of the Damascus Gate and Herod's Family Tomb, near the King David Hotel. From 1000 BC, David's reign, until 590 BC, 22 kings of Judah reigned and were buried in the City of David. It appears that these 'royal tombs' have not survived or have just not been discovered. Most Bible scholars believe David is buried in the City of David *[I Kings 2:10; 11:43, II Kings 8:24; 9:28, 12:21, 14:20; 15:7,38; II Chronicles 16:14; 28:27]*. Peter told the men of Israel that David's tomb was still with them and could be seen *[Acts 2:29]*. This is further evidence of his burial in the City of David, as opposed to the tomb on Mt. Zion which is from Crusader times. Jesus accused the Pharisees of being like tombs that cannot be seen *[Luke 11:44]*. Proceed down to Silwan **SE** from the Dung Gate to the City of David. Future extensive archaeological digs are being planned here.

Tombs of the Kings This site, in the eastern section of Jerusalem, is really misnamed and it is actually the tomb of Queen Helena of Adiabene. She was a convert to Judaism during Herod's time and the time of the great famine in the land prophesied by Agabus *[Acts 11:28]*. Out of her personal wealth, according to Josephus, *[Ant. 20:51-52;101]* she supplied grain to a starving population. The site is **N** of St. George's Cathedral at the intersection of Salahadin and Nablus roads.

Topheth (the fire place, spit fire) Jeremiah went out by the Potsherd Gate to the Valley of Ben Hinnom and it was in this Valley where the Canaanites offered their children up to the god, Molech. Drums were used to drown out the cries of the little children. The men of Judah followed this practice and the Lord said, "...they burn their sons and daughters in the fire, which I did not command nor did it enter My mind" *[Jeremiah 7:30-32; 19:6,11-14]*. Jeremiah cried out here against these abominations and foretold the fall of the Temple and the destruction of Jerusalem which occurred several years later in 586 BC. See Hinnom, Valley of, **SW** of Jerusalem's Old City.

Tower of Ascension   The most prominent structure on the Mt. of Olives, which is a Russian Orthodox church, marks the spot on Mt. Olivet where Jesus ascended to heaven *[Acts 1:9-12]*. The huge bell in the tower was made in Russia and brought to the mount in 1885, by boat from the port of Jaffa. The church is not generally open to visitors. Located 2 kms. from Jerusalem's Old City on **E**. See Mt. of Olives.

Tower of David Museum   This museum located at Jaffa Gate is also called 'The Citadel' but it is erroneously named David's Tower and has been since the Byzantine time. The nearby Jaffa gate was also named after King David. There are large unhewn stones in the middle of the courtyard; from King Hezekiah's time. *[II Chronicles 29:3;32:5]*. Herod the Great built three towers here in order to strengthen the defense of his palace which was adjacent and those enormous ashlars (stones) on the lower course can be seen today. Go to Jaffa Gate, in Jerusalem's Old City, to museum's entrance.

Tower of the Flock   See Shepherd's Field

Tower of Siloam   See Siloam, Pool of

Treasury   (place for treasure, values GK) This was the woman's court in the Second Temple where 13 trumpet-shaped offering pails and 4 lamp stands stood for the Feast of Tabernacles, next to the Beautiful Gate. See Temple Plan at the end of this book. Men were allowed here but the women did not enter the inner courtyard. Jesus took note of the poor widow here *[Mark 12:41-44; Luke 21:1]*. Jesus taught the people here *[John 8:20]*. See model of the Second Temple at the Holyland Hotel, West Jerusalem.

Tribes of Israel Sites   These were the sons of Israel (Jacob): Reuben, Simeon, Levi, Judah, Issachar, Zebulun, Dan, Joseph, Benjamin, Naphtali, Gad, and Asher *[I Chronicles 2:1-2]*. The land was divided by tribe under Joshua. See Tribes at the end of this book.

Tyropoeon Valley   (valley of the cheese makers) It was also called the Outer Valley. However, cheese making was an important industry for the Jews of antiquity as it was a great part of their daily diet. At one time the industry took place here. This valley was partly filled in by Herod the Great, by constructing new support walls in the **SW**, and **N** for the Second

Temple platform. The area was elevated, thereby, the Temple Mount area was doubled. See Herod's Temple, Second Temple. Go to the archaeological excavations on the **S** side of the Western Wall in Jerusalem for further understanding of this project. See maps.

Upper Room   (lofty, 'aliyah') Sometimes these rooms were cool rooftop chambers and used in the summer but during the time of Jesus, this particular room seemed to be rented out for people to have guests. Jesus told His disciples to go and make preparations for His last supper with them in the 'upper room' *[Matthew 26:17-19; Mark 14:12-16; Luke 22:7-13]*. The miracle of Pentecost took place here when the disciples were gathered together *[Acts 2:1-4]*. Many structural changes have taken place here in the past 2000 years but it is generally agreed that the site was here. It is located on Mt. Zion in the Armenian quarter, near Zion Gate, close to the Dormition Abbey. The bottom floor is the 'Tomb of David' site. The Upper Room is also called 'the Cenacle or Coenaculum'. Enter near Zion gate.

I give you a new commandment: love one another as I loved you. JOHN 13:34

Uzza, Garden of   (strength) Both Manasseh and Amon were buried here before the year 643 BC *[II Kings 21:18-26]*. Most of the kings of Israel, as recorded, more than 21, are buried in the City of David. However these wicked kings, Manasseh and his son Amon are buried in their own house. The location is most likely in the city of Silwan, near the Valley of the Kings but the exact location is not identifiable. See Tombs in the City of David. Go **SE** from Dung Gate.

Valley of Achor   See Achor, Valley of

Valley of Aijalon   See Aijalon, Valley of

Valley of the Arava   See Arava, Arabah

Valley of Booths, Succoth   See Succoth

Valley of Decision   See Jehosh'aphat, Valley of

Valley of Elah   (emek of the oak, terebinth trees) Here Goliath was killed at the hands of David *[I Samuel 17:2;21:9]*. The Wadi es-Sunt runs through the valley and is the site of tel-es-Safiyeh. It is 12 kms. **SW** from Jerusalem. Many pilgrims pick up small pebbles here and take them home for keepsakes.

Valley of Giants   See Reph'aim, Valley of

Valley of Hebron   See Hebron, Valley of

Valley of Jehoshaphat   See Jehosh'aphat, Valley of

Valley of Jezreel   See Jezreel, Valley of

Valley of Kings, Valley of the Kings   See Shevah, Valley of

Valley of the Monastery of the Cross   Here, in the Rehavia neighborhood of Jerusalem, is the traditional site where the tree in which Jesus was crucified was cut *[Matthew 27:32,40; Acts 5:30; 10:39]*. A large, impressive Greek Monastery from the Byzantine times stands on the site. A fifty minute walk from the Jaffa Gate, proceeding **W**, directly down Ramban Street, will take you there.

Valley of the Oak   See Valley of Elah

Valley of Salt   See Dead Sea

Valley of Shevah   See Shevah, Valley of

Valley of Shittim   See Dead Sea, Shittim

Valley of Weeping   See Jehoshaphat

Valley Gate   See Gates of the Old City at the end of this book

Via Delorosa   (the way of sorrows LT.) The 14 stations of the cross mark this route beginning in the Moslem quarter of Jerusalem's Old City. Enter through St. Stephen's

(Lion's Gate) on the eastern side of the Old City. Begin station 1 at the <u>Moslem school</u> on your left, which is only open on Friday afternoon, for the weekly processional of the Franciscans through the Via Delorosa, onto station 2 to <u>Chapels of Condemnation & Flagellation.</u>

Continue to station 3, the <u>Polish Chapel</u>, onto the corner of El-Wad Rd., then to station 4, to the <u>Armenian Catholic Chapel</u>. Station 5 is marked by the Franciscan sign over the door of <u>Simon, the Cyrene</u>, station 6, <u>Convent of the Little Sisters of Jesus</u>, station 7, <u>Franciscan Chapel</u>. Station 8 is marked by a Latin cross on the wall of the <u>Greek Monastery</u>, station 9 is approached by going to the <u>roof of the Church of the Holy Sepulcher</u> and stations 10 through 14 are inside the <u>Church of the Holy Sepulcher</u>.

The Franciscans, Roman Catholic monks, came to the Holyland in 1229 but it wasn't until 1458 when they started to guide pilgrims 'on the way of the cross'. Under the Turks, the pilgrims were forbidden to openly pray but the custom of walking the 'way of sorrows, the way of the cross,' took hold in the 17th C. The stations were confirmed in 1731, by Pope Clement XII in Rome. The prayers and scriptures for each station are at the end of this book.

Via Maris (way of the sea LT.) The mountainous nature of the lands dictated the course of the principal routes. Israel, known as Palestine, is in the center of 3 continents, Europe, Africa and Asia. The crossroads of the Ancient East, was an international route from Egypt, connecting it with northern Syria and Mesopotamia, from **S** to **N**. The route followed the line of the seacoast, from Egypt, to Gaza, to Ashkelon, up to Yavneh, then turning **E** to the foothills of Aphek. It skirted the eastern edge of the northern Sharon Plain to Megiddo, through the Jezreel Valley. It continued to Beth-shean then past the sea of Galilee, **N** to Hazor and the Lebanese border to Damascus. The Romans coined it the 'Way of the Sea, Via Maris' but it was known as the 'International Route.' Caravans laden with commercial goods and military campaigners passed through, often leaving much destruction and desolation along the way *[Isaiah 9:1; 24:15; Jeremiah 25:22; Ezekiel 26:18; 39:11; Matthew 4:15]*. See the Roman Via Maris stone marker at Capernaum.

Virgin's Fountain See En-Kerem

Virgin's Well See Gihon Spring

Visitation Church   See Church of the Visitation

Wadi Kelt   See Cherith Brook and St. George's Monastery

Walls of Jerusalem   See illustrated maps at the end of this book.

Warren's Shaft   (peer warren) This was the ancient city's water conduit dug during the First Temple Period so that, in a time of siege, it would be possible to bring water into the city. It was also known as the Jebusite Tunnel as they may have been the first to cut away the natural 'karstic rock'. It was discovered by Sir Charles Warren in 1867. Similar water systems were discovered at Megiddo, Hazor and Gezer. Hezekiah could have executed this particular work, or further improved it *[II Kings 20:20; II Chronicles 32:30]*. Go **SE** from Dung Gate a few meters, sign on the left to Warren's Shaft. See Gihon, Hezekiah's Tunnel, Pool of Siloam.

Water Tunnel   (sinnor) King David wanted his men to strike against the Jebusites through this tunnel *[II Samuel 5:8; I Chronicles 11:6]*. It appears that there was a natural water shaft opening in the rocks but Hezekiah expanded and made a tunnel to divert the waters from the Gihon Springs *[II Kings 20:20]*. Located in Silwan, Jerusalem. Go **S** from Dung Gate to Hezekiah's Tunnel and Pool of Siloam. See Hezekiah's Tunnel, Gihon and Warren's Shaft.

Waters of Merom   See Merom

Well of Abraham   See Beersheva

Well of Bethlehem   (bir shel Bet Lehem; house of bread) David expressed his desire to drink from this well and, in spite of the danger, three of his devoted men went to the well and drew water *[I Chronicles 11:16-19]*. It was located next to the ancient gate but there are no remains today. See Bethlehem, 7 kms. **S** from Jerusalem.

Western Wall   (kotel) The retaining wall of the Second Temple built by Herod, the Great, still remains in the Jewish Quarter of the Old City of Jerusalem. Judaism's holiest 'shrine' and 'open-air synagogue'. Orthodox Jews believe that God's ear is behind this wall. These large limestone blocks are the same Herodian blocks that were laid in place during the time of Jesus, when He and His disciples came to the Temple.

There are more than 15 meters (45 ft.) of additional stones lying underneath our feet, at ground level, as we pray at this wall built by Herod, the Great. *[Matthew 2:1]* See Second Temple, Jesus in Jerusalem.

Wilderness   (midbar, desert) A large tract of land, uninhabited desert, not suitable for human life but often used for pasturing flocks *[Psalm 107:4; Job 24:5]*. Isaiah tells us that the desert shall blossom like a rose *[Isaiah 35:1-2]*. Today, due to great advances by Israeli agricultural technology, the deserts are being recaptured for productive use. See Arava, Negev and 'How to Plant a Tree' page.

Wilderness of Preparation   (midbar, desert of firming up) The northern end of the Dead Sea, the desert just **E** of Jerusalem. From Mt. Scopus, the observation point just **E** of the Hebrew University, you can stand and see the wilderness on a clear day. The prophet Isaiah speaks of this preparation *[Isaiah 40:3]*.

Wilderness of Wanderings   (midbar of the 'nodedim', wanderers) For 40 years, the children of Israel wandered in the great wilderness under Moses, all within the Sinai Peninsula, which is present day Egypt. The year was 1250 BC and these 'wanderings' began when they left Kadesh *[Numbers 14:33; 32:13]*. The Lord blessed them there and provided food and drink *[Deut. 2:7]*. See Kadesh, Paran. See map of 'Desert Wanderings'.

Za'anan, Zenan   (the place of flock) Micah, the Prophet pronounces judgment on the inhabitants of Judah, 735-710 BC. *[Micah 1:11]*. It is in the low lands of Judah, just **N** of Jerusalem but the exact location is not identifiable.

Zair   (small) In present day Jordan, just **E** of the Dead Sea, where the Israelites defeated the Edomites *[II Kings 8:21]*. It is not identifiable.

Zalmon, Mount of   (to be on the dark side; to shade) The mount on the **S** side of Shechem where Abimelech (son of Gideon) went up with the people and fought against the inhabitants *[Judges 9:48]*. King David speaks of the snow on Zalmon *[Psalm 68:14]*. **N** from Jerusalem 60 kms.

Zalmo'nah   (shades of darkness) One of the stages of the children of Israel in the wilderness, just **SE** of Edom, now in present day Jordan which runs in the Wadi el-Amran close to the Gulf of Aquaba, just **E** of Eilat *[Numbers 33:41-42]*.

Zano'ah   (prim. root; to reject) This site in Judah is where the Judeans lived after the return from Captivity under Nehemiah *[Joshua 15:34,56]*. These residents assisted Nehemiah in rebuilding the ancient city walls of Jerusalem *[Nehemiah 3:13;11:30]*. It is Kiryat Zanuh, 18 kms. **W** of Jerusalem in the Wadi Ismail.

Zar'ephath   (a smelting, refining place) Elijah, the Prophet, lived here during the drought and the widow woman provided for him here *[I Kings 17:9-10]*. Jesus mentions it in his homily, in the synagogue at Nazareth *[Luke 4:24-26]*. It lies on the seashore just **N** of Tyre in present day Lebanon and was on a public road next to the sea. 45 kms. **N** from Israel's northern border at Rosh Hanikra.

Zar'ethan   (unclear translation) The city is next to Adam, where the waters rose up in a heap and allowed the children of Israel to cross the Jordan River *[Joshua 3:16]*. It is Tel es-Sarem near Beisan and archaeologists have found an abundance of clay here in the soil, claiming this clay suddenly stopped the flow of waters. 25 kms. **NE** from Jericho on the eastern shore of the River Jordan in present day Jordan.

Zebulun, tribe of   (habitation, dwelling) See Tribes at back of this book

Zedekiah's Cave   See Solomon's Quarries

Zefat   (zafa, observe, watch) There are no Biblical references to this city which only had its beginnings in the Second Temple Period, 2nd C. Josephus mentions it first as one of the cities of the Jewish Revolt against Rome. I mention it only in connection with the Second Temple. After the Temple was destroyed in 70 AD, Zefat became one of the 'Holy Cities' where the Priests who were dispersed from Jerusalem came and resided. The Kabbalists began here in the 2nd C. 188 kms. **N** from Jerusalem in the mountains of Meron.

Zelah (side, slope) Kish, the father of Saul, is buried here. David took the bones of Saul and his sons here for burial *[II Samuel 21:12-14]*. It is Khirbet Salah, 3 kms. **NW** from Jerusalem.

Zel'zah (translation unclear) Two men met Saul near Rachel's Tomb on the road to Bethlehem as foretold by Samuel, the Prophet *[I Samuel 10:2]*. The site on the border of Benjamin is present day Beit Jala, 6 kms. **S** from Jerusalem.

Zemara'im (double fleece) The town belonging to the tribe of Benjamin on the eastern border together with Beth-el and Beth-arabah *[Joshua 18:22]*. It is on the road from Jerusalem to Jericho, identified as Khirbet es-Samrah, 27 kms. **NE** from Jerusalem.

Zemara'im Mountain (mount of double fleece) The king of Judah, Abijah, addressed Jeroboam and the army of Israel from this site *[II Chronicles 13:4]*. It is in the hill country of Ephraim, 10 kms. **S** of Shechem. The exact location is not identifiable.

Ze'nan See Zaanan

Ze'phath (watchtower) Judah and Simeon destroyed this town and renamed it Hormah *[Judges 1:17]*. It is Tel es-Saba 5 kms. **E** of Beersheva in the Negev desert.

Zeph'athah, Valley of (emek of the watchtower) Asa fought against Zerah and the Ethiopian army *[II Chronicles 14:10]*. It is near Marashah, a very deep valley, which runs from Beit Jibrin to the coastlands. The middle of the valley is near Beit Guvrin, 30 kms. **ESE** of Ashkelon.

Zered, Brook of (unclear translation) This wadi, dry river bed, **E** of the Dead Sea is the brook which separated Moab from Edom. Here, the children of Israel encamped before crossing over into the Promised Land *[Numbers 21:12; Deut. 2:13-14]*. It is in Jordan, called Wadi el-Hesa, at the **SE** corner of the Dead Sea, emptying itself here. 150 kms. **SE** from Jerusalem.

Zer'erah See Zarethan

Zerubbabel's Temple   (he who was begotten in Babylon) After the destruction of Solomon's Temple (First Temple) in 586 BC and the exile of the Jewish people in Babylon, the Lord raised up Zerubbabel, a "prince of Judah", to return and rebuild the temple and walls which were fallen. In 520 BC, Cyrus, the Persian king, approved the rebuilding *[Ezra 1:2;2:2;3:1-2;4:2]*. Nehemiah the prophet, who also found favor with the Persian king, also returns and helps rebuild the temple and the 'people ' *[Nehemiah 7:7; 12:1,47]*. This rebuilt Temple is not considered the Second Temple but a rebuilding of Solomon's. The Second Temple is Herod's, which began in 20 BC. See Herod's Temple, Solomon's Temple, Second Temple.

Zik'lag   (unclear translation) Here in the **S** country of Judah in the Negev. It was assigned to the tribe of Simeon *[Joshua 15:31;19:5]*. The King of Gath gave David a home here for a few months *[I Samuel 27:6]*. David was living here when he heard about Saul and his sons' deaths *[II Samuel 1:1;4:10]*. The Jews resettled here after the exile under Nehemiah *[Nehemiah 11:28]*. It is Tel-esh-Sharia in the Negev, between Beersheva and Gaza and covers approximately 4 acres (16 dunam), 105 kms. **S** from Jerusalem.

Zin, Wilderness of   (unclear translation) This large desert plain lies along the eastern shore of the Israel/Jordanian border in the Negev, extending from the land between the Dead Sea and the Gulf of Aqaba. Moses sent Caleb and Joshua here to spy out the land. They came here and the congregation later arrived *[Numbers 14:31;20:1]*. They camped here in the wilderness *[Numbers 33:36]*. Here, was the southern border given to the Israelites *[Numbers 34:3; Joshua 15:1,3]*. Go **S** from Jerusalem to Beersheva 81 kms. and continue **S**. The extent of this desert, from ancient times to present, is not clearly defined. See Ein Avdat Nature Reserve which is next to Wadi Zin.

Zion   See Mount Zion

Zion Gate   See Gates of Jerusalem

Zi'or   (smallness) This site is the mountainous area of the tribe of Judah and is mentioned together with Hebron *[Joshua 15:54]*. It is today Sair, 8 kms. **NE** from Hebron.

Ziph, Wilderness of   (unclear translation) David fled from Saul and sought refuge in this wilderness *[I Samuel 23:14-15;26:2-3]*. After the death of Solomon when the kingdom was divided, it was fortified by Rehoboam *[II Chronicles 11:8]*. It is Tel Zif, 7 kms. **SE** from Hebron, 43 kms. from Jerusalem.

Zippori   (like a bird) This site is believed to be the birthplace and home of Joachim and Anne who were the parents of Mary, the mother of Jesus *[Matthew 1:16,18]*. Tradition tells us that they both lived here in this Jewish village before they moved to Nazareth, where Mary was born. It was called Diocaesarea, in honor of Caesar Augustus, during the reign of Herod. After the destruction of the Temple by Titus in 70 AD, the Sanhedrin (Jewish court of law) moved here and the town flourished under Rabbi Judah Hanassi who compiled the Mishnah. It is one of the more interesting archaeological sites and a National Park in Israel today. 145 kms. **N** from Jerusalem through Nazareth.

Ziz Ascent   (something bright or shining; flower going up) This wadi, dry river bed, leading from the western shore of the Dead Sea, near Ein Gedi, is surrounded by these hills of Ziz, ascending to Jerusalem through the tableland of Judea. The battle where Jehoshaphat fought with the Moabites and Ammonites took place here *[II Chronicles 20:16-20]*. 45 kms. **SE** of Jerusalem.

Zoar   (smallness) Abraham took Lot, his nephew, to the land of promise but there was strife between Abraham's and Lot's herdsmen. Abraham offered Lot the whole land and, "Lot chose the 'well watered spot, like the Garden of Eden… as you go to Zoar", *[Genesis 13:7-11]*. The original name of Zoar was Bela *[Genesis 14:2,8]*. This city was temporarily spared the destruction of Sodom and Gomorrah as it provided shelter for Lot *[Genesis 19:23,30]*. Today, it is believed to be under the southern part of the Dead Sea and archaeologists and geologists confirm this area was once a 'well watered fertile valley' but there was a cataclysmic explosion of some kind several thousand years ago. 100 kms. **S** from Jerusalem on Dead Sea road.

Zo'heleth   (slippery or serpent like) One of the cliffs or ledges "beside En-rogel" in the original City of David, where David's rebellious son, Adonijah, declared himself king *[I Kings*

1:9]. It is an overhanging cliff in the Kidron Valley in the village of Silwan. Go **E** from Dung Gate down to Silwan.

Zophim   (the lookout point, watchers) Here, Balak brought Balaam to this high 'look out point' so he could see all of Israel and curse the Jews *[Numbers 23:14]*. It is Tailat es Sufa in Jordan on Mt. Nebo, opposite Jericho, 19 kms. **E** from where the Jordan River empties itself into the northern tip of the Dead Sea. See Nebo, mountain of.

Zo'rah   (scourge, hornet) A town which was assigned to Dan, within the boundary of Judah *[Joshua 19:41; Judges 18:2]*. Here Samson was born and then buried. *[Judges 13:2,24-25; 16:31]*. After Solomon's death, Rehoboam fortified this city *[II Chronicles 11:10]*. 10 kms. SW from Jerusalem on the hills above the Sorek River.

Zuph   (honeycomb) This site is not far from Rachel's Tomb in the district of Benjamin, where Saul and his servants came looking for their lost donkeys. *[I Samuel 9:5]*. Samuel, the prophet, also lived here *[I Samuel 9:6]*. It has not been exactly identified but some scholars believe it is Beit Jala, 6 kms. from Jerusalem.

SPECIFIC SITES WHERE JESUS WALKED

Abu-Dis   The stone of meeting in Bethany, El Eizariyya *[John 11:20-21]*

Aenon   The baptism of John's site *[Matthew 3:13; John 3:23]*

Antonio's Fortress   Jesus was brought before Pilate *[Matthew 27:2]*.

Banias   See Caesarea Philippi

Barracks   Roman army camp inside the Antonio *[Matthew 27:2]*.

Basilica of the Agony   See Gethsemane

Bethabara   Another name for John's baptismal site *[John 1:28]*.

Bethany   Home of Mary, Martha and Lazarus *[John 11:1-44]*. Home of Simon, the leper *[Matthew 26:6-13]*.

Bethany Beyond the Jordan   See Bethabara

Bethesda   Jesus healed the crippled man *[John 5:1-9]*.

Bethlehem   The city of Jesus' birth *[Luke 2]*.

Bethphage   Jesus enters the city of Jerusalem *[Matthew 21:1-11]*.

Beth-Sahur   See Shepherd's Field

Bethsaida   Jesus rebuked this town *[Luke 10:13]*.

Caesarea Philippi   Banias, where Jesus speaks to His disciples *[Mark 8:27-33]*

Caiaphas' House   See Peter of Galicantu

Calvary   See Golgotha

Capernaum   Jesus' hometown, where He was comforted *[Matthew 4:13]*.

Capernaum Octagon Church   Built over Peter's house *[Luke 4:38-39]*.

Capernaum Synagogue   Jesus entered here and preached *[John 6:24-59]*.

Cenacle   See Upper Room

Chamber of the Last Supper   See Upper Room

Chorazin   Jesus spoke out against the inhabitants *[Matthew 11:21]*.

Church of the Nativity   See Bethlehem

Church of St. Mark   Syrian Orthodox site of the Last Supper *[Matthew 26:17-19]*.

Church of the Eight Apostles   Jesus called His disciples *[Matthew 4;18-22]*.

City of Palms   See Jericho

Coenaculum   See Upper Room

Decapolis   Jesus traveled here *[Matthew 4:23-25]*.

Dominus Flevit Church   Jesus wept over the city of Jerusalem *[Luke 19:41]*.

Eastern Gate   Called the Golden Gate. See Ancient gates back of book.

Ecco Homo   Jesus stands before Pilate *[John 19:5]*.

El-Eizariyva   See Bethany

Emmaus   Jesus reveals Himself to the two men *[Luke 24:13-32]*.

En-Kerem   Mary, pregnant with Jesus comes here *[Luke 1:39]*.

Ephratha   Another name for Bethlehem.

Gadarenes   Jesus heals the demon-possessed man *[Matthew 8:28]*.

Galilee   See all the entries on Jesus in the Galilee.

Galilee, the Sea of   He spent seventy five percent of His ministry here. *[Matthew 14:22-32; Mark 6:45-52; John 6:14-21; Matthew 8:23-27; Mark 4:35-41; Luke 8:22-25]*

Garden of Agony   See Gethsemane

Garden of Gethsemane   See Gethsemane

Garden Tomb   One of the sites honored for Jesus' burial *[Matthew 27:57-65]*.

Gennes'aret   They begged Jesus to heal them here *[Matthew 14:34-36]*.

Gethsemane   Jesus is exceedingly sorrowful here *[Matthew 26:36-46]*.

Golgatha   The place of the skull where Jesus is crucified *[Matthew 27:33]*.

Grotto of Gethsemane   He came with His disciples *[Luke 22:39; John 8:1]*.

Hermon, Mt   Some believe this is the Mt. of Transfiguration *[Matthew 17:1]*.

Herod's Palace   See Pilate's Judgment Hall

Herod's Temple   See Jesus in Jerusalem and Herod's Second Temple.

Herod's Caesarea Philippi   See Caesarea Philippi

Herodion House Mansion   Some beleive that this might have been the home of Caiaphas *[Matthew 26:57]* See Peter of Galicantu

Holy Sepulcher Church   The site of Calvary *[Matthew 27:33,59; Mark 15:22,46]*.

House of Caiaphas   See Herodion House and Peter of Galicantu.

Jacob's Well   Jesus speaks to the Samaritan woman *[John 4:1-26]*.

Jericho   Jesus heals the blind man *[Mark 10:46]*.

Jerusalem   See Jesus in Jerusalem page.

Jordan River   Jesus is baptized in these waters *[Matthew 3:13-17]*.

Jordan, Valley of   Jesus fasted and prayed here in this area *[Matthew 4:1]*.

Judea, land of   Jesus was born here and had His ministry here *[Luke 4:44]*.

Julias   See Bethsaida

Kings's Pool   See Siloam, Pool of

Lake Gennes'aret   See Sea of Galilee

Last Supper Site   See Upper Room

Lazarus Tomb   Jesus raises Lazarus from the dead *[John 11:1-44]*.

Lithostrotos   The pavement stones where Jesus may have been brought inside of the Antonio Fortress *[Matthew 27:26-31]*.

Lord's Prayer Site   Jesus teaches 'The Our Father' *[Luke 11:1-4]*.

Magadan, Mag'dala   Also called Dalmanutha *[Matthew 15:39; Mark 8:9-10]*.

Mary's Well   See En Kerem and Nazareth

Moriah, land of   The mountain over which the Second Temple was built. See Jesus in Jerusalem and Temple sites.

Mount of Ascension   See Mount of Olives and Mt. Olivet

Mount of Beatitudes   Jesus delivers His greatest sermon *[Matthew 5 thru 7]*

Mountain of God   See Moriah

Mount Moriah   See Moriah, land of

Mount of Olives   Jesus came here many times to be with friends and to pray. He taught His disciples from here *[Matthew 24; Luke 21]*.

Mount Olivet   The little hill on the Mt. of Olives, where Jesus ascended *[Luke 24:50; Acts 1:9-12]*.

Mount Sion   See Hermon

Mount Tabor, Tavor   The mount where Jesus was transfigured *[Matthew 17:1-2]*.

Mount of Temptation   The mount where Jesus was tempted *[Matthew 4:1-5]*.

Mustard Seed Site   Jesus makes a point using the mustard seed *[Matthew 13:32]*.

Mount Zion   See Jesus on Mt. Zion

Naim   Jesus raises up the weeping widow's son *[Luke 7:11-15]*.

Nazareth   See Jesus in Nazareth and in the Nazareth Synagogue

Old City of Jerusalem   See Jesus in Jerusalem

Old City Gates   See maps, from the Second Temple Period, of ancient gates

Ophel Archaeological Garden   See streets here from Second Temple period.

Palm Sunday Path   Jesus makes an entry into the city *[Mark 11:1-10]*.

Palm Trees, City of   See Jericho

Peter of Galicantu   Jesus is arrested and brought here *[Matthew 26:34,57]*.

Peter's House   Peter lived here with his family, Jesus came *[Matthew 8:14]*.

Pilate's Judgment Hall   Jesus is brought here, also called the Praetorium *[Matthew 27:2,13,17, 22,24; Mark 15:1-44]*.

Pinnacle of the Temple   Jesus was brought here by the devil *[Matthew 4:5]*.

Pool of Bethesda   See Bethesda

Pool of Siloam   Jesus sends the blind man to wash here *[John 9:7]*.

Portico of Solomon   Jesus casts out the moneychangers *[John 2:13-17]*.

Praetorium   Pilate lived here and Jesus was brought here *[Matthew 27:27]*.

Primacy of Peter   Jesus multiplies the loaves and fishes. He also appears to His disciples after the Resurrection *[Matthew 14:13-21; Mark 6:30-44; John 21]*.

Roads up to Jerusalem   Jesus walked these ancient paths *[Matthew 21;8; Luke 9:57]*.

Robinson's Arch Site   Jesus must have viewed this arch in His comings and goings in the Second Temple.

Rock of Agony   See Gethsemane

Samaria, City of   Jesus was here speaking to the Woman at the Well *[John 4:7]*.

Sea of Galilee   See Galilee and all the entries and scriptures

Sea of Tiberias   See Galilee, Sea of

Second Temple Jesus was brought here as a baby *[Luke 2:22]*. He came here many times during His ministry. See Jesus in Second Temple.

Sheep Gate Jesus heals the man next to this gate *[John 5:1-9]*.

Shepherd's Field See Bethlehem

Siloam, Pool of Jesus opens the eyes of the man born blind *[John 9:1-7]*.

Silwan The city where the Pool of Siloam is located *[John 9:1-7]*.

Sion, Mount See Hermon

Skull, Place of See Golgotha

Solomon's Porch Jesus walked here and taught *[John 10:23; Acts 3:11; 5:12]*.

Stations of the Cross See Via Delorosa

Struthion Pools These pools are underneath the Antonio Fortress where Jesus was brought. See Antonio Fortress and Praetorium.

Sychar See Shechem

Synagogue See Capernaum and Nazareth Synagogues

Tabgha Jesus feeds the multitudes *[Matthew 14:13-21; Mark 6:30-44]*.

Tabor See Mt. Tabor

Tear Drop Church See Dominus Flevit

Temple Mount See Moriah, Mount of

Temptation, Mount of See Mount of Temptation

Tower of Ascension Another site on the Mt. of Olives where Jesus may have ascended into heaven *[Acts 1:9-12]*.

Tyropoeon Valley   Herod filled in this valley to build the Second Temple where Jesus walked. See Herod's Temple and Jesus in Jerusalem.

Upper Room   Jesus held His last supper here *[Matthew 26:17-19]*

Via Delorosa   The 'Way of Sorrows' was the way Jesus walked on His way to Calvary *[Matthew 27:33]*.

Virgin's Fountain   See En-Kerem

Water Tunnel   See Pool of Siloam

Western Wall   See Herod's Second Temple

Zion   See Mount Zion and Jesus on Mt. Zion

THE ARK OF THE COVENANT
AND ITS WANDERINGS
(WHERE IS IT TODAY?)

The Ark of the Covenant was one piece of furniture, most holy to the Jews of Biblical times. It was given by God to Moses. Today, some Orthodox Jews and Evangelical Christians are still looking for it. They believe it will be found at the end of the age. It was a box 1.2 meters (4 ft.) in length by one half meter (2.5 ft.) high, made of acacia wood. This was overlaid with gold both within and without and it was a symbol of God's presence. No one was allowed to touch it, therefore, poles were made, also of gold, which slipped through the rings that were attached to the ark. Only the Levites, the Cohenim who were the Priests, were allowed to move the Ark. The first mention of this Ark is the Lord speaking to Moses in Exodus. "And they shall make an Ark of acacia wood…" *[Exodus 25:10-25]*. When this Ark was in the Tabernacle or the dwelling place in the desert, the cloud of the 'Presence of the Lord' hovered over the Mercy Seat. This Mercy Seat, also made of pure gold, was on top of the Ark as its cover. The stone tablets of the ten commandments, which was given by the Lord, to Moses was inside the Ark of the Covenant *[Exodus 40:20; Deut. 10:2]*. Aaron's rod was also kept inside the Ark for a period of time *[Numbers 17:10]*. The letter to the Hebrews also speaks of the Ark *[Hebrews 9:4]*. This Ark was with the children of Israel throughout their wanderings in the desert from Sinai to the Promised Land. From Acacia Grove, on the eastern side of the Jordan River, opposite Jericho, the Ark of the Covenant headed the 'parade' of the children of Israel into the Promised Land *[Joshua 3:3]*.

Shiloh Joshua stood before the Lord and divided the land and the Ark entered the Promised Land with the children of Israel *[Joshua 3:1-17]*. They set up the Ark here *[Joshua 18:1]*. The Ark rested here for 369 years.

Ebenezer   The Israelites were encamped here against the Philistines, together with the Ark while the Philistines camped at Afek *[I Samuel 4:1-11]*.

Afek   The Philistines fought against Israel and every man fled to his tent. There was a great slaughter and the Ark was captured. The two sons of Eli, Hophni and Phinehas, died at this site *[I Samuel chapter 4]*. The Ark was here for seven months.

Ashdod   The Philistines brought the Ark here after fighting the Israelites in the battle at Afek *[I Samuel 5:1-7]*.

Gath   From Ashdod, it rested here before being taken to Ekron *[I Samuel 5:8]*.

Ekron   The Philistines captured the Ark and took it here but the people were very much afraid *[I Samuel 5:10-12]*.

Beth Shemesh   Fifty thousand people were killed here because they dared to look into the Ark *[I Samuel 6:18,19]*.

Kiriat-jearim   Also called Gibeath, the Ark rested here for twenty years in the house of Abinadab *[I Chronicles 13:6-12]*.

Gath   The Ark remained in the house of Obed-edom, a Gittite, a Philistine from Gath, for three months before it was removed to Jerusalem. It was the second time it rested in Gath *[I Chronicles 13:12-14]*.

Jerusalem   Solomon became King and removed the Ark from the tent in Jerusalem to the First Temple which was built on the threshing floor of Araunah which his father, David, had purchased for this purpose *[II Samuel 24:24; I Chronicles 21:18; II Chronicles 3:1]*. The Ark rested, at last, in the 'Most Holy Place' in the Temple. *[I Kings 8:1-13,21; II Chronicles 5:2-14]*.

The Ark was placed in its most holy place in Jerusalem, its last recorded resting place and then there is no mention of it from the time of the destruction of Jerusalem on the 9th of Av, in 586 BC, by the Babylonians, until this day.

Orthodox Jews believe it is still buried underneath the Temple Mount. They believe that when God gave His instructions to Solomon for the building of the First Temple then He also gave instructions concerning the Ark. They believe, because Solomon knew that the Temple Mount was earthquake prone that there were secret vaults made for the Ark, underneath the First Temple. They believe that it will be discovered and come to light in the near future. Today, one may take a tour of the Temple Tunnels and see part of the retaining walls of the Second Temple and perhaps behind these walls are the vaults from Solomon's period. Time will tell.

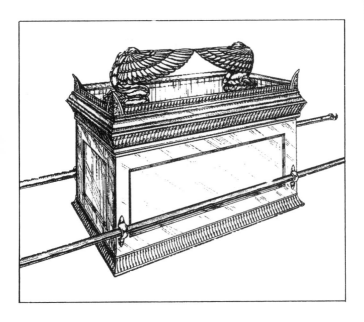

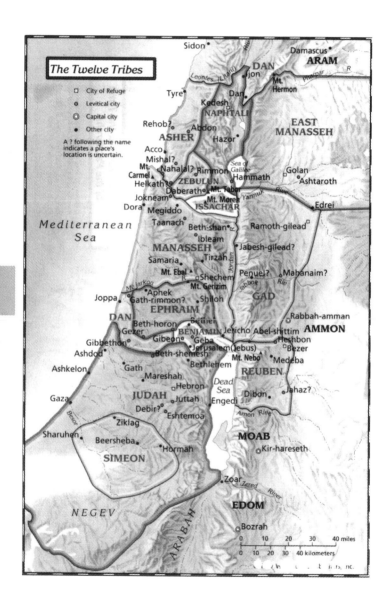

The Twelve Tribes

□ City of Refuge
◉ Levitical city
◎ Capital city
● Other city

A ? following the name
indicates a place's
location is uncertain.

THE BIRTH ORDER OF JACOB'S (ISRAEL'S) SONS AND THEIR TRIBES

Mother	Son	The Tribes and Their Land Allotmentsn
Leah	Reuben (born 1921 BC)	"Their territory was from Aroer which is on the bank of the Arnon, and the city that is in the midst of the ravine and all the plain of Medeba; Heshbon and all the cities in the plain: Dibon, Bamoth Baal, Beth Baal Meon, Jahaza, Kedemoth, Mephaath, Kirjathaim, Sibmah, Zereth Shahar …Beth Peor, slopes Pisgah and Beth Jeshimoth – all the cities of the plain and all the kingdom of Sihon, king of the Amorites…" *[Joshua 13:15-23]*.
Leah	Simeon	"They had in their inheritance Beersheva, Moladah Hazar, Shual, Balah, Ezem, Eltolad, Bethul, Hormah, Ziklag, Beth Marcaboth, Hazar Susah, Beth Lebaoth, and Sharuhen: 13 cities and their villages; Ain, Rimmon Ether, and Ashan: 4 cities and their villages: and all the villages that were around these cities, as far as Baalath Beer, Ramah of the South…" The inheritance of the children of Simeon was included in the portion of the children of Judah…" *[Joshua 19:1-9]*.
Leah	Levi	"Only to the tribe of Levi He had given no inheritance; the sacrifices of the Lord God of Israel made by fire are their inheritance, as He said to them" *[Joshua 13:14]*.
		Levi received no share of the land. God said to him simply, "I am thy part and thine inheritance." and by those words made him richer than all his brethren, richer than all the kings and rulers who ever lived in the world. The spiritual principle implied here is that the man who has God for his treasure, has everything!
Leah	Judah	"…the border of Edom, at the Wilderness of Zin south-ward, was the extreme southern boundary. Their southern border began at the shore of the Salt Sea, from the bay that faces southward. Then it went out to the southern side of the Ascent of Akrabbim, passed along to Zin, ascended on the south side of Kadesh Barnea, passed along to Hezron, went up to Adar, and went around to Karkaa. From there, it passed toward Azmon and went out to the Brook of Egypt and the border ended at the sea…, The **E**

Mother	Son	The Tribes and Their Land Allotmentsn
		border was the Salt Sea, as far as the mouth of the Jordan. The border went up to Beth Hoglah and passed north of Beth Arabah; and the border went up to the stone of Bohan the son of Reuven. Then, the border went up from Debir from the Valley of Achor, and it turned northward toward Gilgal which is before the Ascent of Adummim, which is on the **S** side of the valley. The border continued toward the waters of En Shemesh and ended at En Rogel. And the border went up by the Valley of the son of Hinnom to the southern slope of the Jebusite city (Jerusalem) The border went up to the top of the mountain that lies before the Valley of Hinnom westward, which is at the end of the Valley of Rephaim northward. Then, the border went around, from the top of the hill to the fountain of the water of Nephtoah, and extended to the cities of Mount Ephron. And the border went around to Baalah (which is Kirjath Jearim). Then the border turned westward from Baalah to Mount Seir, passed along to the side of Mount Jearim on the **N**, went down to Beth Shemesh, and passed on to Timnah. And the border went to the side of Ekron northward. Then the border went to Shicron, passed along to Mount Baalah, and extended to Jabneel; and the border ended at the sea. The **W** border was the coastline of the Great Sea (Mediterranean)…" *[Joshua 15:1-12]*
Bilhah (Rachel's maid)	Dan	"And the territory of their inheritance was Zorah, Eshtaol, Ir Shemesh, Shaalabbin, Aijalon, Jethlah, Elon Timnah, Ekron, Eltekeh, Gibbethon, Baalath, Jehud Bene Barak, Gath Rimmon, Me Jarkon, and Rakkon, with the region near Jaffa. And the border went beyond these, because the children of Dan went up to fight against Leshem and took it… called Leshem, Dan…" *[Joshua 19:40-48]*
Bilhah	Naphtali	"And their border began at Heleph, enclosing the territory from the terebinth tree in Zaanannim, Adami Nekeb, and Jabneel, as far as Lakkum; it ended at the Jordan. From Heleph, the border extended westward to Aznoth Tabor, and went out from there toward Hukkok It adjoined Zebulun on the **S** side and Asher on the **W** side, and ended at Judah, by the Jordan, toward the sunrise. The fortified cities are Ziddim, Zer, Hammath, Rakkath, Chinnereth, Adamah, Ramah, Hazor, Iron, Migdal El, Horem, Beth Anath, and Beth Shemesh: 19 cities with their villages…" *[Joshua 19:32-39]*

Mother	_Son_	_The Tribes and Their Land Allotmentsn_
Zilpah (Leah's maid)	Gad	"Their territory was Jazer, and all the cities of Gilead, and half the land of the Ammonites as far as Aroer, which is before Rabbah, and from Heshbon to Ramath Mizpah and Betonim, and from Mahanaim to the border of Debir, and in the valley Beth Haram, Beth Nimrah, Succoth, and Zaphon, the rest of the kingdom of Sihon, king of Heshbon, with the Jordan at its border, as far as the edge of the Sea of Chinnereth (Sea of Galilee) on the other side of the Jordan east-ward *[Joshua 13:24-28]*.
Zilpah	Asher	"And their territory included Helkath, Hali, Beten, Achshaph, Alammelech, Amad and Mishal; it reached to Mt. Carmel westward, along the Brook Shihor Libnath. It turned toward the sunrise to Beth Dagon; and reached to Zebulun and to the Valley of Jiphthah El, then northward beyond Beth Emek and Neiel, by-passing Cabul, which was on the left, including Ebron, Rehob, Hammon, and Kanah, as far as Great Sidon. And the border turned to Ramah, to the fortified city of Tyre; then the border turned to Hosah, and ended at the sea, by the regions of Achzib. Also Ummah Aphek, and Rehob were included: 22 cities with their villages *[Joshua 19:24-31]*.
Leah	Issachar	"And their territory went to Jezreel, and included Chesulloth, Shunem, Haphraim, Shion, Anaharath, Rabbith, Kishion, Abez, Remeth, En Gannim, En Haddah and Beth Pazzez. The border reached to Tabor, Shahazimah, and Beth Shemesh; their border ended at the Jordan: 16 cities with their villages *[Joshua 19:17-23]*.
Leah	Zebulun	"Their border went toward the **W** to Maralah, went to Dabbasheth, and extended along the brook that is east of Jokneam. Then, from Sarid, it went eastward toward the sunrise along the border of Chisloth Tabor, and went out toward Daberath, bypassing Japhia. And from there, it passed along on the **E** of Gath Hepher, toward Eth Kazin, and extended to Rimmon, which borders on Neah. Then, the border went around it on the **N** of Hannathon, and it ended in the Valley of Jiphthah El. Included were Kattath, Nahallal, Shimron Idalah, and Bethlehem: 12 cities with their villages *[Joshua 19:10-16]*.

Joseph and His Sons' Land Allotment

Although there were twelve sons of Jacob, Joseph's allotment for the land fell to his two sons, Manasseh, was the oldest and Ephraim, the youngest. Joseph presented his two sons to Jacob on his deathbed. Jacob leaned over and blessed his grandsons. "And Joseph took them both, Ephraim, with his right hand toward Jacob's left hand, and Manasseh, with his left hand toward Israel's right, and brought them near him (to Jacob). Then Jacob stretched out his right hand and laid it on Ephraim's head, who was the younger, and his left hand on Manasseh's head, guiding his hands knowingly, for Manasseh was the firstborn," *[Genesis 48:13-14]*.

"Now when Joseph saw that his father laid his right hand on the head of Ephraim, it displeased him; so he took hold of his father's hand to remove it from Ephraim's head to Manasseh's head. And Joseph said to his father, "Not so, my father, for this one is the firstborn; put your right hand on his head." But his father refused and said, "I know, my son, I know. He shall also become a people and he also shall be great; but truly his younger brother shall be greater than he, and his descendants shall become a multitude of nations." *[Genesis 48:17-19]* Jacob also told Joseph, "…I have given you one portion above your brothers…" *[Genesis 48:22]*. Therefore there appears to be 13 divisions of the land because Joseph's share goes to Manasseh and Ephraim.

Ezekiel, the Prophet said, "Thus says the Lord God: "These are the borders by which you shall divide the land as an inheritance among the twelve tribes of Israel. Joseph shall have two portions" *[Ezekiel 47:13]*.

Rachel	Joseph's (Manasseh and Ephraim)	"The lot fell to the children of Joseph from the Jordan, by Jericho, to the waters of Jericho on the east, to the wilderness that goes up from Jericho through the mountains to Beth-el, then went out from Beth-el to Luz passed along to the border of the Archites at Anaroth, and down westward to the boundary of the Japhletites, as far as the boundary of Lower Beth Horon to Gezer, and it ended at the sea (Med. Sea). So the children of Joseph, Manasseh and Ephraim took their inheritance." *[Joshua 16:1-4]*.

Rachel   Benjamin   "Their border on the **N** began at the Jordan, and went up to the side of Jericho on the **N**, and went up to the mountains westward; it ended at the Wilderness of Beth Aven. The border from there to Luz (Beth-el) southward; and the border descended to Ataroth Addar, near the hill that lies on the **S** side of Lower Beth Horon. Then, the border extended from there around the west side to **S**, from the hill that lies before Beth Horon southward; and it ended at Kirjath Baal, a city of the children of Judah. This was the west side. The south side began at the end of Kirjath Jearim, and the border extended on the **W** and went out to the springs of the waters of Nephtoah. Then, the border came down to the end of the mountain that lies before the Valley of the Son of Hinnom, which is in the Valley of Rephaim on the **N**, descended to the Valley of Hinnom, to the side of the Jebusite city on the **S**, and descended to En Rogel. And it went around from the **N**, out to En Shemesh, and extended toward Geliloth, which is before the Ascent of Adummim, and descended to the stone of Bohan, the son of Reuven. Then it passed along to the **N** side of Arabah, and went down to Arabah. The border passed along to the **N** side of Beth Hoglah; then, the border ended at the **N** bay at the Salt Sea (Dead Sea) at the **S** end of the Jordan. This was the southern border. The Jordan was its border on the **E** side *[Joshua 18:11-20]*.

"Now the cities of the tribe of the children of Benjamin, according to their families, were Jericho, Beth Hoglah, Emek Keziz, Beth Arabah, Zemara'im, Beth-el, Avim, Parah, Ophrah, Chephar Haammoni, Ophni, and Gaba; 12 cities with their villages; Gibeon Ramah, Beeroth, Mizpah, Chephirah, Mozah, Rekem, Irpeel, Taralah, Zelah, Eleph, Jebus *[Joshua 19:21-18]*.

* * *

Joshua summed it up "...Joshua took the whole land according to all that the Lord had said to Moses; and Joshua gave it as an inheritance to Israel according to their divisions by their tribes. Then the land rested from war *[Joshua 11:23]*.

In the NT, the Apostle Paul speaks of the tribe allotment "...and when He had destroyed seven nations in the land of Canaan, He distributed their land to them by allotment," *[Acts 13:19]*.

Ezekiel's Vision of the Borders of Israel

The Prophet Ezekiel, in the year 570 BC beheld a vision, given to him from God, showing the borders of Israel. See the entire *chapter 48 of the Prophet Ezekiel* (Yehezke'l, God strengthens) and the map below.

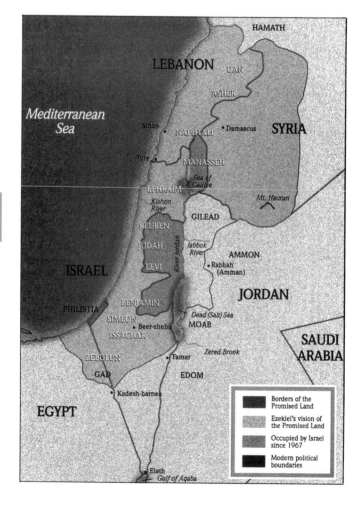

THE VIA DELOROSA, THE WAY OF THE CROSS, THE WAY OF SORROWS

The Franciscan Fathers came to the Holyland in 1229 and their first residence was the site where the Fifth Station of the Cross is now honored. The site of the Antonio Fortress was identified by the Franciscans. A Dominican Catholic, named William Wey, came as a pilgrim in 1458 and the traditional story is that the Franciscan Fathers toured him through the sites. The term 'Stations of the Cross' was then used for the first time. Since 1458, many have followed this 'Way of the Cross'.

The Political situation under the Turks did not allow the pilgrims to pray openly. In the beginning of the 17th C. the custom of praying at the sites was widely adopted and the political situation eased. The Catholic Church, under Pope Clement XII, issued a decree in the year 1731 and the Stations were then confirmed, accepted and marked as they are today. The main procession begins at 3:00 PM every Friday afternoon, from the courtyard of the Omariya Moslem College, just inside of St. Stephen's Gate. All the fourteen stations are marked by chapels or churches.

Station One Jesus is condemned *[Mark 15:1; John 18:28]*. The Al Omariya Moslem School

Station Two Jesus receives the cross *[John 19;1,16]* The two chapels of the Flagellation and Condemnation, next to Ecco Homo Church

Station Three Jesus falls for the first time *[Lamentations 1:16]*. At the corner of El Wad St. stands the Polish Chapel with a high-relief sculpture over the door which depicts Jesus falling.

Station Four Jesus meets His mother *[Luke 2:34; Lamentations 1:12]*. The Armenian Catholic Church of Our Lady marks this site.

Station Five Simon, the Cyrenean helps Jesus carry the cross *[Mark 15:21]*. A Franciscan Chapel stands here and the ascent to Golgotha begins here, to the Church of the Holy Sepulcher.

Station Six Veronica (like an image LT) wipes the face of Jesus. "May the Lord's face shine upon you…" *[Numbers 6:25]*. The convent of the Little Sisters of Jesus marks this site.

Station Seven	Jesus falls the second time *[Isaiah 63:9]*. A Franciscan Chapel houses a Roman column here.
Station Eight	Jesus speaks to the daughters of Jerusalem *[Luke 23:28]*. A Latin cross on the wall of the Greek Monastery stands here.
Station Nine	Jesus falls for the third time *[Psalm 40:8]*. On the top of the Church of the Holy Sepulcher Basilica is a Roman column. It is next to the entrance of the Coptic Church. One must go to the rooftop of the Church.

These next five Stations of the Cross, from the tenth through to the fourteenth stations, are inside the Church of the Holy Sepulcher. There is a staircase from the Coptic Church leading down to the main courtyard of the Church.

Station Ten	Jesus is stripped of His garments *[Mark 15:24]*. A small stairway of stone outside once led to the Chapel of Divestiture. Proceed inside the Holy Sepulcher Church and go up the stone steps to the right and up.
Station Eleven	Here, Jesus is nailed to the cross *[Psalm 22; Luke 23:33]*; "He came to the Place of the Skull (in Hebrew Golgotha), where they crucified Him *[John 19:17]*. The main Roman Catholic (Latin) shrine commemorates the site here.
Station Twelve	Jesus dies on the cross, "Jesus when He had cried again with a loud voice, yielded up His spirit" *[Matthew 27:50]*. The Greek Orthodox Altar stands here where the cross stood on the 'Rock of Calvary'.
Station Thirteen	Jesus' body is taken down from the cross. "Joseph of Arimathea…went to Pilate and asked for the body of Jesus. Then he took the body down." *[Luke 23:53]* Returning to the lower level, we come to the 'Stone of Anointing,' in the main entrance hall of the Church.
Station Fourteen	Jesus is placed in the tomb. "And when Joseph had taken the body, he wrapped it in a clean linen cloth, laid it in his own tomb which he had hewn out of the rock" *[Matthew 27:59]*. The tomb of Joseph of Arimathea is a chapel in the center, and is the focal point of the Church of the Holy Sepulcher underneath the rotunda. It marks Christendom's most sacred place, as the burial and the Resurrection of Jesus. The remains are from the first Byzantine chapel, built by Helena in 325 AD.
	"And the angel said to the women: 'He has risen, He is not here,'" *[Mark 16:6]*

THE GATES OF THE OLD CITY OF JERUSALEM
Present and Former Names

Present Name	Former Names
Present Name	**Former Names**
1. Jaffa Gate	The ancient road by Jaffa Gate once led to the port city of Jaffa, thus, the gate was called Jaffa Gate. Gate of David (Byzantine and Crusader times); Western Gate Bab Mihrab David Gate (Arab period); Hebron Gate (Bab el Kahlil; (Arabic name).
2. New Gate	It is the newest gate, built in 1889. Bab es-Sultan (Turkish era) The Europeans, the French mainly, obtained permission from the Turkish Sultan to build this gate so easy access would be possible to the Old City from the new Christian buildings.
3. Damascus Gate	The ancient road here led to the capital city of Damascus, thus, its name. Gate of the Column (Crusader times); Ban al Amud (Turkish era); and St. Stephen's Gate during Byzantine times.
4. Flower Gate Herod's Gate	Bab es-Zahra Gate, a corruption of Sahira which means "the place where people stay awake," as the Moslems to Mecca once passed here 'watchfully'. The Byzantine pilgrims called it Herod's Gate, as they believed it was here where Jesus came to the palace of Herod Antipas *[Luke 23:7]*. The entrance is decorated with carvings of flowers.
5. St. Stephen's Gate Lion's Gate	This gate marks the traditional site where Stephen was stoned *[Acts 7:58-60]* thus its name. A legend has it that two pairs of lions were ordered engraved on either side of the gate, as the Sultan had a dream that he would be eaten by lions if he didn't rebuild the gates and the walls, which he did, in 1538. Gate of Jericho and Gate of Jehoshaphat during Crusader times.
6. Eastern Gate Golden Gate	This beautiful double-arched gate was closed in 1541, by the Turks, for fear of the Jewish Messiah coming through it. It is the only gate that is part of the city wall. One part is called the Mercy Gate and the other, the Gate of Repentance. The Jews believe it will open with the advent of the Messiah. It was called Golden Gate in Jesus' time, as He entered through the lower gate on Palm Sunday *[Mark 11;9; John 12:13]*. It was called Beautiful Gate during Peter and John's time *[Acts 3:2]*. Ezekiel called it the

	Eastern Gate, for it faces **E** *[Ezekiel 10:19; 44:2]*. It was repaired during Nehemiah's time *[Nehemiah 3:29]*. Shushan Gate is its Arabic name.
7. Dung Gate	The trash was taken out through this gate and, thus, its name. Gate of Jeremiah's Pit, named during the Crusader's time and Gate of Siloam, for from here, one goes **S** to the village of Siloam. Bab Silwan is its Arabic name.
7a. Pedestrian Gate	This gate was opened in the summer of 1996, for the convenience of pedestrians in the area going to and from the Western Wall.
8. Zion Gate	This gate is located on Mt. Zion, thus it's name. The Crusaders named it the Prophet David's Gate because of its close proximity to the tomb of King David, when they was here in the 12th century.

The Ancient Gates and Towers of the Old City From David's time to Nehemiah's time

It appears that the Jebusites were the first to build walls around the City of Jerusalem. These Jebusites, the descendants of the Canaanites held the 'stronghold of Zion' that is Jerusalem and David conquered them and the city *[II Samuel 5:6-9; I Chronicles 11:4-7]*. David bought the threshing floor (Temple Mount, Mt. Moriah) *[II Samuel 24:21-15]* He built the city around the Temple Mount area (by building walls and gates) *[I Chronicles 10:8]*. King Solomon, the son of David was the one chosen by the Lord and commissioned by his father to build a Temple to the Lord *[I Kings 1:35;5:5, I Chronicles 17:10-15; 29:19]* In the year 950 BC Solomon formed a marriage alliance with Pharoah, the king of Egypt and married Pharaoh's daughter. He built the wall around Jerusalem at this time *[I Kings 3:1]*. We only know the names of the towers and gates from the book of Nehemiah and the prophets. Almost 400 years passed but on that fateful day on the 9th of Av 586BC Nebuchadnezzar came and destroyed the city, walls and Temple in Jerusalem *[II Kings 24:10;25:1-2]* Jeremiah told of the breaking down of the walls *[Jeremiah 39:8]* The exiled Jews went to Babylon but the Lord raised up the prophet Nehemiah in 444 BC who had found favor with the King of Persia in Babylon. He was granted permission to return and rebuild the walls *[Nehemiah chapters 2 and 3]*. The Prophet Ezekiel prophesied his vision of the gates *[Ezekiel 48:30-35]*. Only the Water Gate has been identified in recent archeological excavations. The other gates and towers have not been identified with certainty and most likely have been completely destroyed by the ravages of time. Unfortunately there is no precise descriptions of the work done by Herod, the Great on the walls and gates of Jerusalem. The following gates had several names and are the listed with their most popular name first and their other names directly underneath.

1. Sheep Gate
   Benjamin Gate

   See Sheep Gate in main entry. The goldsmiths and merchants carried out repairs here *[Nehemiah 3:32]*. This gate was also called the Benjamin Gate, the Gate of the Guard or Prison *[Nehemiah 12:39]*, and the Inspection Gate.

2. Muster Gate
   Captain Gate

   Muster (gadad) The gate to gather or penetrate into. This gate on the **NE** side of the upper Ophel and Temple Mount may have been used as the main entry into the city. Micah speaks of 'mustering (gathering) the troops' *[Micah 5:1]*. Also called its Hebrew name HaMifkad Gate.

3. East Gate
   Eastern Gate

   See Eastern Gate in main entry. Shemaiah… was the keeper of this gate and he carried out the repairs *[Nehemiah 3:29]*. See Present Gates of the Old City.

4. Horse Gate

   This gate was near the king's house *[II Chronicles 23:15]*. It was used to bring in the horses from the eastern hill. The priests of the Temple who returned with Nehemiah carried out repairs on this gate, in front of their homes *[Nehemiah 3:28]*. Jeremiah foretold a day when the valley and the fields from the Kidron to the corner of the Horse Gate would be holy unto the Lord *[Jeremiah 31:40]*.

5. Water Gate
   Casemate Gate

   The Temple servants who lived in the Ophel (mound or tower) which was the original City of David occupied by the Jebusites repaired this area near the Water Gate *[Nehemiah 3:26]*.

6. Fountain Gate
   Spring Gate

   "The Gate between two walls" Here on the southern border of the Ophel lies the Fountain Gate next to the King's Pool (Pool of Siloam). The men of war fled here from Nebuchadnezzar's army *[II Kings 25:4; Jeremiah 39:4]*. Nehemiah returned from Babylon, he started his inspection work for the repair of the walls and gates near here *[Nehemiah 2:14]*. Shallum… repaired the Fountain Gate *[Nehemiah 3:15]*. The leaders of Judah came to the repaired walls and gates for their dedication. Here at the Fountain Gate they went directly up the steps to the City of David *[Nehemiah 12:27, 37]*.

7. Refuse Gate

   See Refuse Gate in main entry *[Nehemiah 2:13; 3:14;12:31]*.

8. Valley Gate

Nehemiah entered by night here on his inspection tour of the broken walls and gate *[Nehemiah 2:13,15]*.

9. Tower of Furnaces

See Furnace, Tower of, in main entry. Malchijah and Hasshub repaired another section (of the wall) and this Tower of Furnace *[Nehemiah 3:11; 12:38]*.

10. The Old Gate
Ephraim Gate
First Gate
Middle Gate

This Old Gate may have simply been the oldest of the gates and Jooiada and Meshullam repaired this gate, laid the beams and hung the doors *[Nehemiah 3:6]*. This gate was next to an open square *[Nehemiah 8:16]*. King Jehoash broke down the wall by this gate *[II Kings 14:13]*. Zechariah speaks of the kingdom of the Messiah returning here *[Zechariah 14:10]*.

11. Fish Gate
Corner Gate

See Fish Gate in main entry. This gate was located on the **W** side of the Gihon Spring *[II Chronicles 33:14]*. The sons of Hassenaah rebuilt this gate *[Nehemiah 3:3]*. Zephaniah foretold of a cry of mourning here *[Zephaniah 1:10]*.

12. Tower of Hananel
Hanan-el
(God has favored)

A tower in the main wall in the **N** was located next to the Fish Gate. No doubt because of the great deal of activity through the Fish Gate, the tower was an excellent guardhouse or watchtower. Jeremiah spoke of the rebuilding that would take place here *[Jeremiah 31:38]*. It was sanctified and rededicated by the high priest Eliashib *[Nehemiah 3:1]*. The second choir rejoiced here *[Nehemiah 12:39]*. Zechariah also speaks of a time of restoration from this tower *[Zechariah 14:10]*.

13. The Tower of
the Hundred
(mea migdalim)

The watchtower (migdal) also was built in a strategic place next to the Sheep Gate and the Tower of Hananel in the **N**. The Sheep gate also had a large guard room and an upper room and we might assume since it was located next to the this watchtower they both served to secure the city. The high priest Eliashib also blessed and sanctified this tower *[Nehemiah 3:1]*.

BIBLIOGRAPHY

Arav, Rami & Rousseau, John J., *Jesus and His World*, Augsburg Fortress Press, Minneapolis, MN 55440

Carta's Official Guide to Israel, Carta Press, Jerusalem 1983

Geva, Hillel, *Ancient Jerusalem Revealed*, Israeli Exploration Society, 1994, Ben-Zvi Printing Enterprises, Jerusalem

Gonen, Rivka, *Biblical Holy Places*, Palphot Ltd., Herzlia 1987

Josephus, *The Jewish War* translated by G.A. Williamson, Penguin Books, Baltimore, Maryland 1959

Shanks, Hershel, *The City of David*, Biblical Archeology Society, Washington 1973

Strong's Exhaustive Concordance, Baker Book House, Grand Rapids, Michigan

The Complete Works of Josephus, translated by William Whiston, Kregel Publications, Grand Rapids, Michigan 49501, 1995

The Israel Road and Touring Guide, The Stephen Greene Press, Lexington, Massachusetts, 1985

The Life and Works of Flavius Josephus, translated by William Whiston, A.M.; Holt, Rhinehart and Winston Publishers, Grand Rapids, Michigan

The MacMillan Bible Atlas, MacMillan Publishing Co., New York, Carta Press, Jerusalem 1993

The New American Standard Exhaustive Concordance, The Lockman Foundation 1981, Holman Bible Publishers, Nashville, Tennessee

The New King James Version, The Open Bible; Thomas Nelson Publishers, 1985

Unger, Merrill F., *The New Unger's Bible Dictionary*, Moody Press, Chicago, Illinois 1988

Wager, Eliyahu, *Illustrated Guide to Jerusalem*, Jerusalem Publishing House, Jerusalem 1988

Trees
By Joyce Kilmer 1886-1918

I think that I shall never see
A poem as lovely as a tree
A tree whose hungry mouth is pressed
Upon the earth's sweet smelling breast
A tree that looks at God all day
And lifts its leafy arms to pray
A tree that may in summer wear
A nest of robins in her hair
Upon whose bosom snow has lain
Who intimately lives with rain
Poems are made by fools like me
But only God can make a tree.

* * *

You can plant a tree with your own hands and leave your fingerprints in the land of the Bible. Israel is the only country in the world which has a national afforestation program that invites participation from all the peoples of the world. Many peoples have come and taken the opportunity to sink their hands into this Biblical soil, a moving occasion to honor and commemorate dear ones thereby creating an emotional link with the Land of the Bible.

I invite you the reader to contact the KEREN KAYEMETH LEISRAEL, the JEWISH NATIONAL FUND at 00972-2-6707402 and make plans today to plant a tree in the soil as you walk in the footsteps of Jesus and the Prophets.

ACKNOWLEDGEMENTS

I would like to acknowledge and thank the following persons for their kind help and assistance in the preparation of this guide book. First of all to my loving and thoughtful husband Fredrick for his insight, patience, proofreading talents and his love and devotion without which I could not attempt to do this work. My dearest and best friend of over twenty five years, Dr. Norma Neal Gause who critiqued my work and offered many interesting comments, corrections and suggestions. Joni Arden, a fellow tour guide, who offered comments and corrections from a guide's point of view. Dr. Larry Hawks whose computer and technical knowledge allowed me to set up the computer and program to produce this work. His patience and endurance and help through out the years cannot be measured. Ruth Moore, a former editor from the US who proofread the final version and offered additional suggestions and comments. She is counted among the ones who long endure and expect nothing in return. I am so grateful. To all of these I thank you from the very bottom of my heart. Thank you for helping me make this work possible.

Hela Crown-Tamir 5759/1999

JERUSALEM, GOD'S NAME IS HERE

As we stand on Mt. Scopus, the northern part of the Mt. of Olives, overlooking the Jordan Valley toward the East, next to the Hebrew University, we say and reflect.

Stand here with me in Jerusalem. Sooner or later the entire world will pass by — not only people from other times and other places but all the nations, gowns, garbs, dress, tongues and the religious. The religious and everyone who is looking for God. The searches, the contented, the discontented and the ecstatic, they all come. This is odd because Jerusalem is a rather smallish place, off the beaten path, perched on a ridge between the desert on one side and the rocky hillside on the other. She is beautiful but she is not exquisite. Jerusalem bears God's name.

II Chronicles 6:6,20
II Chronicles 12:13b
Nehemiah 1:9
Jeremiah 3:17
Jeremiah 25:29

See attached drawing and illustration of the topography of Jerusalem. The land surrounding the Old City clearly shows the Hebrew letter 'shin' in the topography.

God's Name is here, see the Hebrew letter shin ש

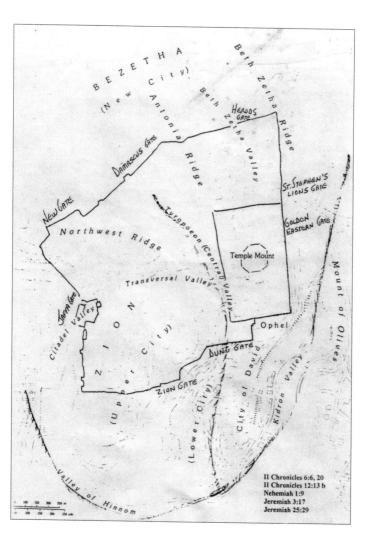

II Chronicles 6:6, 20
II Chronicles 12:13 b
Nehemiah 1:9
Jeremiah 3:17
Jeremiah 25:29

Solomon's Temple

This possible reconstruction of Solomon's Temple is based on Old Testament and some archaeological evidence. [I Kings 5:5; 12-18; II Chronicles 2:1; II Chronicles 3:5].

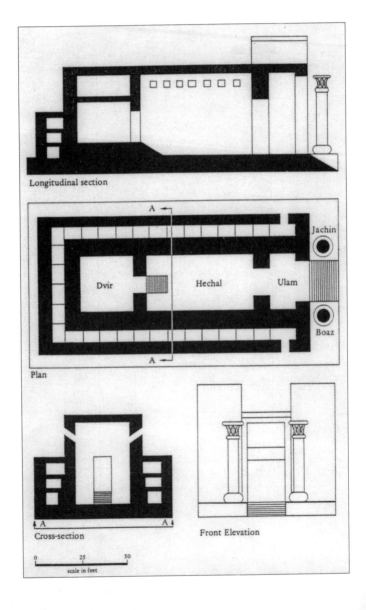

Longitudinal section

Plan

Dvir   Hechal   Ulam

Jachin

Boaz

Cross-section

Front Elevation

0   25   50
scale in feet

Herod's Temple during the Time of Jesus

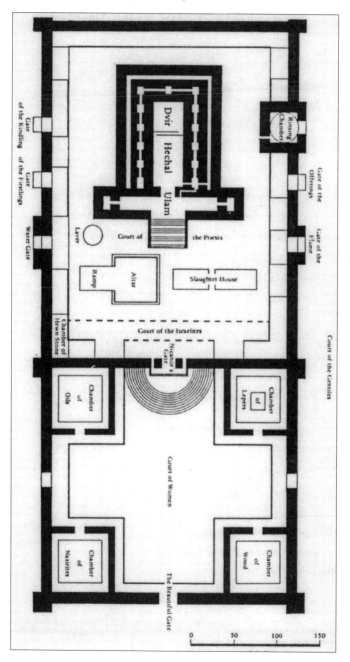

GEOGRAPHY OF THE BIBLE TIMELINE

a) Beginning with Adam and Eve (Genesis 2)

b) Noah and the flood (Genesis chapters 6, 7, 8)

c) Abraham comes from Ur, his encampments, settlements (Genesis 11:31) Age of the Patriarchs 2200 BC–1550 BC (Middle Bronze Age)

d) Isaac and his settlements (Genesis 21)

e) Ya'acov (Jacob) and his encampments, his wanderings and settlements Joseph and his brothers (Genesis 25:20–Genesis 50)

f) Moses leads the children of Israel 1250 BC (all the book of Exodus) The children of Israel enter the Promised Land under Joshua 1210 BC

g) King David 1004 BC–968 BC (Samuel 24:24; I Chron. 21:25)

h) King Salomon 968–928 BC First Temple Period (I Kings 5:5)

i) The Kingdom is divided after Salomon's death 930–586 BC (I Kings 16:21)

j) The destruction of the First Temple 586 BC, 9th day of Av (II Kings 24:10, 11; 25)

k) The Persian Period 538–333 BC Return of the Jews to Judah (Ezra 2)

l) Alexander de Great enters, Hellenistic Period 333 BC

m) The Maccabeans (Hasmonean Dynasty) 142–63 BC

n) The Roman Period (63 BC–324 AD) Herod the Great 37–4 BC The Second Temple 18 BC

o) Jesus of Nazareth is born (4 BC–30 AD)

p) The Second Temple is destroyed 70 AD, 9th day of Av

q) The Byzantine Period (324–640 AD)

r) The Arab Period (640–1099 AD)

s) Crusaders (1099–1291 AD)

t) Mamlukes (1250–1517 AD) Suliman rebuilds the walls of Jerusalem (1520–1566)

u) Turkish Rule (1517–1917 AD)

v) British Mandate (1917–1948 AD) General Allenby enters Jaffa Gate on Dec. 11, 1917 (Hannucah)

w) Israel is established May 14, 1948 (Isaiah 66:8)